YOU ARE MY SUNSHINE

The WWII V-Mail Cartoons of Harry E. Chrisman:
"LOVE LETTERS TO THE WACS"

Volume Two

Heep! Sheryl Jones

SHERYL JONES

HELLGATE PRESS   ASHLAND, OREGON

YOU ARE MY SUNSHINE
©2014 Sheryl Jones

Published by Hellgate Press
(An imprint of L&R Publishing, LLC)

Hellgate Press
PO Box 3531
Ashland, OR 97520
email: sales@hellgatepress.com

Editor: Harley B. Patrick
Cover design: L. Redding

Library of Congress Cataloging-in-Publication Data available on request.

Printed and bound in the United States of America
First edition 10 9 8 7 6 5 4 3 2 1

For Harry and Catherine

Contents

Acknowledgments

As always, many people help get a project such as this along the way until it reaches a reader whom I hope will enjoy Harry's cartoons as much as I do.

I could never get any of this done without the love and support of my husband, Don. He reads every word, passes judgment on content and feasibility and I know that he will not give strokes unless they are deserved. So when he says, "That's good, that's good," I know he means it.

And, of course, my sister, Judy Slothower, who sends encouragement over the cell phone every morning and when necessary, during the day also. She's eight hundred miles away, but that phone and e-mail attachments are my favorite tools! Well, next to my computer, of course.

To Major Thomas G. Grandin, retired, 82nd Airborne, who can answer all those Army questions, my loving gratitude and hugs. He's one heck of a good cook too!

And my new favorite Army guy, my grandson, Specialist Erik K. Jones, 82nd Airborne stationed at Ft. Bragg, North Carolina. What a delight to learn the ins and outs of today's Army.

And many gracious thanks to three friends who continually support my efforts, with all my writing: Rita Friedman, Colleen Lautenbach, and Chuck Lautenbach. It makes life so much more enjoyable to have friends like them who encourage, congratulate, and, perhaps most importantly, laugh with you!

Special thanks to Ryan Henry, editor of the *Brownsville Herald* and the first newsman who saw the worth in Harry's cartoons and did a front page spread on "Harry's Legacy." Thank you so much, Ryan. How Harry would have loved meeting you.

And, as always, it's great to have an editor and publisher who is also a friend. Thank you Harley Patrick for your judgment and encouragement and patience as these volumes come together.

And lastly, but of course, not last, my two sons, Scott and Steven Jones. Scott is my walking WWII encyclopedia and can do things like stop mowing the lawn, mower on pause, and answer a question immediately and explain why this and that happen during that war. And Steve who thinks everything I write is terrific and is my best encourager! Don and I have raised good sons!

Catherine and Harry Chrisman, circa 1945.

Harry's Original Introduction

THIS WORK IS DEDICATED TO THE PRESIDENT AND OUR COMMANDER-IN-CHIEF, Franklin D. Roosevelt, and to our First Lady of that time, Eleanor Roosevelt, both of whom played predominant roles in the leadership of the American people in our struggle against Japanese Imperialism and Nazi-Fascism in World War II.

Although our great leader died before the victory came, his inspiring life and the guidance he gave us lives on in a time when the nation sorely needs it.

To all who followed this democratic path through the pains of World War II, and survived, and to all born since, we learn that the beaten path is the safe one. Let us continue to appreciate and follow the philosophy laid down by this masterful architect of the Good Neighbor Policy in all of our relations, foreign and domestic.

—Harry Chrisman, 1982

"They never needed anyone else. You know, they were just so content with each other," a niece of Catherine's once told me. And it was true. They were two of the most content, compatible people I ever met. I never heard a harsh word, a complaint, a gripe—nothing but loving, caring words between them. And laughter. A lot of laughter. What wonderful role models they were!

In addition, they were both handsome people. The photo above, from 1935 when they had been dating for a few years, is proof of their good looks.

Catherine in summer uniform. Until the summer uniform was issued the WACs at Victorville were wearing their winter Olive Drabs or the men's pants issued to them to wear when they climbed the radio towers. Before the end of the war, however, they were issued pants and shirts designed for women.

Preface

THIS VOLUME WAS DRAWN AND WRITTEN IN THE FALL OF 1982 when Harry and I began to search out possible publishers to print his collection of V-Mails. We were unsuccessful, not because the interest was not there, but because the expense of duplicating and photographing 403 cartoons/v-mails plus several pictures was too prohibitive.

I have chosen most of the V-Mails he drew especially with the Women's Army Corp (WACs) in mind and considered appropriate for his wife, Catherine, and her WAC friends. Some were meant just for her and those she did not share with her fellow soldiers; but many were placed on the bulletin board in "Hysteria Haven," the name she and her mates chose for their barracks. She told me remembering those V-Mails helped bring a smile or, often, laughter as she spent night after lonely night without Harry, wondering where he was and what he was doing, and was he safe.

Several years after Harry's death, Catherine and I were cleaning out the trunk of his 1966 Buick, the first new car he ever bought, and there was his Army first aid kit. She told my husband, Don, to open it. He began that process and looked up at her and said, "Why, Catherine, this has never been opened." She smiled and said, "Thank goodness!"

For the first year after he died, she cried a lot and spent a good deal of time reading the autobiography he wrote while recuperating from four heart attacks. We saw her often because Don helped her with financial and personal matters from the time Harry died. After the first year she began to take an interest in life again and began to talk about Harry and their life together. But most of what I knew about her years as a WAC I learned as she wrote her book, My War, WWII—As Experienced by One Woman Soldier. It was written while Harry was still alive and published in 1989 by Maverick Publica-

Catherine with actor Randolph Scott. According to Catherine, "I met Scott at a golf tournament at San Bernardino in November 1943. I had met his WAC sister earlier in Florida, at Daytona Beach."

tions, Harry's own publishing house, just as the 50th anniversary of that war approached. As she wrote the book she shared her experiences with me. We often dropped by the house on our way home from school and she would talk about what she wrote that day while Don and Harry visited in another room. I asked her once how she could remember so much and she said once she started writing, one incident lead to another and so on and so on.

Harry was so proud of her book, he had been after her for years to take her thumbs out of her fists and write it, that we had several celebrations for her. First, a signing party at my house and then a big celebration for her 80th birthday with a picnic in their backyard. My son, Scott, filmed it so we have it all on a DVD. What fun it is now after all these years to see them both once again, happy and smiling.

Introduction

CATHERINE WAS GOOD FOR HARRY. Harry sowed many a wild oat BEFORE he met her. He was a good looking traveling salesman and liked women, wine, and song. But Catherine changed all that. He gave his total love and respect to her. He told me once that without Catherine he would have undoubtedly taken a different road in life. They remained faithful to each other for the rest of their lives, although many an airman looked longingly at Catherine while she served in the WACs at the air base in Victorville, California. This photo, taken when she finished basic training, explains why she received many a second look during her time in the service.

This is Catherine's story as much as Harry's because he enjoyed drawing all the cartoons. He knew the WACs in Hysteria Haven waited every day to see if Catherine got a V-Mail cartoon she would share with them. Usually the cartoon was posted on the bulletin board in the barracks and officers often "inspected" the barracks to check out the latest cartoon.

The Women's Army Corps (WAC) was the women's branch of the Army until it disbanded in 1978 and women joined whatever branch of the Armed Forces they chose. In May of 1942 the WAAC, Woman's Army Auxiliary Corps, was created by several branches of the U. S. government. It was soon apparent that the expected 11,000 enlistees was a very inaccurate number because 150,000 women eventually served during WWII. So many woman applied for the Corps that in 1943 WAAC was changed to WAC, Woman's Army Corp, and granted full status as a branch of the Armed Forces. The first Director was Oveta Culp Hobby from Texas. She served in that position from 1942 to 1945.

The first women to enlist began training at Fort Des Moines in late 1942. Catherine began her training there as one of the first WAACs in November of 1942. There were

800 women in that first contingent. The first day of basic training they were fitted for uniforms, interviewed, assigned to companies and barracks and inoculated against disease. Catherine was just beginning to learn "The Army Way" that day when she finally was assigned a cot in the barracks and got only two hours of sleep before a "Roll Out!" call found her on the snowy parade ground of the fort in ten minutes.

Harry's first V-Mails to her were addressed to WAAC and he, as well as others, used the term interchangeably for the first year of Catherine's service.

So here they are—Harry's "love letters" to the WACs—and, when I know it, the back story of the cartoon as told to me by Harry, and often by Catherine. In addition, Harry wrote a line or two about some of them, and those are designated with an "H". When I clarify or add background information, it will be indicated with an "S".

Catherine Chrisman in uniform during WWII (*above*) and at home in 1992 (*right*).

PART ONE

LOVE, ROMANCE AND THE WAC

Catherine was sworn in to the WAAC (Women's Army Auxiliary Corps) on November 12, 1942, just four weeks after Harry's swearing in to the Army. He knew she had joined but did not know the date she would be sworn in. He told me he was so proud of her, but worried, of course, how she would be treated by the men she would be working with. Many men resented the WAAC as they felt the women were replacing men who would eventually end up on the front lines. They warned their wives and sisters that people would think they were prostitutes or lesbians and many a father forbade his daughter enlisting. Not every enlistee was like Harry and Catherine, doing what they could to win the war. This V-Mail was Harry's way of looking at the situation with humor. (S)

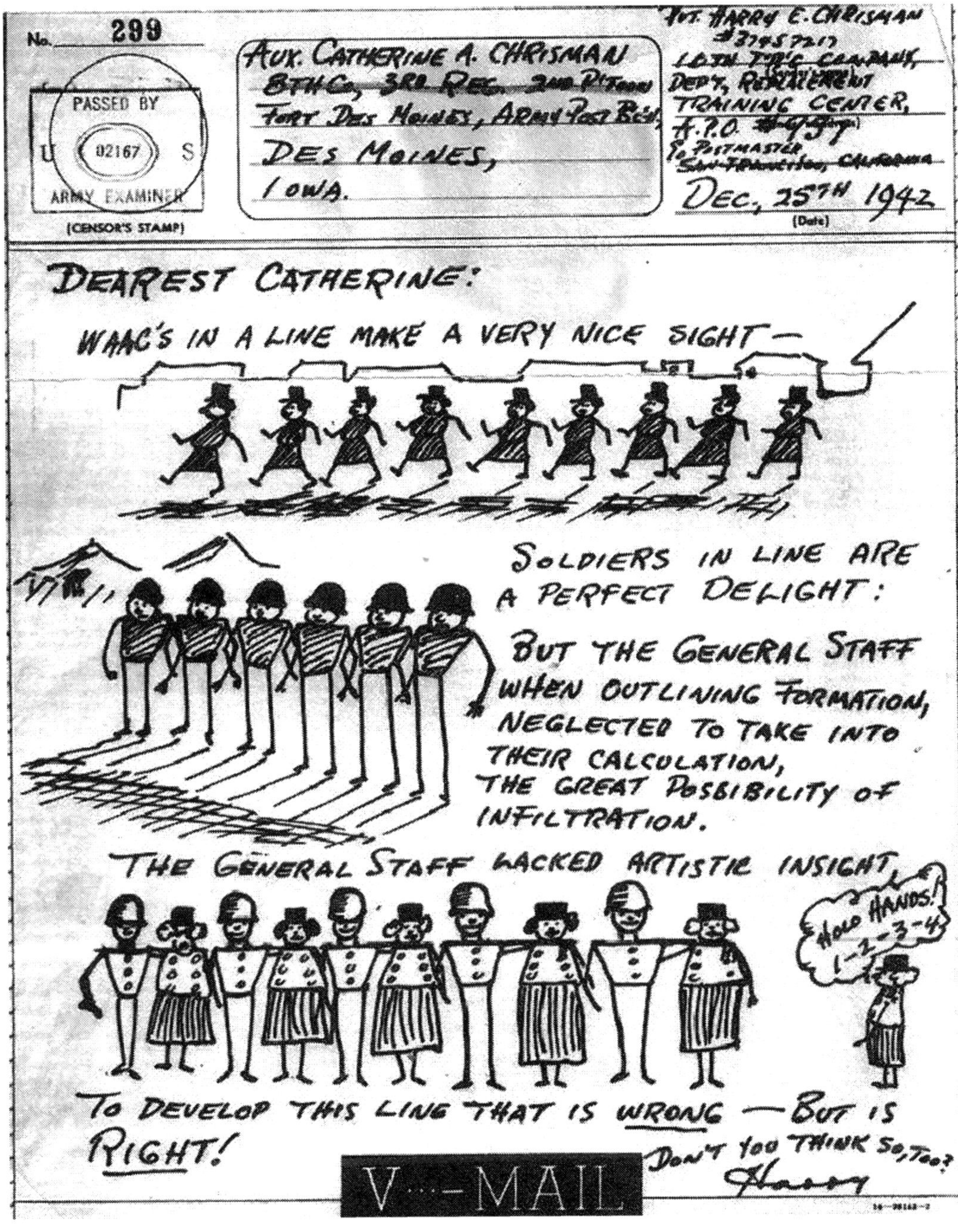
No. 299

PASSED BY
U 02167 S
ARMY EXAMINER
(CENSOR'S STAMP)

AUX. CATHERINE A. CHRISMAN
FORT DES MOINES, ARMY POST BR.,
DES MOINES,
IOWA.

PVT. HARRY E. CHRISMAN
TRAINING CENTER,
A.P.O.
DEC, 25TH 1942
(Date)

DEAREST CATHERINE:

WAAC'S IN A LINE MAKE A VERY NICE SIGHT—

SOLDIERS IN LINE ARE A PERFECT DELIGHT:

BUT THE GENERAL STAFF WHEN OUTLINING FORMATION, NEGLECTED TO TAKE INTO THEIR CALCULATION, THE GREAT POSSIBILITY OF INFILTRATION.

THE GENERAL STAFF LACKED ARTISTIC INSIGHT,

HOLD HANDS! 1-2-3-4

TO DEVELOP THIS LINE THAT IS WRONG — BUT IS RIGHT!

DON'T YOU THINK SO, TOO?

Harry

V—MAIL

WACs in a Line-12-25-42

All of the sayings Harry wrote on this V-Mail were true. And he had yet to see a WAC. Catherine was the first woman from Scottsbluff, Nebraska, to join the Women's Army Auxiliary Corps (WAAC) and the second from that state. It wasn't long before Catherine became a member of the Women's Army Corps (WAC) rather than the WAAC. (S)

What Does a WAC Look Like? 1-27-43

Catherine knew Harry was at an island location somewhere in the Pacific because of the palm tree and the water movement onto the shore. She knew he was no longer in training camp because of the change in the APO (Army Post Office) address. She always wanted to go to Hawaii and see where Harry had served but somehow they never got there. Harry had me take pictures of Sand Island and the bunkers and beaches of Maui when Don and I went there to celebrate our 25th anniversary. It was as though he could not experience "Island Fever" again just like he would never go camping again! We offered to take Catherine after Harry's death but she could not bear to go without him. (S)

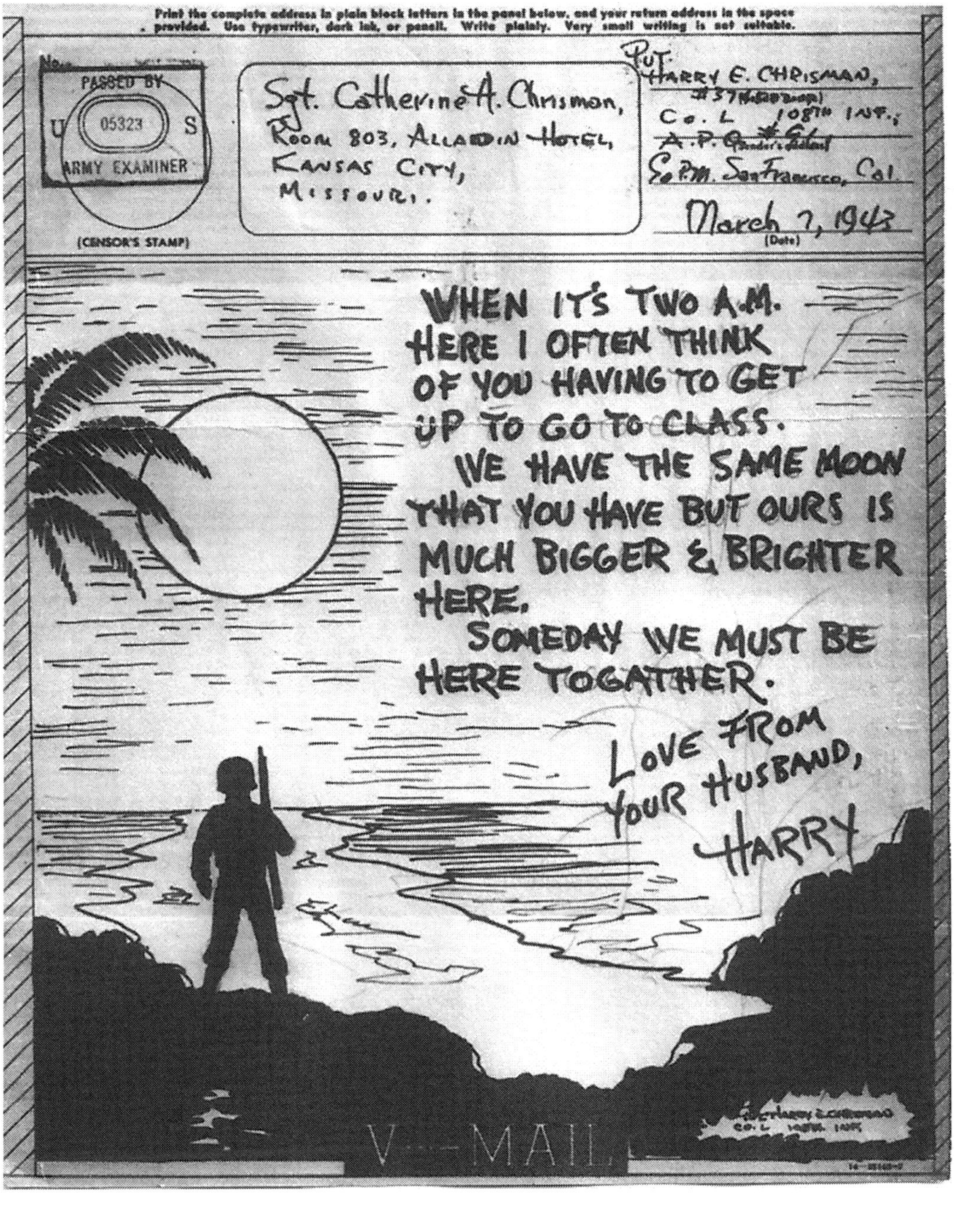

Print the complete address in plain block letters in the panel below, and your return address in the space provided. Use typewriter, dark ink, or pencil. Write plainly. Very small writing is not suitable.

No.

PASSED BY
U 05323 S
ARMY EXAMINER

(CENSOR'S STAMP)

Sgt. Catherine A. Chrisman,
Room 803, Alladin Hotel,
Kansas City,
Missouri.

Pvt. Harry E. Chrisman,
Co. L 108th Inf.,
A.P.O.
c/o P.M. San Francisco, Cal

March 7, 1943
(Date)

WHEN IT'S TWO A.M.
HERE I OFTEN THINK
OF YOU HAVING TO GET
UP TO GO TO CLASS.
WE HAVE THE SAME MOON
THAT YOU HAVE BUT OURS IS
MUCH BIGGER & BRIGHTER
HERE.
SOMEDAY WE MUST BE
HERE TOGATHER.

LOVE FROM
YOUR HUSBAND,
HARRY

V-MAIL

When It's Two AM 3-7-43

This was not only an item of interest, but an indication to Catherine that Harry was going to another station. The sailor in the center of all the G.I.s was a signal that he would probably be going somewhere on a ship. His next cartoon V-Mail listed him in the 108th instead of 102nd so she knew he was probably in a different location. Although she did not know this at the time, he had volunteered for the Birch Task Force and was headed to Christmas Island, one of the Line Islands off the coast of Australia. It was feared that the Japanese might try to use these islands as refueling points for both aircraft and ships. Christmas Island had an airfield and a harbor, perfect for both functions.

In October 1942, the United States Army placed a contingent of twenty-five engineers on Christmas Island in order that they might build an airfield. They had several graders plus other equipment they might need to build the field. Christmas Island was occupied at that time, but after the bombing of Pearl Harbor the civilians were evacuated. The Corps of Engineers remained and served duty after the Birch Task Force arrived in the summer of 1943. (S)

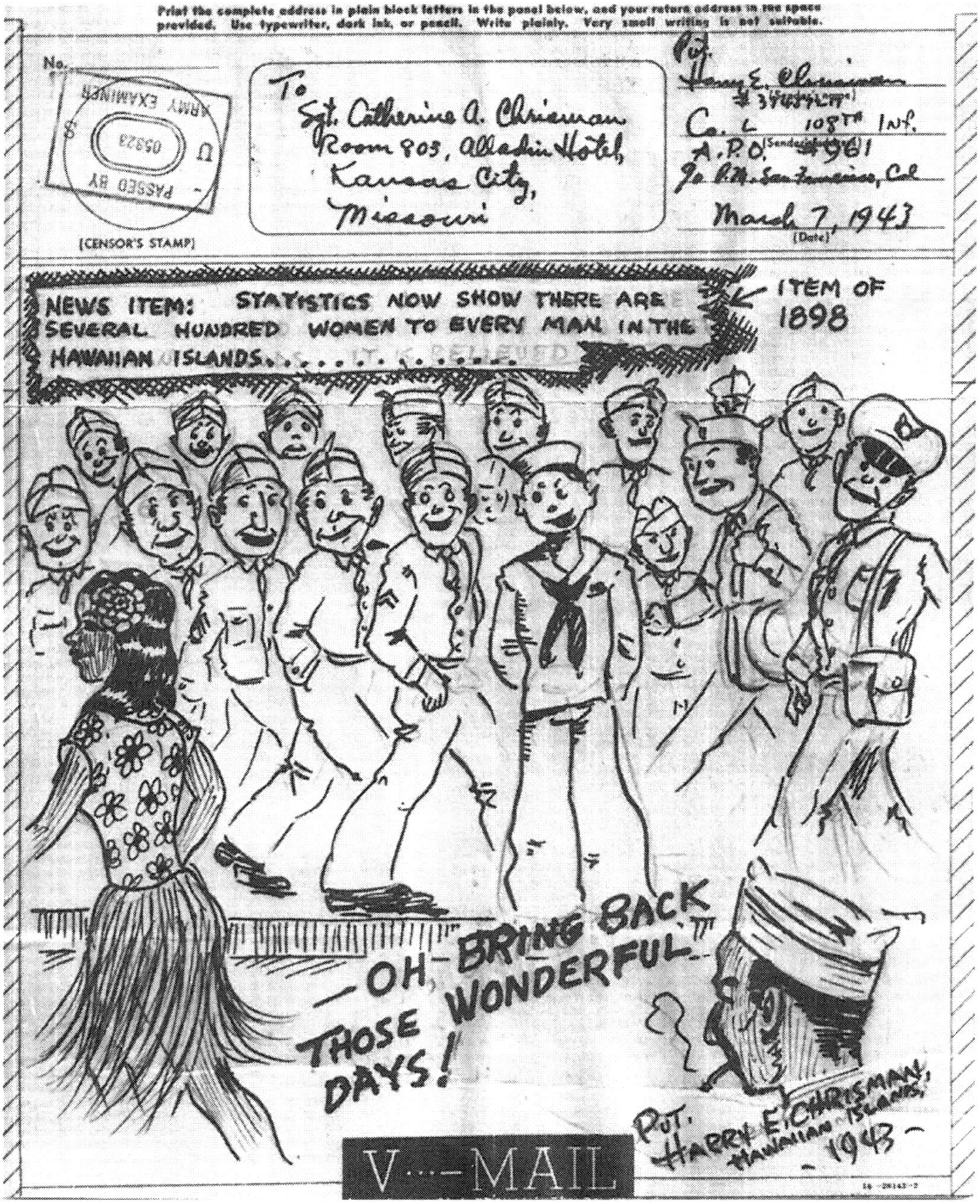
Print the complete address in plain block letters in the panel below, and your return address in the space provided. Use typewriter, dark ink, or pencil. Write plainly. Very small writing is not suitable.
No.
PASSED BY ARMY EXAMINER 05323
(CENSOR'S STAMP)
To Sgt. Catherine A. Chrisman
Room 803, Alladin Hotel,
Kansas City,
Missouri
Co. L 108th Inf.
A.P.O. #961
March 7, 1943
(Date)
NEWS ITEM: STATISTICS NOW SHOW THERE ARE SEVERAL HUNDRED WOMEN TO EVERY MAN IN THE HAWAIIAN ISLANDS.........
ITEM OF 1898
—OH, BRING BACK THOSE WONDERFUL DAYS!
PVT. HARRY E. CHRISMAN, HAWAIIAN ISLANDS, 1943
V-—MAIL

Item of 1898 3-7-43

The first impression of Christmas Island as we approached it that morning of March 26, 1943 was of a flat line of coral on the horizon, bedecked with a fringe of the greenest of green coconut fronds, and with a background of gigantic cumulus clouds forming in the east. The sea was a deep blue, that contrasted greatly with the pale green of the large inner lagoon as we approached closer. A trade wind of about twenty-five miles per hour wafted to us the scent of land as we sailed in from the northwest and took a position some mile or so westward from the single harbor, a place they called London town. South from the port city, across the neck of the lagoon, was the place known to the local population as "Paris." (H)

This is the first V-Mail Harry sent from Christmas Island. The APO (Army/Air Post Office) number for there was 915. Harry's family knew by the number change that he was in a different location, but did not know where. Catherine's address is marked out and the V-Mail forwarded. She had joined the WAC and was inducted in Kansas City, MO, and then trained at Fort Des Moines, Iowa, and at Daytona Beach, FL, before being sent to Victorville, CA. She loved the WAC and felt she was doing her part for the war effort while still able to support her mother. (S)

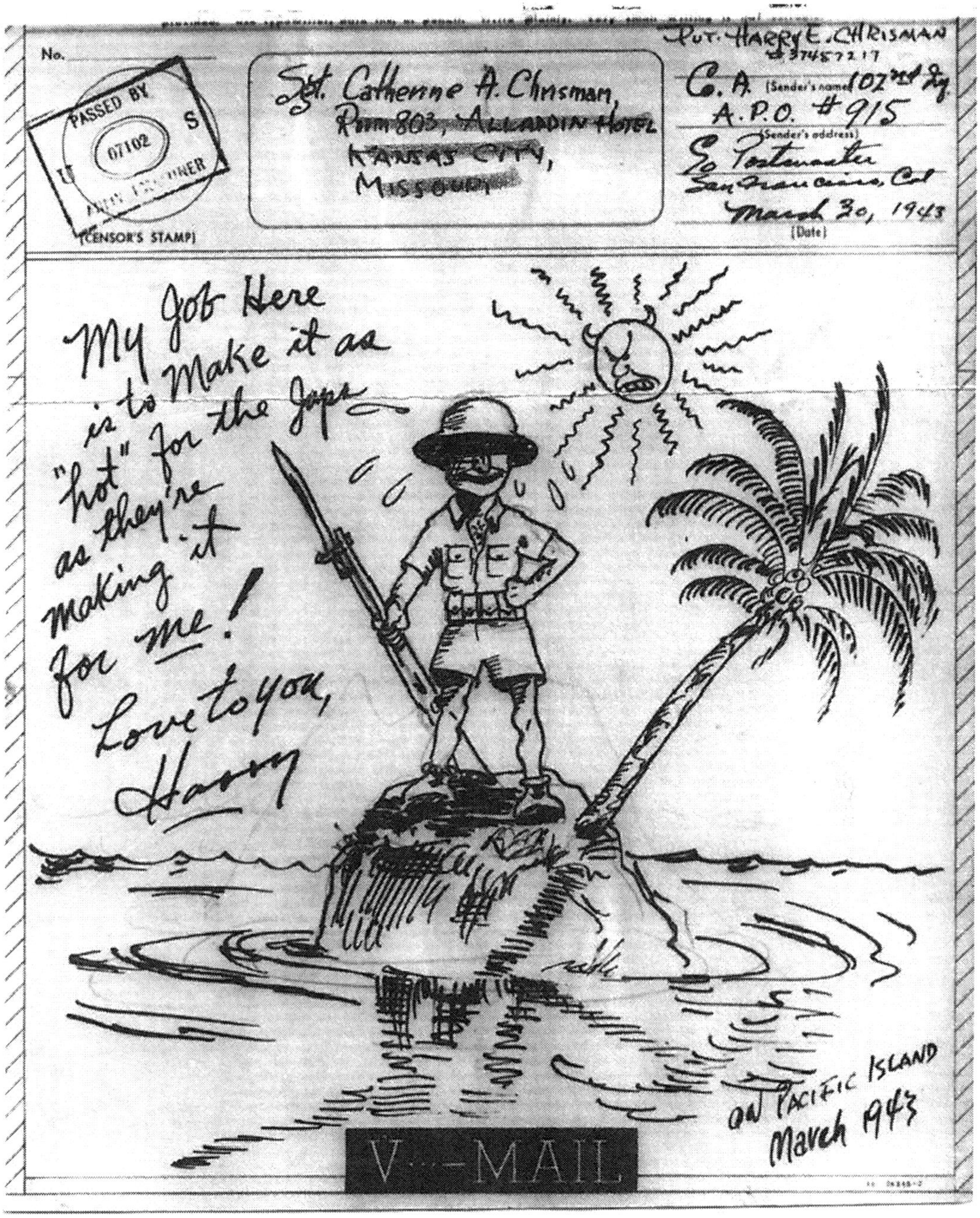
No.
PASSED BY
U S
07102
(CENSOR'S STAMP)
Sgt. Catherine A. Chrisman,
Kansas City,
Missouri
Pvt. Harry E. Chrisman
C.A. (Sender's name) 102nd Inf.
A.P.O. #915
(Sender's address)
c/o Postmaster
San Francisco, Cal
March 30, 1943
(Date)
My Job Here is to Make it as "hot" for the Japs as they're making it for me!
Love to you,
Harry
On Pacific Island
March 1943
V-MAIL

On Pacific Island 3-30-43

The letter in Harry's hands reads, "Dances, parties, and formals." Harry was a jealous husband and it shows in this V-Mail. Notice the change from "Sgt." to "Cpl." in the address. Catherine was only a temporary sergeant, which Harry knew, but he did not approve of her attending the camp shindigs. All of the V-Mails were sent on to Harry's mother for safe-keeping and she was upset and disappointed with her son for berating Catherine. She sent him a letter really chewing him out, explaining that Catherine needed her fun and entertainment just as he did. Harry told me his ears stung for a week after that letter and he apologized to Catherine in a long letter of his own.

But for a while Catherine ceased going to the camp dances and get-togethers until one of her officers asked her why she chose to stay in the barracks rather than attend a dance. "I'm married," said Catherine. "Most of us are," the officer replied, "but that doesn't mean we can't enjoy ourselves a bit just going to a dance. It doesn't mean anything but a twirl or two around the floor." (S)

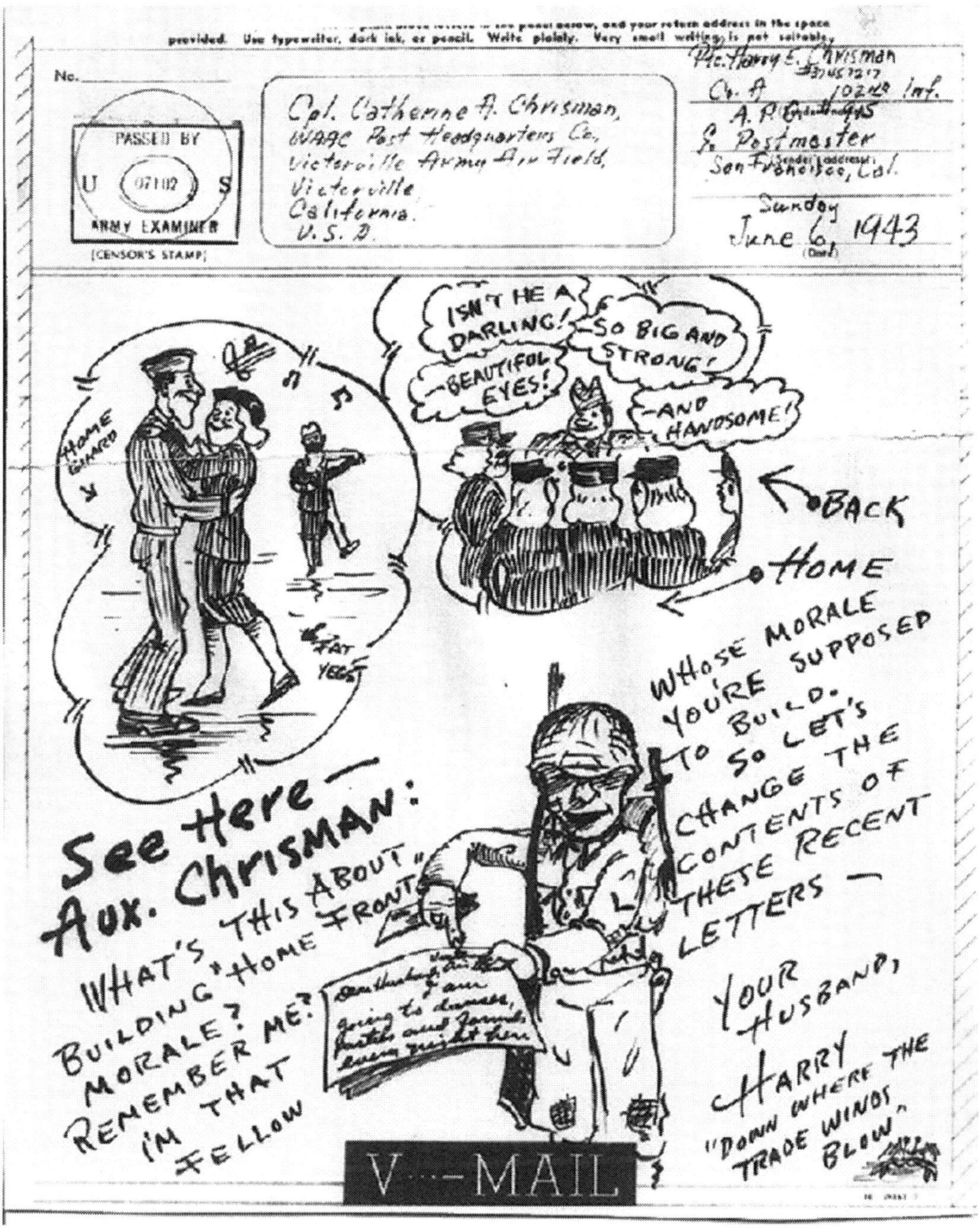
provided. Use typewriter, dark ink, or pencil. Write plainly. Very small writing is not suitable.
No.
PASSED BY
U S
ARMY EXAMINER
(CENSOR'S STAMP)
Cpl. Catherine A. Chrisman,
WAAC Post Headquarters Co.,
Victorville Army Air Field,
Victorville
California.
U.S.A.
Pfc. Harry E. Chrisman
Co. A 102nd Inf.
A.P.O.
% Postmaster
San Francisco, Cal.
Sunday
June 6, 1943
ISN'T HE A DARLING!
SO BIG AND STRONG!
BEAUTIFUL EYES!
AND HANDSOME!
HOME GUARD
FAT YEGG
BACK HOME
See Here — Aux. Chrisman:
WHAT'S THIS ABOUT BUILDING "HOME FRONT" MORALE? REMEMBER ME? I'M THAT FELLOW WHOSE MORALE YOU'RE SUPPOSED TO BUILD. SO LET'S CHANGE THE CONTENTS OF THESE RECENT LETTERS —
YOUR HUSBAND,
Harry
"DOWN WHERE THE TRADE WINDS BLOW"
V-MAIL

See Here 6-6-43

Harry and Catherine's song was "Paradise," written in 1931 by Nacio Herb Brown, a movie songwriter, and Gordon Clifford, a lyricist. It was featured in a 1932 film, "A Woman Commands." The lyrics said it all:

> *And then she holds my hand, mm mm mm mm,*
> *And then I understand, mm mm mm mm,*
> *Her eyes afire with one desire,*
> *Then a heavenly kiss;*
> *Could I resist?*
>
> *And then she dims the light, mm, mm, mm, mm*
> *And then she holds me tight, mm, mm, mm, mm*
> *Her kiss each fond caress,*
> *They lead the way to happiness,*
> *She takes me to Paradise.*

It was recorded by many artists, including Nat King Cole, Bing Crosby, and Frank Sinatra.

Harry often sang it while he worked at his desk years later. He helped one of the engineers on base build a radio station on Christmas Island. They hooked into the radio tower on the airfield and ran the wire to the clerk's hut. Harry took his turn as D.J. several nights a week. During daylight working hours, the station would only broadcast emergency information; but at night, they could broadcast music and news. (S)

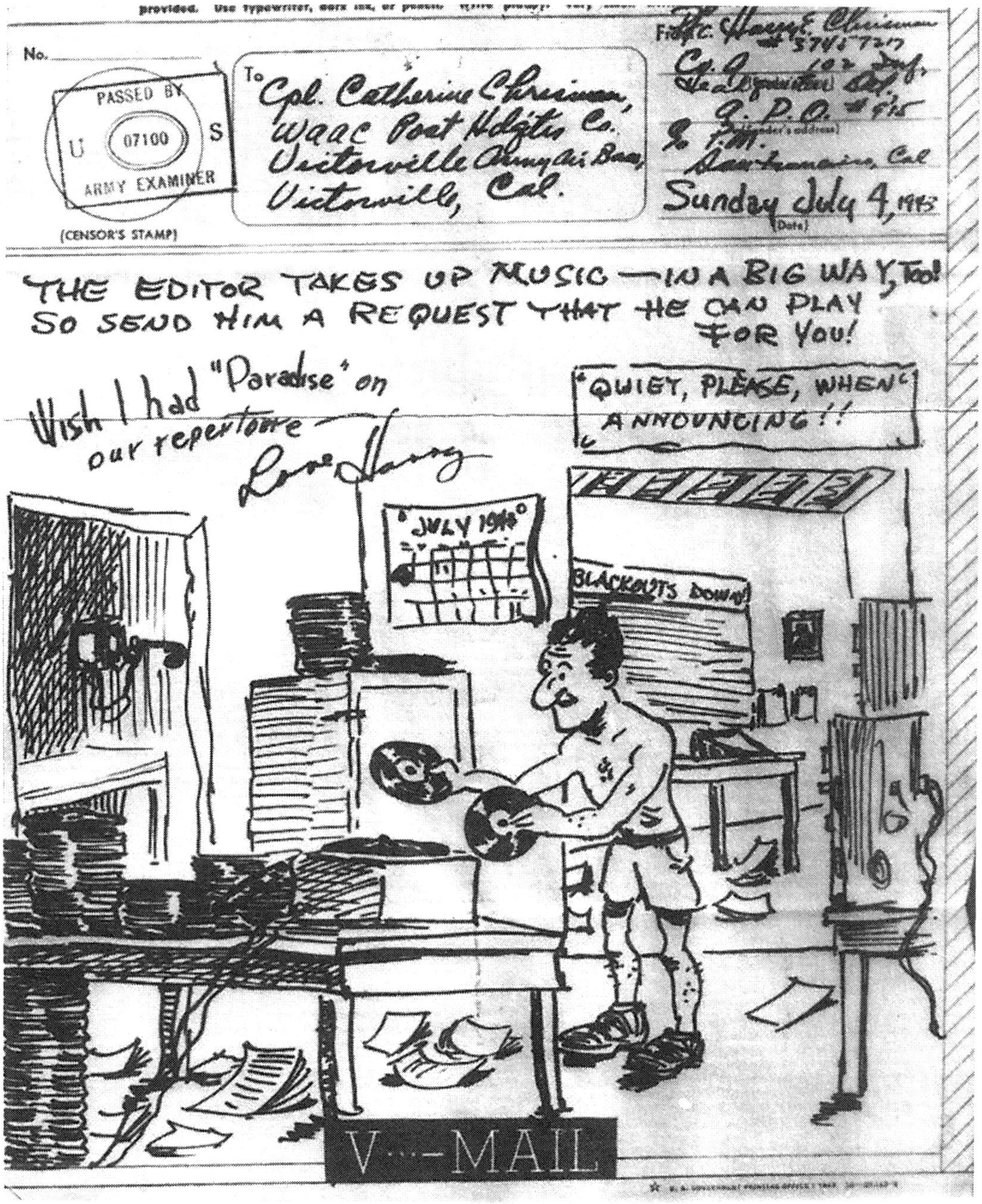
No.
PASSED BY
U 07100 S
ARMY EXAMINER
(CENSOR'S STAMP)
To Cpl. Catherine Chreiman,
WAAC Post Hdqtrs Co.
Victorville Army Air Base,
Victorville, Cal.
Sunday July 4, 1943
(Date)
THE EDITOR TAKES UP MUSIC — IN A BIG WAY, Too!
SO SEND HIM A REQUEST THAT HE CAN PLAY FOR YOU!
Wish I had "Paradise" on our repertoire —
Love Harry
"QUIET, PLEASE, WHEN ANNOUNCING!!
JULY 1943
BLACKOUTS DOWN!
V---MAIL

Music-Radio 7-4-43

Catherine sent Harry a new radio from Victorville using money she and Harry's family saved for it, as they knew that he loved music almost as much as he loved Catherine. Sixty dollars was a lot of money since both Harry and Catherine supported their mothers. Harry's pay base for overseas duty was about $60 a month, Catherine's was $50. The G.I.s could pick up music and even Tokyo Rose on that radio! (S)

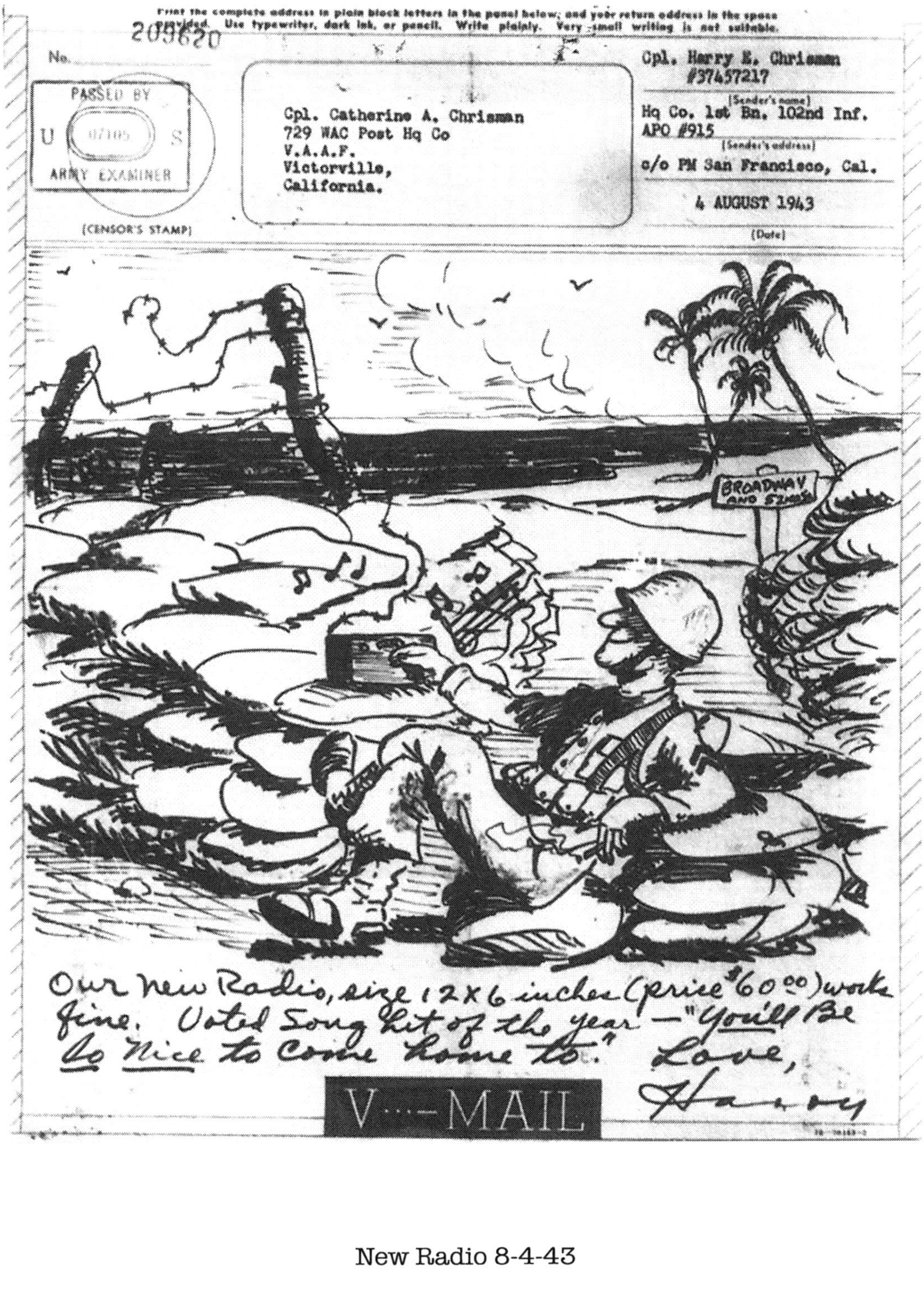

Print the complete address in plain block letters in the panel below, and your return address in the space provided. Use typewriter, dark ink, or pencil. Write plainly. Very small writing is not suitable.

No. 209620

PASSED BY
U 07105 S
ARMY EXAMINER

(CENSOR'S STAMP)

Cpl. Catherine A. Chrisman
729 WAC Post Hq Co
V.A.A.F.
Victorville,
California.

Cpl. Harry E. Chrisman
#37457217
(Sender's name)
Hq Co. 1st Bn. 102nd Inf.
APO #915
(Sender's address)
c/o PM San Francisco, Cal.

4 AUGUST 1943
(Date)

BROADWAY
AND 52ND

Our new Radio, size 12 X 6 inches (price $60.00) works fine. Voted Song hit of the year — "You'll Be So Nice to Come home to." Love,
Harry

V···—MAIL

New Radio 8-4-43

Harry really thought he would move up quickly to Sgt., but several blocks were put in his way. At his interview for Officer Training School (OTS), before basic training, he thought a general wanted a true answer to a question about the railroad in Harry's hometown when in reality he wanted agreement with his statement. Harry and Catherine both felt this episode followed Harry throughout his Army career. And, any CO who had a G.I. on his staff who could type, draw, write, and knew how to layout a newspaper or newsletter made sure that man stayed on his staff. Many COs (often referred to as "90-day wonders") were jerked from well-paying office jobs and sent to out-of-the-way assignments. Many were unhappy and really didn't care if their men did anything but make them look good. (See "Song of the Engineers" in Volume One of this series, This is the Army, Mr. Jones!*) Catherine talked with me at length about this after Harry died. Whether the interview misstep followed him or not, it took him a bit longer than Catherine to get his third stripe, and only temporary ones at that until 1945. (S)*

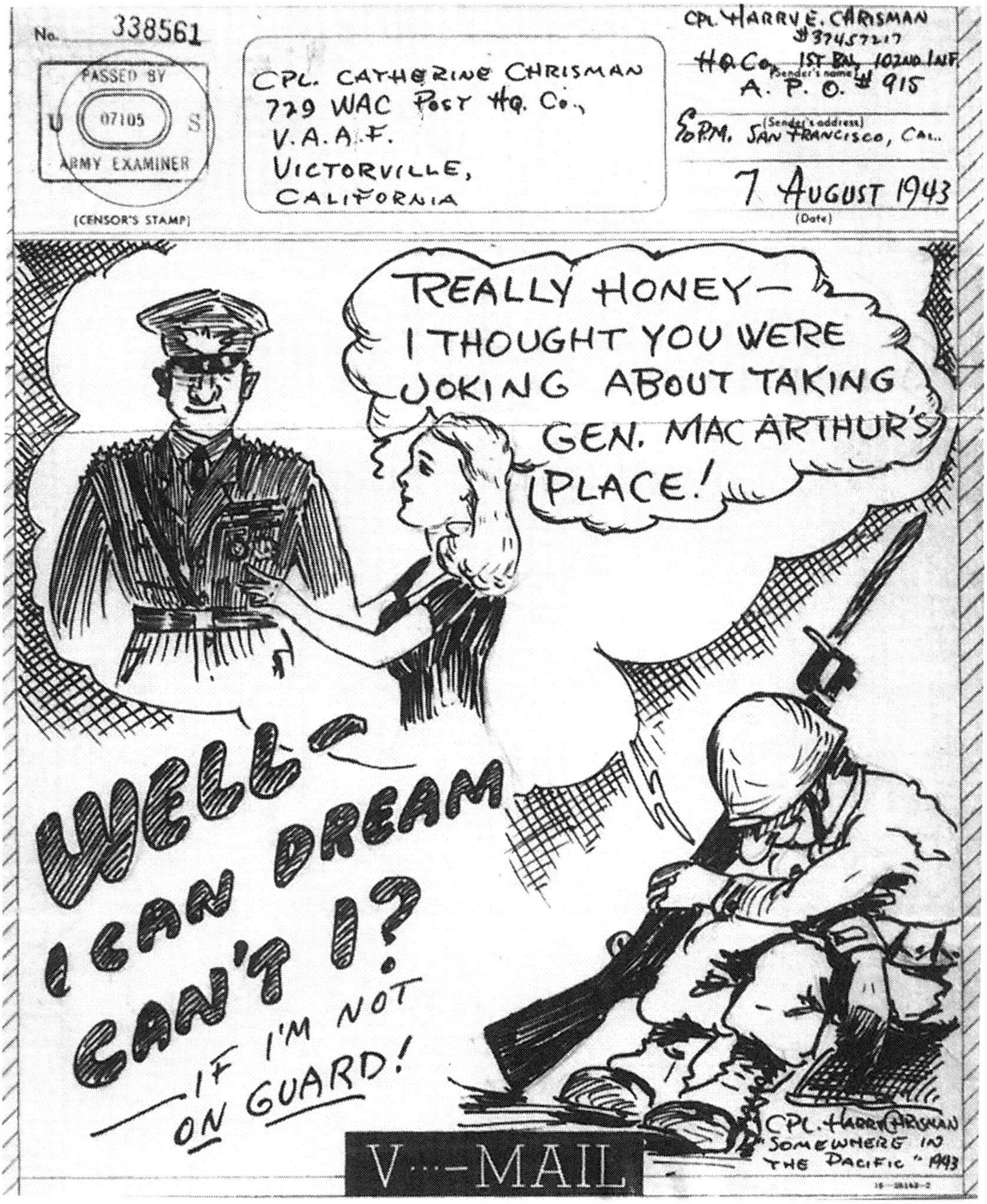
No. 338561
PASSED BY
U 07105 S
ARMY EXAMINER
(CENSOR'S STAMP)
CPL. CATHERINE CHRISMAN
729 WAC POST HQ. CO.,
V.A.A.F.
VICTORVILLE,
CALIFORNIA
CPL. HARRY E. CHRISMAN
#37457217
HQ. CO. 1ST BN. 102ND INF.
(Sender's name)
A. P. O. # 915
% P.M. SAN FRANCISCO, CAL.
(Sender's address)
7 AUGUST 1943
(Date)
REALLY HONEY— I THOUGHT YOU WERE JOKING ABOUT TAKING GEN. MAC ARTHUR'S PLACE!
WELL— I CAN DREAM CAN'T I?
—IF I'M NOT ON GUARD!
V···–MAIL
CPL. HARRY CHRISMAN
"SOMEWHERE IN THE PACIFIC" 1943

Well I Can Dream-8-7-43

Harry was proud of Catherine and readily showed her picture to his fellow G.I.s. Their envy and admiration was apparent when Catherine was nominated for camp sweetheart. Harry was greatly upset about this and in turn nominated Catherine's best friend, Rose Aisenberg. His vote for Rose broke a tie between the two. I asked Harry once why he voted against his wife. "Well," he said in a rather gruff voice, "every time a G.I. passes the camp sweetheart picture they reach out and pat her someplace, usually on the rump. No one pats my wife but me, especially there!" I queried no further. (S)

Dream About Your Own Girl 9-12-43

This picture and article about Rose was printed in the Victorville, California paper.
Don and I met Rose and her husband, Dr. George Markham, a year or so after
Harry died. Rose was still a beauty in 1995! (S)

VICTORVILLE ARMY AIR FIELD

Wac Corporal Here Chosen
Queen of Gooneybird Island

"Gooneybird" Island of the Pacific is in the war zone.

Nevertheless, the men of Gooneybird in keeping with the custom of other soldiers have chosen themselves a pin-up girl——

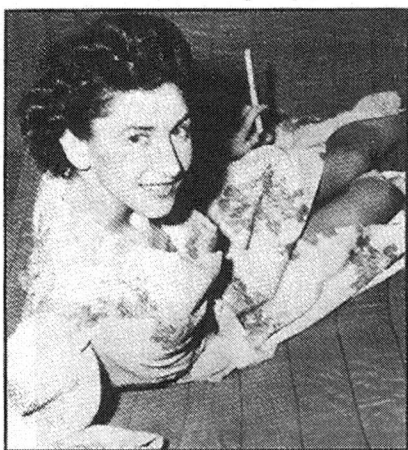

"THE BLUSHING ROSE"

none other than Cpl. Rose Aisenberg, the little lady who answers the phone when you buzz "locator file."

Rose, sweet and demure, was at first loath to release this information to the GI press, and it was only upon persistent demand of her closest associates that she finally consented to publication of the document that has marked her as "one above the others."

The letter which set Cpl. Aisenberg on the pedestal along with such immortals in the art of pleasing the eyes as Hayworth, Rogers and Lamarr follows:

Gooneybird Island,
West Point of the Pacific.

Dear Corporal Aisenberg:

In a contest conducted to determine an Island Pinup Girl—"The Girl With Whom We Would Rather Sweat Out Our Time Here"—you were chosen to fill the position.

Your friend Cpl. Catherine Chrisman of your organization ran you a close second. You were victorious by a single vote--a ballot cast by Cpl. Harry Chrisman, husband of the runner-up. In swinging the contest in your favor, the Corporal went on record as saying, "My wife will love me anyway, and this will mean much both in prestige and self-confidence to Cpl. Aisenberg."

We express our best wishes to you in your victory over all the charmers in Hollywood and in the nation. Imprinted herewith please find the Medal awarded you for your significant achievement.

Signed: Sgt. A.J. Grissilo, Judge of Personality, Head & Shoulders. T/Sgt. L. Hollis Blake, Judge of Torso, Frontal and Posterior; Sgt. R.H. Duquette, Judge of Arms, Limbs and Pedal Extremities.

Rose Aisenberg, Camp Sweetheart - 1943

These are places Harry and Catherine managed to visit before they joined the Army. They had gone together for ten years before they were able to marry since each was the sole support of their parents. They spent their three-day honeymoon at Lake Minatare, a large multi-use lake to the east of Scottsbluff, Nebraska. We drove by it when we took Harry and Catherine on a trip to Broken Bow, Nebraska, to his class reunion in 1990. He never stopped talking the entire trip, pointing out landmarks, telling stories about the land and the people. It was a four-day history lesson! (S)

Things We Could Be Doing 9-14-43

Catherine wrote to Harry every day telling him what she was doing, describing the desert around her, the women she worked with, etc. Most of her letters he could not keep because of space. Any that he was able to return to her, or those Harry was able to carry home, she destroyed after his death, and she also destroyed the ones he sent her. She told me they were personal and not for other eyes. But she did include the following one in her book, My War:

> *My Beloved Husband,*
>
> *The sun hasn't really shone for me since the day you went away—even though it's 110 degrees outside. But the Sun I speak of may never shine again, nor come from behind the clouds that have dimmed its splendor since you left me. For all the deep inner satisfactions of my life went with you. I have the usual outer pleasures, of course, but I never really laugh with all my heart anymore. For the happy, carefree, interested and alive side of me has remained in cold storage more than two years now, awaiting your return. No other person could ever possess me as you do.*
>
> *Yet I have gained something from this experience. I now have a part of you within me. I can keep it forever, come what may. I share every beautiful thought and sight with you. You laugh with me at the silly happenings of each day. I still hold your hand during the tender places in motion pictures, and I get angry along with you at the injustices I see in the world.*
>
> *I have learned that I can live this way, even enjoy life without your physical presence beside me, for I know that you are here, always with me in spirit. I know that when we grow older, and if I should lose you in death, I can go on without you, and still have you beside me every hour of every day and every night, for...*
>
> *"You Are Always In My Heart,"*
> *Catherine*

Catherine showed me this letter, written on her own stationery, and asked if I thought she should include it in her book. I said yes. At Catherine's funeral a niece told me, "They never needed anyone else, just each other." And so it was. (S)

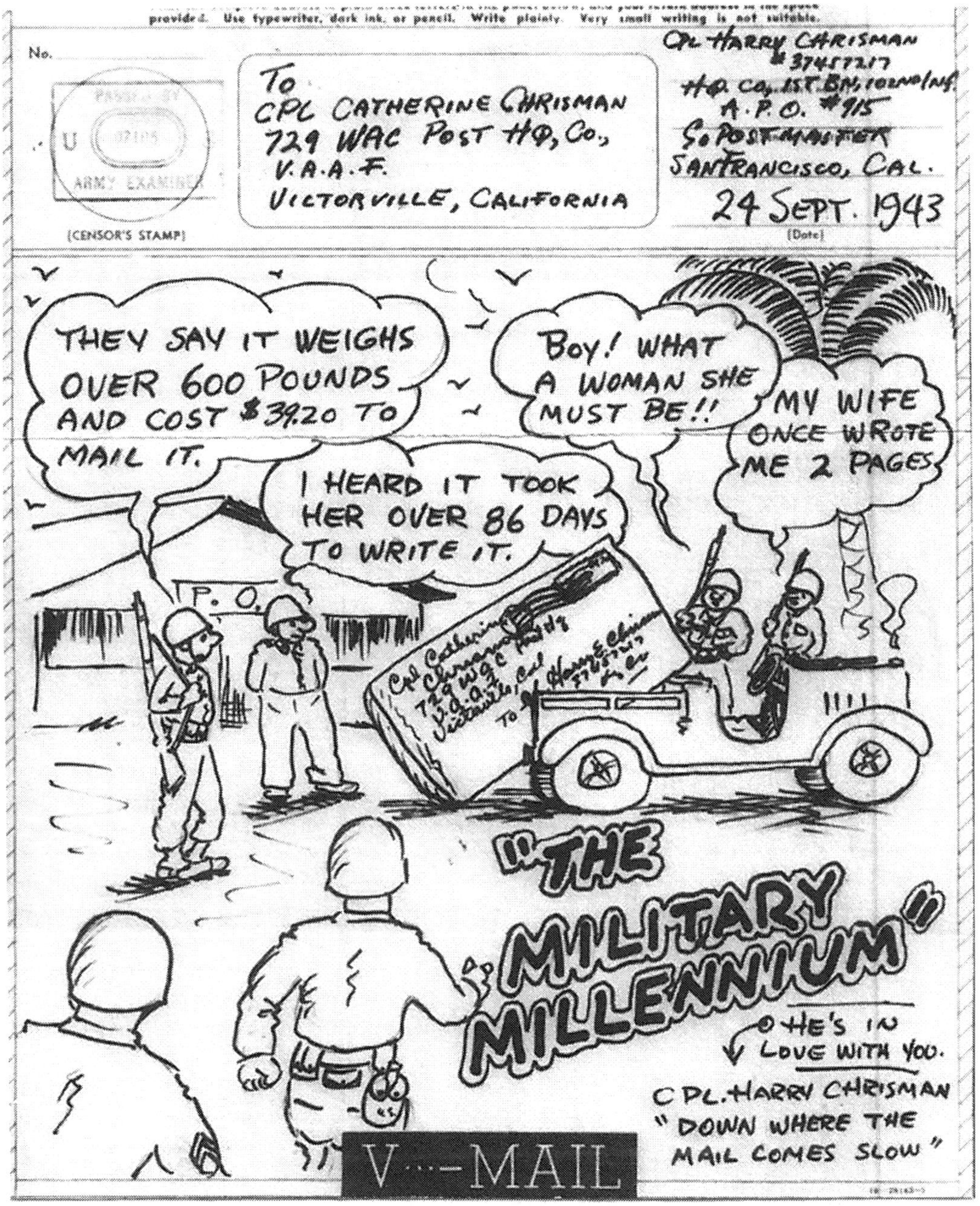

provided. Use typewriter, dark ink, or pencil. Write plainly. Very small writing is not suitable.
No.
(CENSOR'S STAMP)
ARMY EXAMINER
TO
CPL CATHERINE CHRISMAN
729 WAC POST HQ, CO.,
V.A.A.F.
VICTORVILLE, CALIFORNIA
CPL HARRY CHRISMAN
#37457217
HQ. CO. 1ST BN, 102ND INF.
A.P.O. #915
% POSTMASTER
SANFRANCISCO, CAL.
24 SEPT. 1943
(Date)
THEY SAY IT WEIGHS OVER 600 POUNDS AND COST $39.20 TO MAIL IT.
I HEARD IT TOOK HER OVER 86 DAYS TO WRITE IT.
BOY! WHAT A WOMAN SHE MUST BE!!
MY WIFE ONCE WROTE ME 2 PAGES
P. O.
"THE MILITARY MILLENNIUM"
HE'S IN LOVE WITH YOU.
CPL. HARRY CHRISMAN
"DOWN WHERE THE MAIL COMES SLOW"
V-MAIL

Military Millennium 9-24-43

Christmas Mail always came early—in October and November. By Christmas Day, everything had been eaten or worn out. Cathy returned this so I could see how red ink reproduced. It is good I think, much better than black or blue ink. (H)

Harry received many packages, especially for Christmas. Many of his fellow G.I.s did not. Harry took great pleasure in sharing the bounty, especially the food. But he also received writing and painting tools and books. He loved the books and these too were shared. The painting and writing tools he carefully guarded. (S)

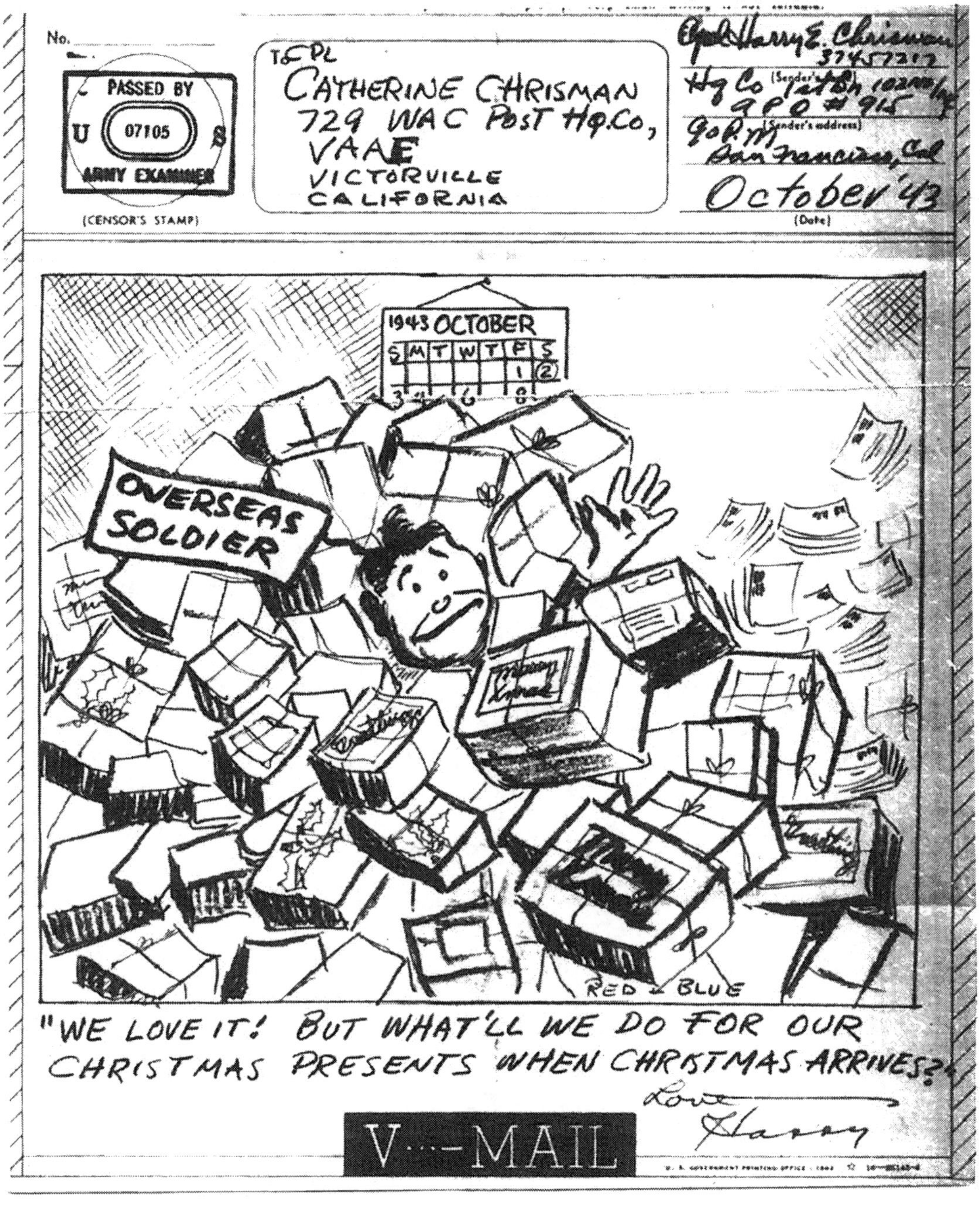

No.
PASSED BY
U 07105 S
ARMY EXAMINER
(CENSOR'S STAMP)
TO CPL
CATHERINE CHRISMAN
729 WAC POST HQ.CO,
VAAF
VICTORVILLE
CALIFORNIA
(Sender's name)
(Sender's address)
October '43
(Date)
1943 OCTOBER
S M T W T F S
OVERSEAS SOLDIER
RED & BLUE
"WE LOVE IT! BUT WHAT'LL WE DO FOR OUR CHRISTMAS PRESENTS WHEN CHRISTMAS ARRIVES?"
Love
Harry
V-MAIL

Packages 10-4-43

This cartoon was drawn and sent to Catherine on their 1st anniversary, a date Harry never forgot. They came to my house for dinner on their 50th anniversary and talked about how difficult those days of separation were. (S)

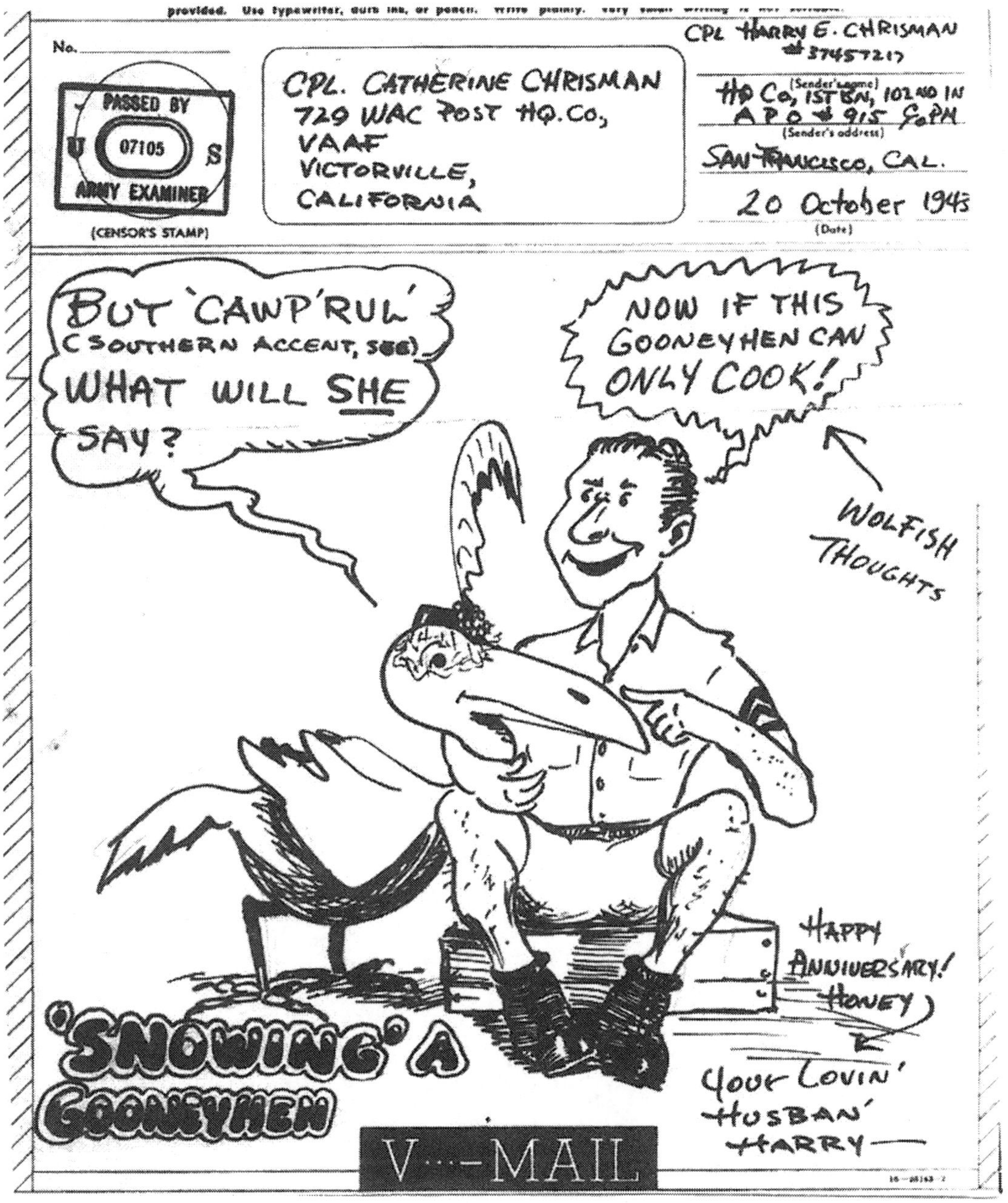
No.
PASSED BY
U 07105 S
ARMY EXAMINER
(CENSOR'S STAMP)
CPL. CATHERINE CHRISMAN
729 WAC POST HQ.Co,
VAAF
VICTORVILLE,
CALIFORNIA
CPL HARRY E. CHRISMAN
#37457217
HQ Co, 1ST BN, 102ND IN
(Sender's name)
APO #915 %PM
(Sender's address)
SAN FRANCISCO, CAL.
20 October 1943
(Date)
BUT 'CAWP'RUL' (SOUTHERN ACCENT, SEE) WHAT WILL SHE SAY?
NOW IF THIS GOONEYHEN CAN ONLY COOK!
WOLFISH THOUGHTS
HAPPY ANNIVERSARY! HONEY
YOUR LOVIN' HUSBAN' HARRY
'SNOWING' A GOONEYHEN
V...-MAIL

Snowing a Gooneyhen 10-20-43

This V-Mail was asking for forgiveness and as usual Harry wrote a poem and hoped that Catherine would understand what he was saying. She did. All I knew about this one is that she sent him that wonderful love letter trying to reassure him of her love then and always, and it reached Harry in time for their first anniversary. Harry was a smart fellow and decided that his southern gooneyhen V-Mail was not quite what a first anniversary called for. (S)

GREMLINS is difficult to read so the transcript follows:

> *"GREMLINS IS WONDERFUL PEOPLE!!"*
>   A GREMLIN, IN A DREAM LAST NIGHT,
>   HELPED ME CORRECT AN OVERSIGHT,
>   AND (FOR THAT SHORT "HEN-PECKY" KISS;
>   THAT ONCE CONVEYED "GOODNIGHT, SWEET MISS)
>   OFFERED TO ME SUFFICIENT TIME
>   TO COMPENSATE MY TURBID MIND
>   FOR FAILING IN MY OVERSIGHT
>   TO PROPERLY <u>KISS MY WIFE</u> GOODNIGHT.
>   SO, QUITE AS SOON AS I'D PERCEIVED
>   OF WHICH HE SPOKE, MY HEART CONCEIVED
>   OF ALL I'D MISSED IN MY PAST LIFE
>   FOR FAILING TO KISS MY DEAREST WIFE......

Two lower lines:

> THIS V-MAIL ESTABLISHES CONTINUITY.
> I KISS YOU <u>NOW</u> <u>IN PERPETUITY</u>.

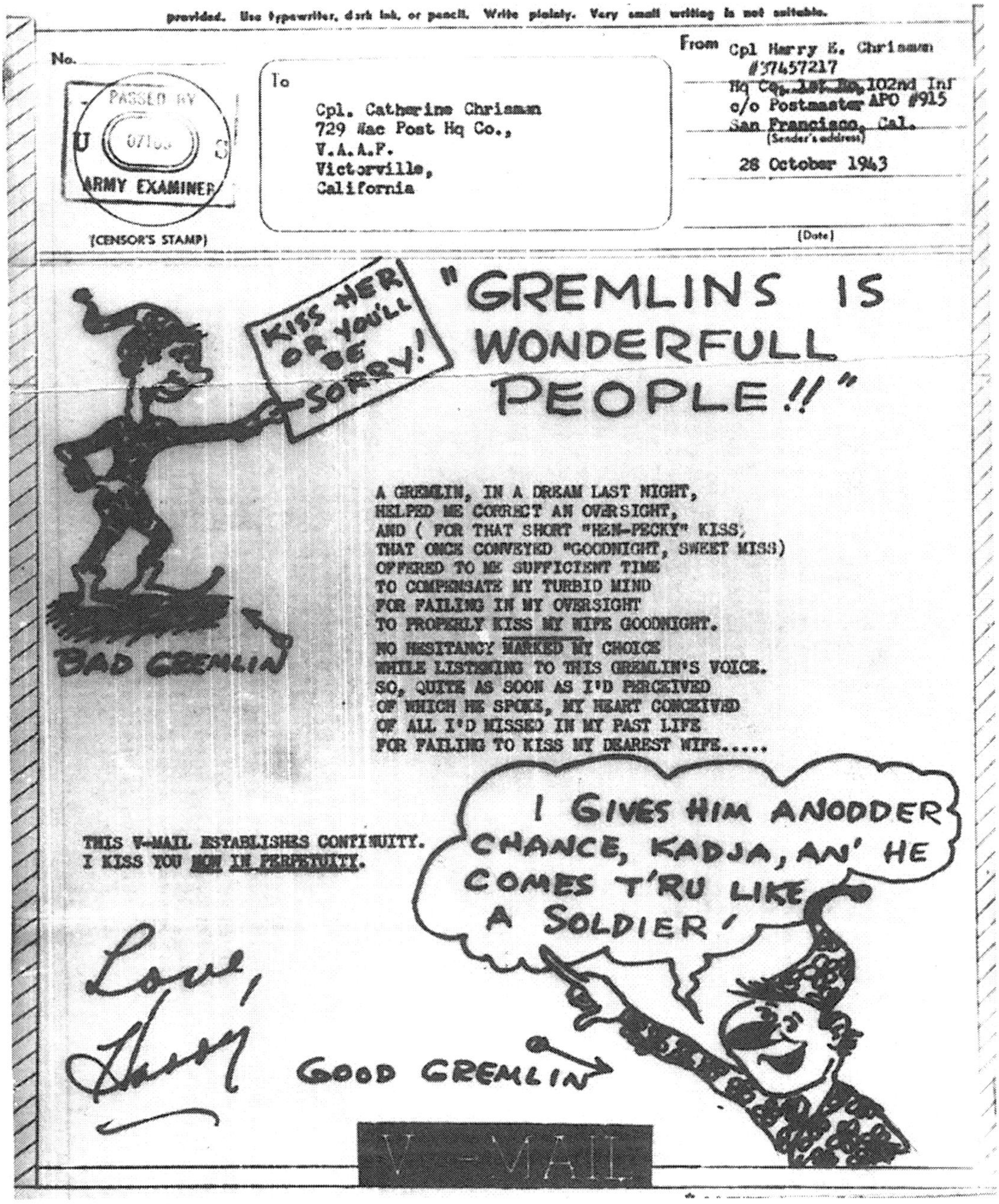

provided. Use typewriter, dark ink, or pencil. Write plainly. Very small writing is not suitable.

No.

PASSED BY
U 07165 S
ARMY EXAMINER

(CENSOR'S STAMP)

To

Cpl. Catherine Chrisman
729 Wac Post Hq Co.,
V.A.A.F.
Victorville,
California

From Cpl Harry E. Chrisman
#37457217
Hq Co. 1st Bn. 102nd Inf
c/o Postmaster APO #915
San Francisco, Cal.
(Sender's address)

28 October 1943

(Date)

KISS HER OR YOU'LL BE SORRY!

"GREMLINS IS WONDERFULL PEOPLE!!"

A GREMLIN, IN A DREAM LAST NIGHT,
HELPED ME CORRECT AN OVERSIGHT,
AND (FOR THAT SHORT "HEN-PECKY" KISS;
THAT ONCE CONVEYED "GOODNIGHT, SWEET MISS)
OFFERED TO ME SUFFICIENT TIME
TO COMPENSATE MY TURBID MIND
FOR FAILING IN MY OVERSIGHT
TO PROPERLY KISS MY WIFE GOODNIGHT.
NO HESITANCY MARKED MY CHOICE
WHILE LISTENING TO THIS GREMLIN'S VOICE.
SO, QUITE AS SOON AS I'D PERCEIVED
OF WHICH HE SPOKE, MY HEART CONCEIVED
OF ALL I'D MISSED IN MY PAST LIFE
FOR FAILING TO KISS MY DEAREST WIFE.....

BAD GREMLIN

I GIVES HIM ANODDER CHANCE, KADJA, AN' HE COMES T'RU LIKE A SOLDIER'

THIS V-MAIL ESTABLISHES CONTINUITY.
I KISS YOU NOW IN PERPETUITY.

Love,
Harry

GOOD GREMLIN

V-MAIL

Gremlins 10-28-43

Catherine wrote to Harry telling him she wanted to put in a request for overseas duty. They had agreed before she joined the WAAC that if he was overseas she could request duty there. She wanted to "See the Elephant," a term that meant she wanted to be a part of all the new activity going on all over the world. Going to "See the Elephant" was a term coined by gold-rushers and pioneers following the Oregon Trail. It was not just any elephant they wanted to see but the experience of new and even dangerous adventures.

Harry wrote: "Stay where you are well off. I have yet to meet anyone here who would not trade places with you on a moment's notice…Don't get adventuresome ideas about these faraway places. All too soon beauty here becomes as commonplace and boring as the charming and exotic desert scenes must have become to you."

The words to the poem he wrote are as follows:

YOU'LL BE SO – R – R – Y !!

Sung to "Put on Your Old Grey Bonnet"

A WAC sat in her lonesome barracks, about to give birth to hysterics
For she wished to travel more,
The Mail Call brought her one fat letter, from her husband who did "sweet her"
From a South Pacific shore.
Said the letter – Chorus:
You think you'd like foreign service and to trouble be impervious
But the truth is, once you've gone across,
There is no spot so glam'rous, so romantic and amorous as the land where you are boss!!
Repeat Chorus:
So put on your funny round bonnet, with the WAC insignia on it
And stay back there in the good old USA –
For there'll be no promotion this side of the ocean 'till our "Golden Wedding Day!"

As usual, Harry tried to convey his concern and dominance through humor. (S)

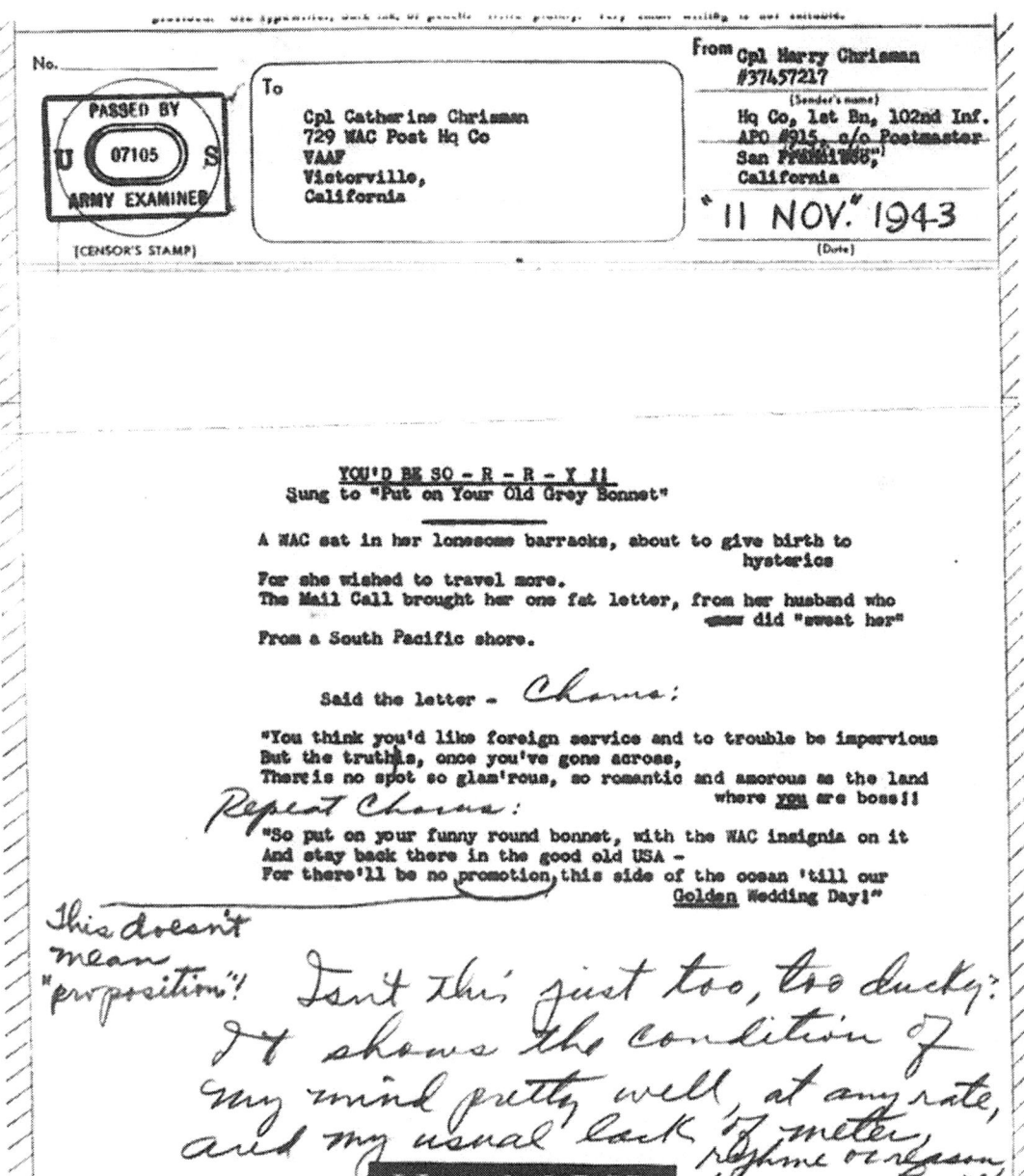

Harry again used humor and a bit of a threat in this V-Mail to convince Catherine not to go overseas. Since she wrote to him everyday, he got her letters saying she wanted to apply for that duty one after the other. His choice of the word "Overmanned", plus the drawing of only one woman apparently was meant to reassure her of his love for her. Hmmm.

In a letter he wrote: "I hate to threaten you, but if you wish to keep my respect, you will be more attentive of my wishes. So—if you go ahead in spite of my feelings, then file your divorce papers at the same time you make application and have them with you when you leaved the States."

Catherine told me she was shocked then mad when she got this letter. She never before had her feelings hurt by Harry and he promised she could go overseas. Needless to say she did not go overseas but chose to remain married to Harry. I asked him why he didn't want her to go overseas and he said, "I was afraid she might get killed." I replied, "Why didn't you tell her that?" He didn't answer but had the decency to look sheepish! I found myself angry for Catherine.

I talked with her about this letter and she said she had to decide what she wanted more, Harry or adventure. She took a long walk in the desert around Victorville Air Base and knew she had to decide what she wanted for the rest of her life, marriage or??? She chose Harry and said she never regretted it and they never spoke of this letter. But she did include excerpts of it in her book. (S)

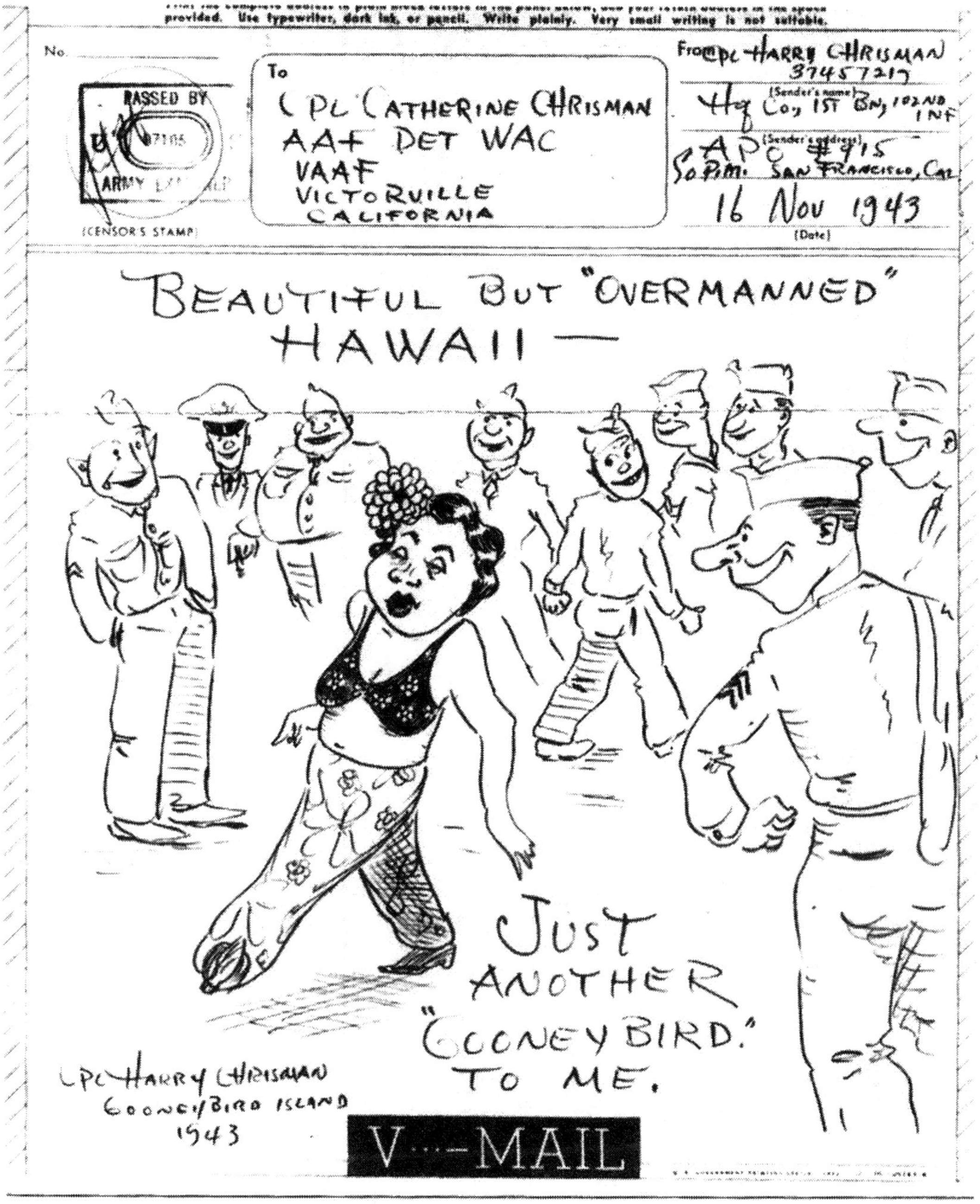
provided. Use typewriter, dark ink, or pencil. Write plainly. Very small writing is not suitable.
No.
PASSED BY
CENSOR'S STAMP
To
CPL CATHERINE CHRISMAN
AAF DET WAC
VAAF
VICTORVILLE
CALIFORNIA
From CPL HARRY CHRISMAN
37457217
(Sender's name)
Hq Co, 1st Bn, 102nd INF
(Sender's address)
APO #915
% P.M. SAN FRANCISCO, CAL
16 Nov 1943
(Date)
BEAUTIFUL BUT "OVERMANNED" HAWAII —
JUST ANOTHER "GOONEY BIRD." TO ME.
CPL HARRY CHRISMAN
GOONEYBIRD ISLAND
1943
V---MAIL

Overmanned 11-16-43

Six weeks passed since the "discussion" about overseas duty for Catherine. Harry wrote to her in September that he injured his back lifting some heavy artillery during a regular drill. Now he was headed to Honolulu for back surgery. His back bothered him the rest of his life but this surgery he was to have helped a great deal. I always thought it interesting that his doctor in Liberal, Kansas, where he worked on the local paper, told him one of the worst positions he could be in was akin to that position one took when washing dishes at the kitchen sink. He never helped Catherine with them again! (S)

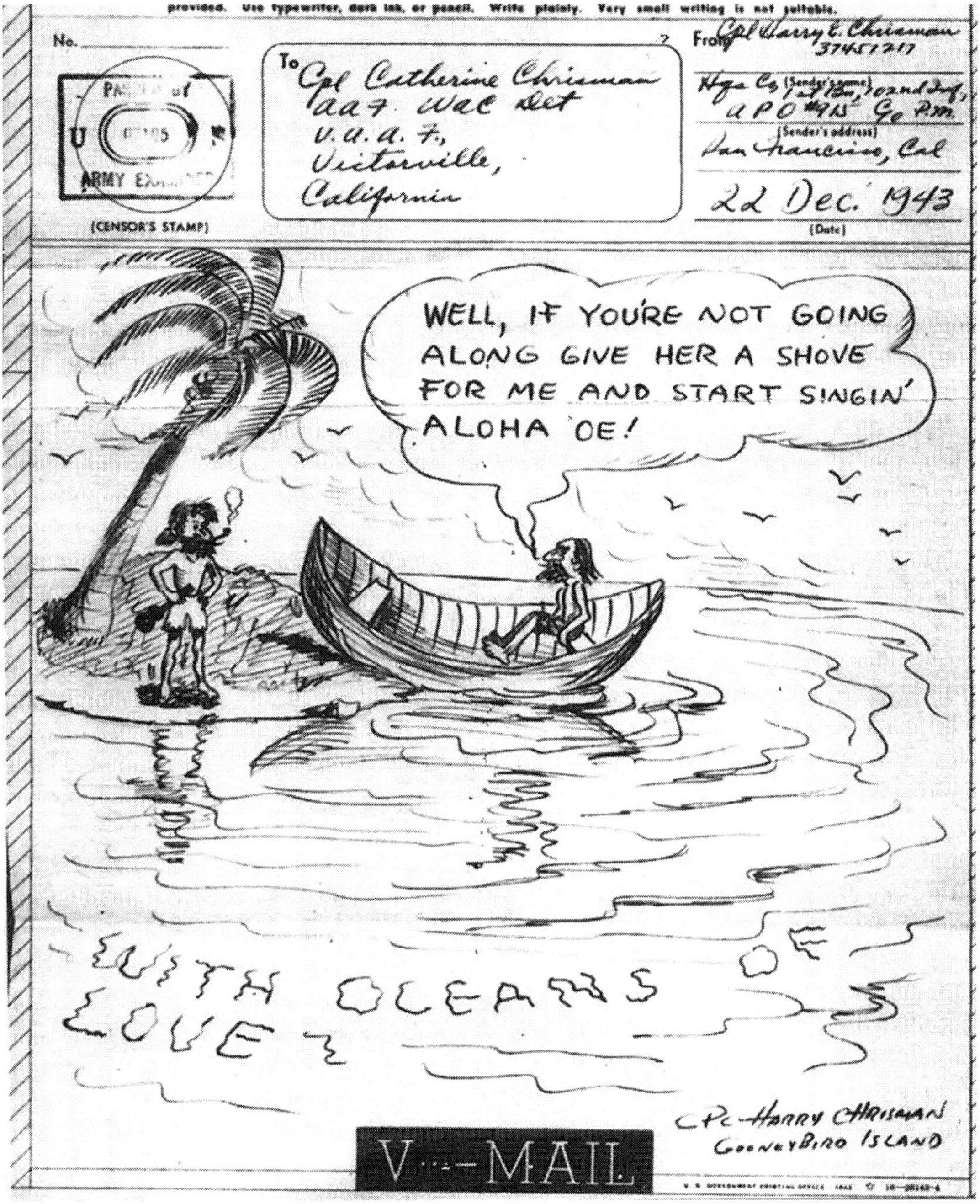
provided. Use typewriter, dark ink, or pencil. Write plainly. Very small writing is not suitable.
No.
To Cpl Catherine Chrisman
AAF WAC Det
Victorville,
California
(CENSOR'S STAMP)
From Cpl Harry E. Chrisman
37451217
San Francisco, Cal
22 Dec. 1943
(Date)
WELL, IF YOU'RE NOT GOING ALONG GIVE HER A SHOVE FOR ME AND START SINGIN' ALOHA 'OE!
WITH OCEANS OF LOVE
CPL HARRY CHRISMAN
GOONEYBIRD ISLAND
V-MAIL

Boat to Hawaii 12-22-43

Note the word "Christmas" is blanked out by the censor. Although Harry was headed to Honolulu for back surgery his A.P.O. was still Christmas Island. For several months Harry sent V-Mails and letters showing how much he loved Catherine. It took a while to make up for that ultimatum letter. (S)

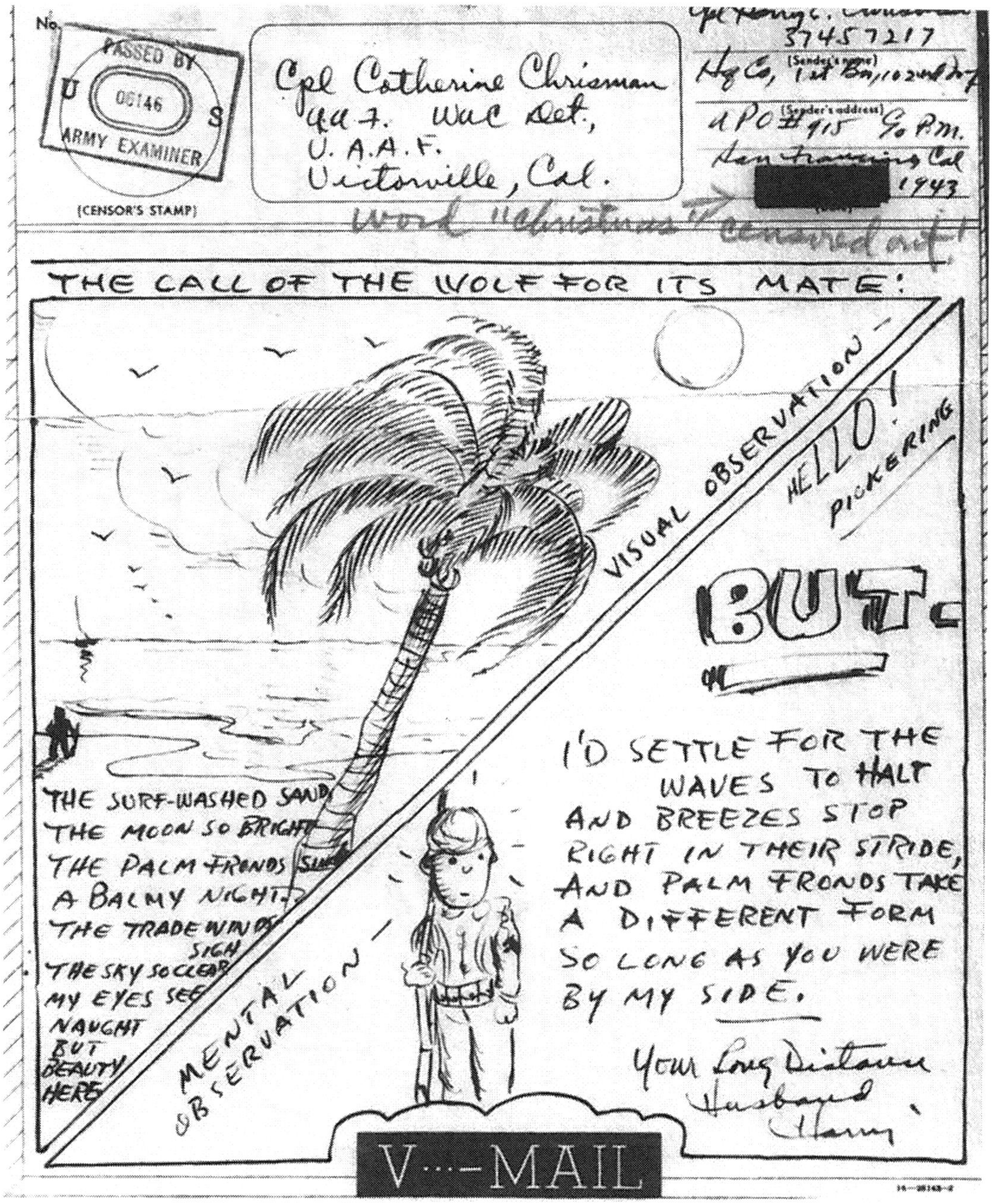
No.
PASSED BY
U 06146 S
ARMY EXAMINER
(CENSOR'S STAMP)
Cpl Catherine Chrisman
44-7. Wac Det.,
U. A. A. F.
Victorville, Cal.
37457217
(Sender's name)
Hq Co, 1st Bn, 102nd Inf
(Sender's address)
APO #915 % P.M.
San Francisco Cal
[redacted] 1943
(Date)
Word "Christmas" censored out!
THE CALL OF THE WOLF FOR ITS MATE:
VISUAL OBSERVATION –
HELLO!
PICKERING
BUT –
THE SURF-WASHED SAND
THE MOON SO BRIGHT
THE PALM FRONDS SU
A BALMY NIGHT.
THE TRADE WIN
SIGH
THE SKY SO CLEAR
MY EYES SEE
NAUGHT
BUT
BEAUTY
HERE
MENTAL OBSERVATION –
I'D SETTLE FOR THE
WAVES TO HALT
AND BREEZES STOP
RIGHT IN THEIR STRIDE,
AND PALM FRONDS TAKE
A DIFFERENT FORM
SO LONG AS YOU WERE
BY MY SIDE.
Your Long Distance
Husband
Harry
V-MAIL

Call of the Wild 12-25-43

This was drawn aboard the ship taking Harry to Honolulu. He mailed it after he arrived. (I noticed that his V-Mails to her after their earlier dispute were more loving than funny.) But while on board, he continued to write letters and draw V-Mails as it was a three-week trip from Christmas Island to Oahu. He also drew V-Mails for the crew and even did a couple for the ship's monthly newsletter. In return he was allowed to sleep on deck, a remedy for the sea-sickness he suffered below decks. (S)

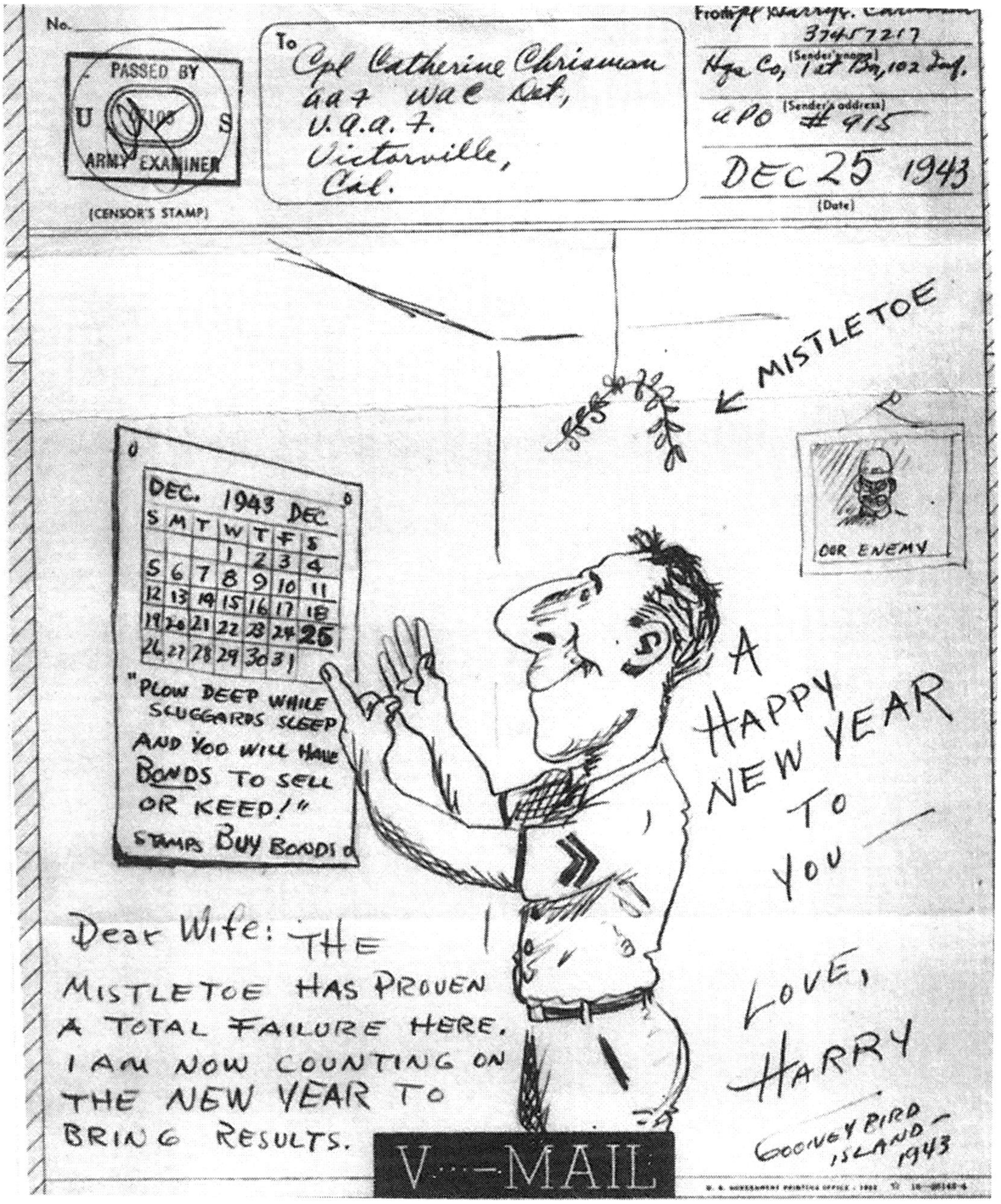
No.
PASSED BY
U S
ARMY EXAMINER
(CENSOR'S STAMP)
To Cpl Catherine Chrisman
AA7 WAC Det,
V.A.A.7.
Victorville,
Cal.
37457217
(Sender's name)
Hqs Co, 1st Bn, 102 Inf.
(Sender's address)
APO # 915
DEC 25 1943
(Date)
MISTLETOE
DEC. 1943 DEC
S M T W T F S
1 2 3 4
5 6 7 8 9 10 11
12 13 14 15 16 17 18
19 20 21 22 23 24 25
26 27 28 29 30 31
"PLOW DEEP WHILE SLUGGARDS SLEEP AND YOU WILL HAVE BONDS TO SELL OR KEEP!"
STAMPS BUY BONDS
OUR ENEMY
A HAPPY NEW YEAR TO YOU
Dear Wife: THE MISTLETOE HAS PROVEN A TOTAL FAILURE HERE. I AM NOW COUNTING ON THE NEW YEAR TO BRING RESULTS.
LOVE, HARRY
GOONEY BIRD ISLAND - 1943
V---MAIL

Mistletoe 12-25-43

Madame Ennui (pronounced in the French, an-we, or ong-we) slept with more soldiers, sailors, and Marines in the Pacific during World War II than any other woman of known history. She spent the nights in every man's tent, or fox hole, or slit trench. She spent her daytime hours sitting upon every desk soldier's lap, as well as making every forced march with every soldier in the service, over the roughest mountain terrain in the volcanic islands of the Pacific. And she languished beside every soldier on every Pacific beach during his rest hours. Once Harry devoted a poem to her, writing:

> *Then cried I out to ask for Love and Life,*
> *From the Black Pit in which I lay entrapped,*
> *Came Madame Ennui there to be my wife,*
> *And slump in perpetuity on my lap.*

From Harry's Webster's Third New International Dictionary, Ennui is described as "A feeling of weariness and dissatisfaction: languor or emptiness of spirit. Tedium or boredom." Harry said many soldiers on Christmas Island wanted to see combat merely to have something to do! Boredom was often more debilitating than being in the thick of battle. (S)

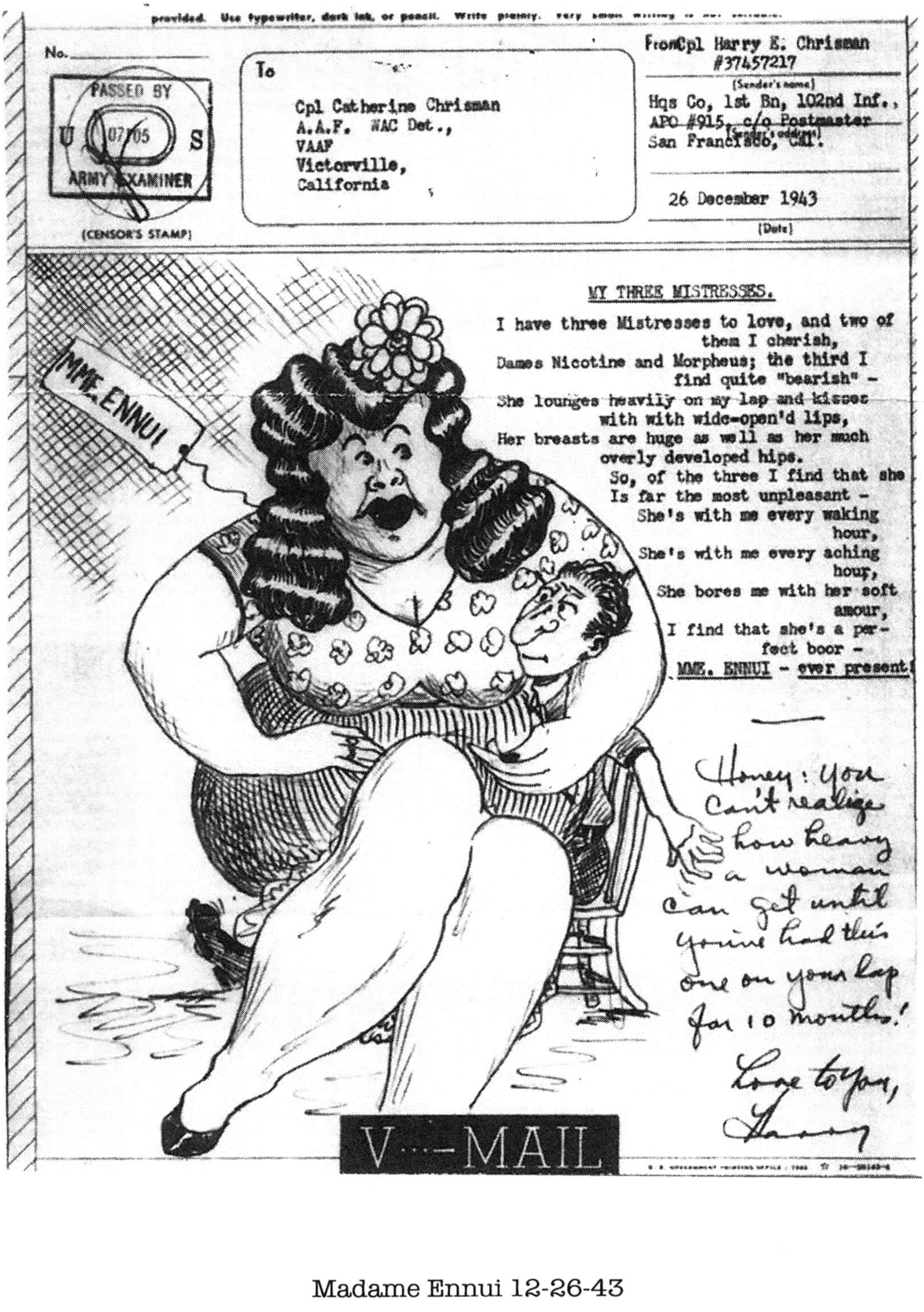
provided. Use typewriter, dark ink, or pencil. Write plainly.

No.

PASSED BY
U 07705 S
ARMY EXAMINER
(CENSOR'S STAMP)

To

Cpl Catherine Chrisman
A.A.F. WAC Det.,
VAAF
Victorville,
California

From Cpl Harry E. Chrisman
#37457217
(Sender's name)
Hqs Co, 1st Bn, 102nd Inf.,
APO #915, c/o Postmaster
San Francisco, Cal.
(Sender's address)

26 December 1943
(Date)

MME. ENNUI

MY THREE MISTRESSES.

I have three Mistresses to love, and two of
them I cherish,
Dames Nicotine and Morpheus; the third I
find quite "bearish" -
She lounges heavily on my lap and kisses
with with wide-open'd lips,
Her breasts are huge as well as her much
overly developed hips.
So, of the three I find that she
Is far the most unpleasant -
She's with me every waking
hour,
She's with me every aching
hour,
She bores me with her soft
amour,
I find that she's a per-
fect boor -
MME. ENNUI - ever present!

Honey: You
can't realize
how heavy
a woman
can get until
you've had this
one on your lap
for 10 months!

Love to you,
Harry

V—MAIL

Madame Ennui 12-26-43

Once again Harry tried humor when he felt overlooked. His ship docked earlier than expected in Honolulu and he was recovering from surgery when he received word that his name was, once again, not on the promotion list. It really bothered him that Catherine made sergeant first! (S)

The Day of the Chevron Shower! 1-6-44

Harry was still anxious that Catherine was satisfied with her decision to remain in the U. S. He was still "sweet talking" her, wanting back into her good graces. (S)

Catherine Drawn from Memory 1-16-44

I found Catherine's Air Base in California loaded with "Saluting Demons." Overseas we usually looked aside at passing Brass. Not There! An officious OD Captain caused her to be confined to Quarters for a day! (H)

Harry thought he might get a furlough after his surgery, but he didn't. Catherine wrote long letters about everything of her day including how many times she had to salute. Catherine said it was the male officers who were sticklers for that observance of their superiority. The female officers always called an "at ease" when they entered the barracks. The airmen on the base evidently wanted to be sure the women noticed them. Catherine's day in Quarters came about because she had equipment in one hand and the first rung of the ladder to the roof in her other hand. She was on her way to repair a roof-top radio. The ladder was located in the officers' mess hall and one who passed her as she readied for the climb was miffed because she didn't salute. She told me her sergeant was horrified that the officer put her on report. Catherine said she thought one of her superiors must have spoken to him because she saw him coming her way once and he about faced and went in another direction. She grinned when she told me this. Of any person I know who would ignore protocol, it was NOT Catherine! (S)

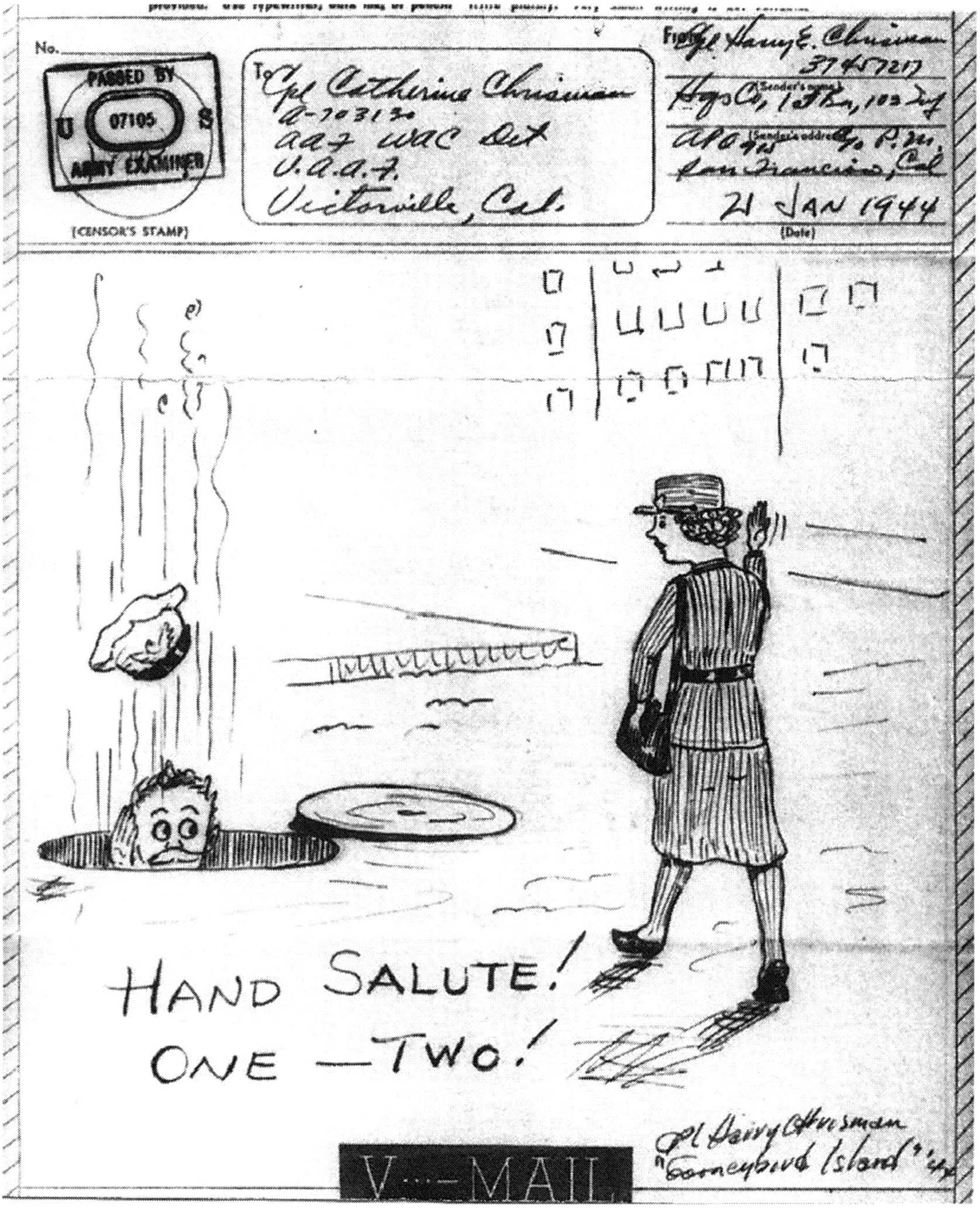
No.
PASSED BY
U 07105 S
ARMY EXAMINER
(CENSOR'S STAMP)
To Cpl Catherine Chrisman
A-703130
AAF WAC Det
U.A.A.F.
Victorville, Cal.
From
37457217
San Francisco, Cal
21 JAN 1944
(Date)
HAND SALUTE!
ONE — TWO!
V—MAIL

Hand Salute 1-21-44

Harry and Catherine often wondered what the U. S. and the world would be like when they returned home. They wrote about it in their letters to each other and to their family members. All letters written by family members were passed to first one and then the other so that each of them knew what was going on in the Army and in Scottsbluff, Nebraska! (S)

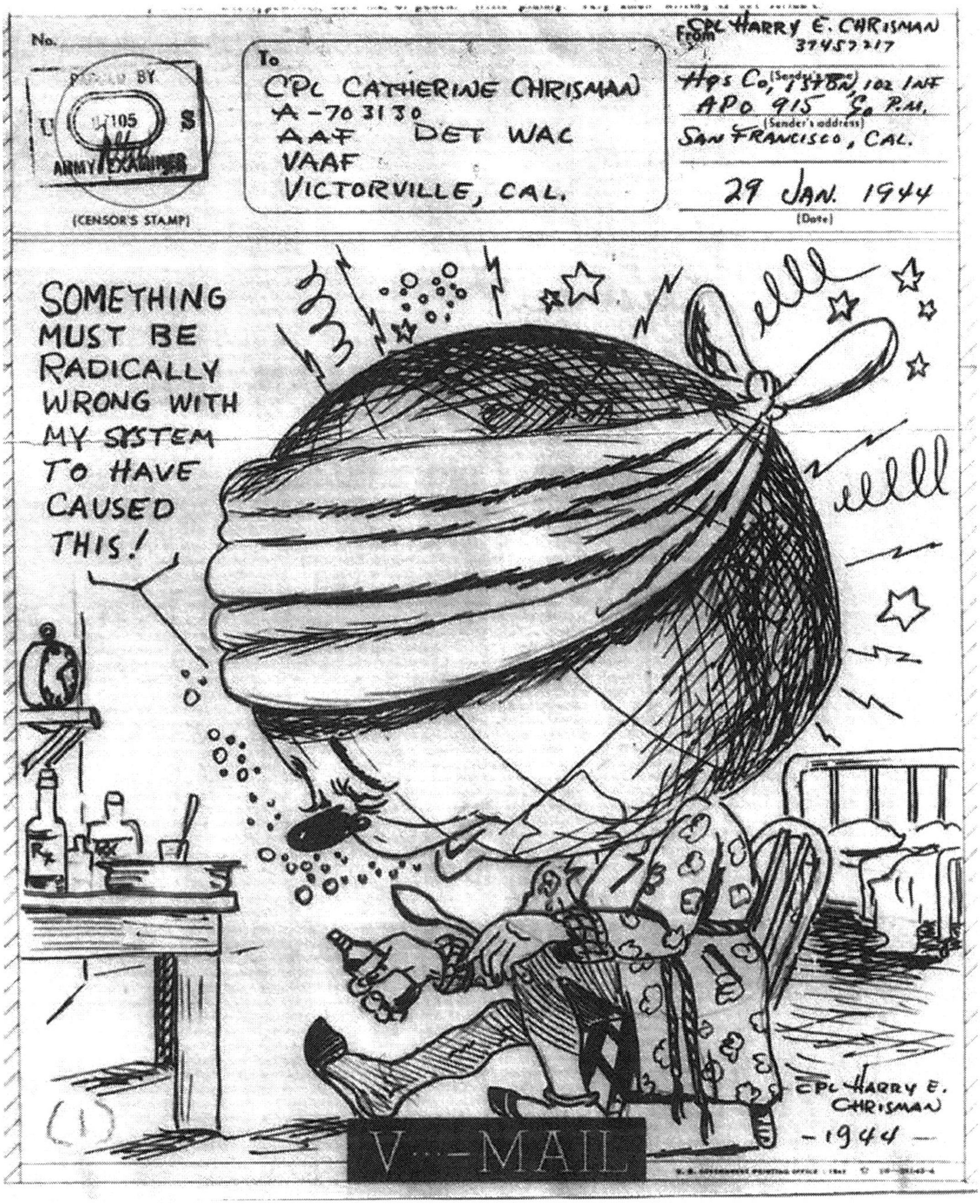
No.
ARMY EXAMINER
(CENSOR'S STAMP)
To
CPL CATHERINE CHRISMAN
A-703130
AAF DET WAC
VAAF
VICTORVILLE, CAL.
From CPL HARRY E. CHRISMAN
37457217
(Sender's address)
SAN FRANCISCO, CAL.
29 JAN. 1944
(Date)
SOMETHING MUST BE RADICALLY WRONG WITH MY SYSTEM TO HAVE CAUSED THIS!
CPL HARRY E. CHRISMAN
-1944-
V-MAIL

Poor World 1-29-44

There was a question whether the overseas soldiers would be "allowed" to vote in the Fall Election of 1944. The GI's overseas were most concerned until Congress and the Military set up a system for our Elections. (H)

Harry was a staunch Democrat as was Catherine, and they often held the primary caucus at their home in Lakewood, Colorado. Neither one of them ever missed voting. Don took Harry to vote in a major election when he seldom left his bed, but, by George, he left it that day! And I requested mail-in ballots for Catherine the last year of her life. Harry always felt voting was a privilege and a responsibility. "Besides," he once told us, "how can I gripe about politics if I don't vote?" (S)

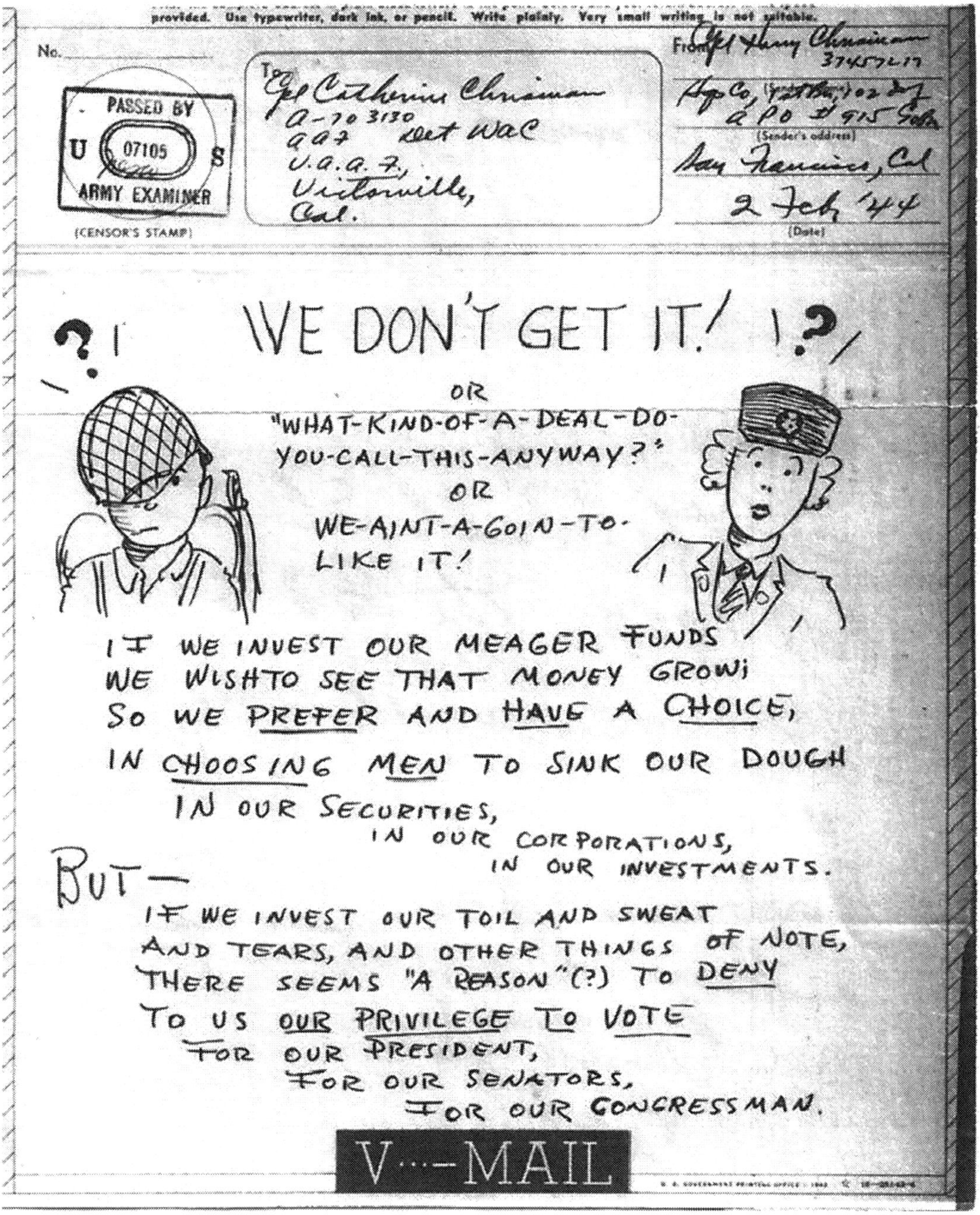
provided. Use typewriter, dark ink, or pencil. Write plainly. Very small writing is not suitable.

No.

PASSED BY
U 07105 S
ARMY EXAMINER
(CENSOR'S STAMP)

To: Cpl Catherine Chrisman
A-703130
AAF Det WAC
U.A.A.F.,
Victorville,
Cal.

From Cpl Henry Chrisman
37457217
Hq Co, 1st Bn, 102 Inf
APO #915 % PM
(Sender's address)
San Francisco, Cal
2 Feb '44
(Date)

WE DON'T GET IT!

OR
"WHAT-KIND-OF-A-DEAL-DO-YOU-CALL-THIS-ANYWAY?"
OR
WE-AINT-A-GOIN-TO-LIKE IT!

IF WE INVEST OUR MEAGER FUNDS
WE WISH TO SEE THAT MONEY GROW;
SO WE PREFER AND HAVE A CHOICE,
IN CHOOSING MEN TO SINK OUR DOUGH
IN OUR SECURITIES,
IN OUR CORPORATIONS,
IN OUR INVESTMENTS.

BUT—
IF WE INVEST OUR TOIL AND SWEAT
AND TEARS, AND OTHER THINGS OF NOTE,
THERE SEEMS "A REASON" (?) TO DENY
TO US OUR PRIVILEGE TO VOTE
FOR OUR PRESIDENT,
FOR OUR SENATORS,
FOR OUR CONGRESSMAN.

V-MAIL

We Don't Get It! 2-2-44

The Island girls call this a "Snow Job!" (H)

Harry disapproved of this type of behavior especially by a married man. But many of the G.I.s he knew thought bamboozling a native girl was great entertainment. However, he noted that when he got back to Honolulu in August of 1944, most of the Island girls avoided the G.I.s! Catherine found herself on the receiving end of a Snow Job or two and laughed later about how pathetic those guys were. (S)

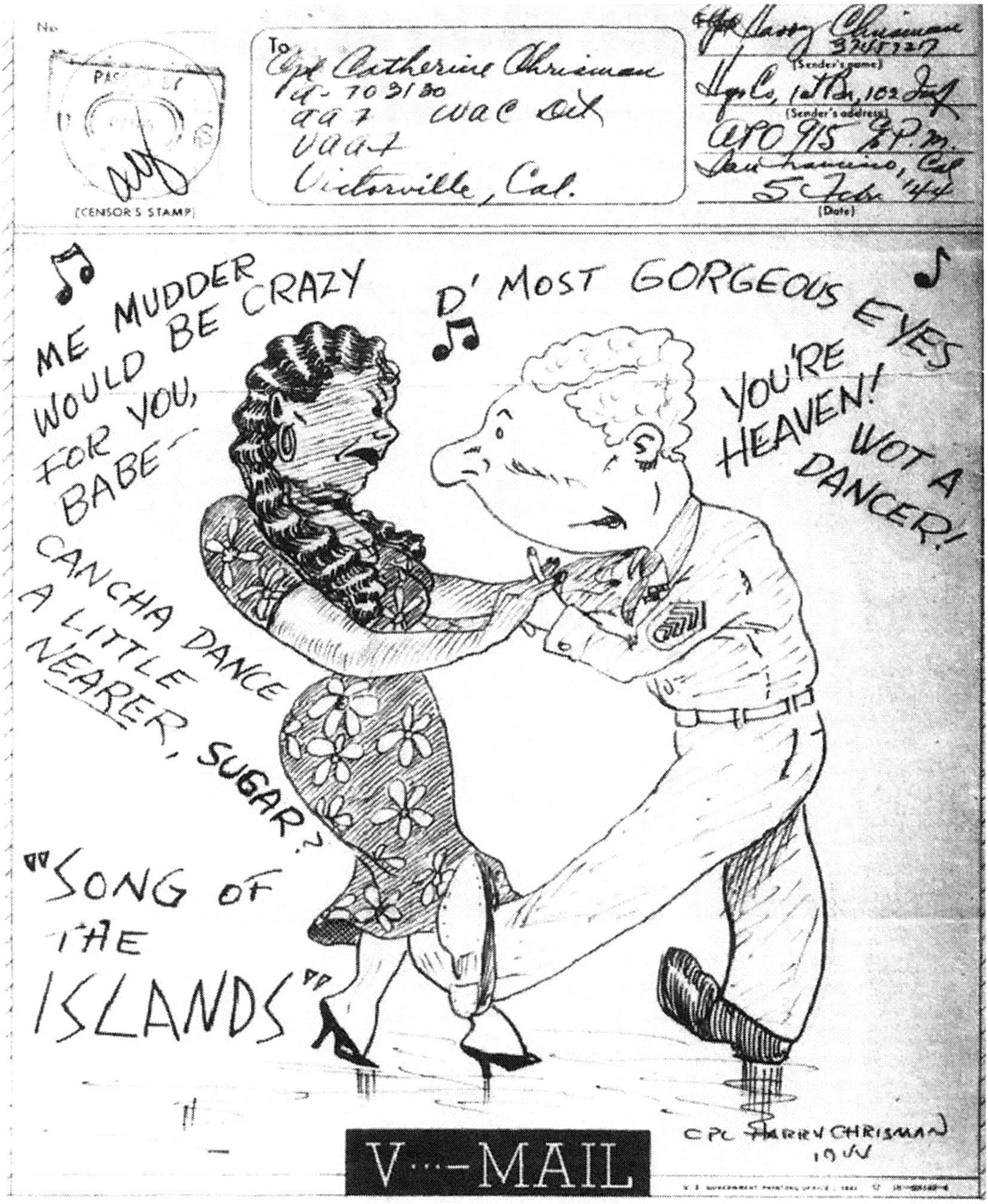
No.
To
Cpl Catherine Chrisman
A-703130
AAF WAC Det
VAAF
Victorville, Cal.
(CENSOR'S STAMP)
(Sender's name)
(Sender's address)
APO 915
5 Feb '44
(Date)
ME MUDDER WOULD BE CRAZY FOR YOU, BABE—
D' MOST GORGEOUS EYES
YOU'RE HEAVEN!
WOT A DANCER!
CANCHA DANCE A LITTLE NEARER, SUGAR?
"SONG OF THE ISLANDS"
CPL HARRY CHRISMAN
V...-MAIL

Snow Job 2-5-44

By this time Catherine had forgiven Harry and was content to stay at Victorville always hoping Harry would get a furlough soon. (S)

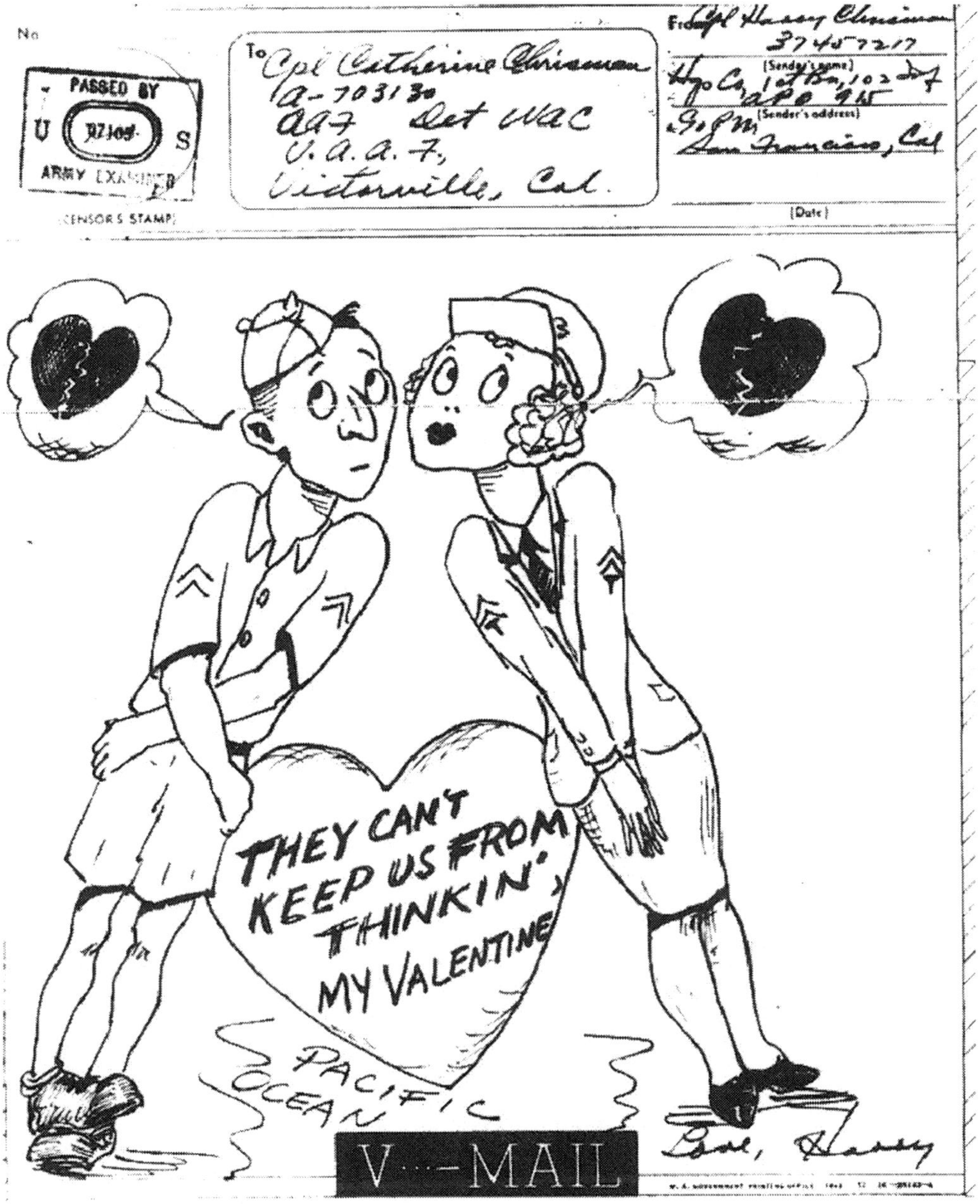
No
PASSED BY
U S
ARMY EXAMINER
CENSOR'S STAMP
To Cpl Catherine Chrisman
A-703130
AAF Det WAC
V.A.A.F.,
Victorville, Cal.
From Cpl Harry Chrisman
37457217
(Sender's name)
(Sender's address)
San Francisco, Cal
(Date)
THEY CAN'T KEEP US FROM THINKIN', MY VALENTINE
PACIFIC OCEAN
V---MAIL
Love, Harry

Valentine 2-14-44

Harry was having fun supposing. But Catherine could still wear her uniform long after his did not fit. She donated her uniform to Colorado State University in Fort Collins, CO. Note: In this V-Mail "A.R." stands for Army Regulation. (S)

WAC PARADE ————— 1964.

(A.R. 600:39 provides that all WAC's honorably discharged from the service may retain their uniforms and their personal accoutrements).

I can't suppress a chuckle when I cast a forward look,
To where I'll be in twenty years — according to this "book";
The "book" is the AR six hundred dash and thirty-nine,
It proves that I'll be lacing up that old sweetheart of mine.
She'll have me gird her corset so the torso will look smooth,
It will not matter that she finds it quite a task to move,
She'll want to show her uniform, her cap, and what is more
To let our neighbors know how she was in the last World War.
I'll stay home with the children (for the darlings are afraid!)
While "Mom" goes out a struttin' with her WAC friends on Parade!

Love,
Harry

WAC '64 2-23-44

Catherine and Harry thought a furlough for both would never come through. This was Harry's way of dealing with the frustration, by poking fun at it. Harry had been on one island or another for eighteen months! (S)

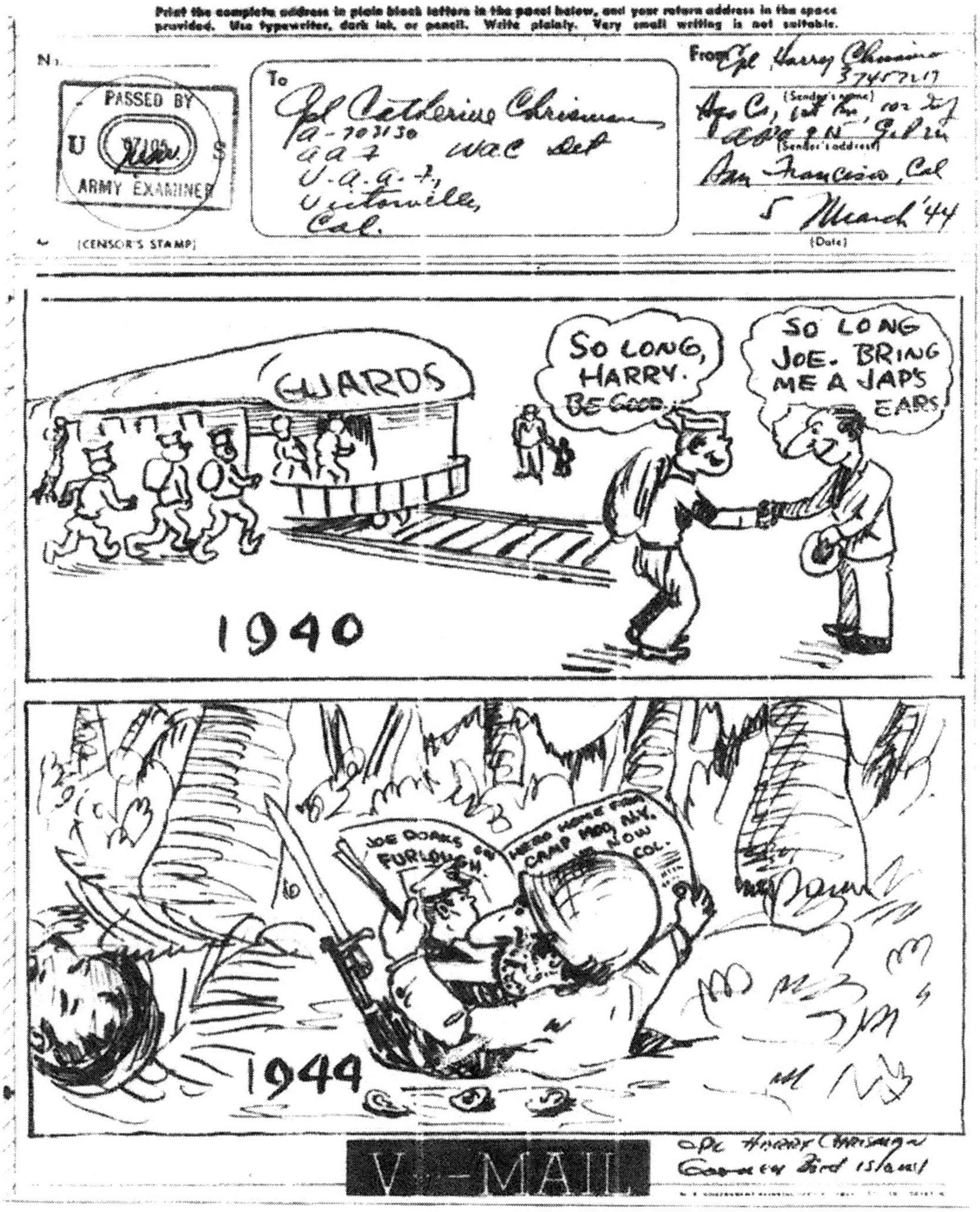
Print the complete address in plain block letters in the panel below, and your return address in the space provided. Use typewriter, dark ink, or pencil. Write plainly. Very small writing is not suitable.
PASSED BY
U S
ARMY EXAMINER
(CENSOR'S STAMP)
To
From
(Sender's name)
(Sender's address)
San Francisco, Cal
5 March '44
(Date)
GUARDS
SO LONG, HARRY. BE GOOD.
SO LONG JOE. BRING ME A JAP'S EARS
1940
JOE DOAKS ON FURLOUGH
1944
V-MAIL

Furlough 3-5-44

Catherine knew Harry was being transferred because he and his buddy are carrying their "A and B bags" in this cartoon. She later got a letter in May telling her he was transferred to the Army Port and Service Command (APSC), in Honolulu. He would be in the Information and Education Section. Until then, she just knew he was transferred to somewhere that was not Christmas Island and she knew his APO had changed. The A and B bags were just a clue that he was leaving Christmas Island, but no cartoon after that, until he could tell her by mail, indicated where he was. He was a stickler for that kind of information NOT getting out. Note: "A" Bags contained all essentials to travel to another place for a time, "B" bags contained personal mementoes such as books and letters, etc., which could be claimed when the soldier returned to that particular place. (S)

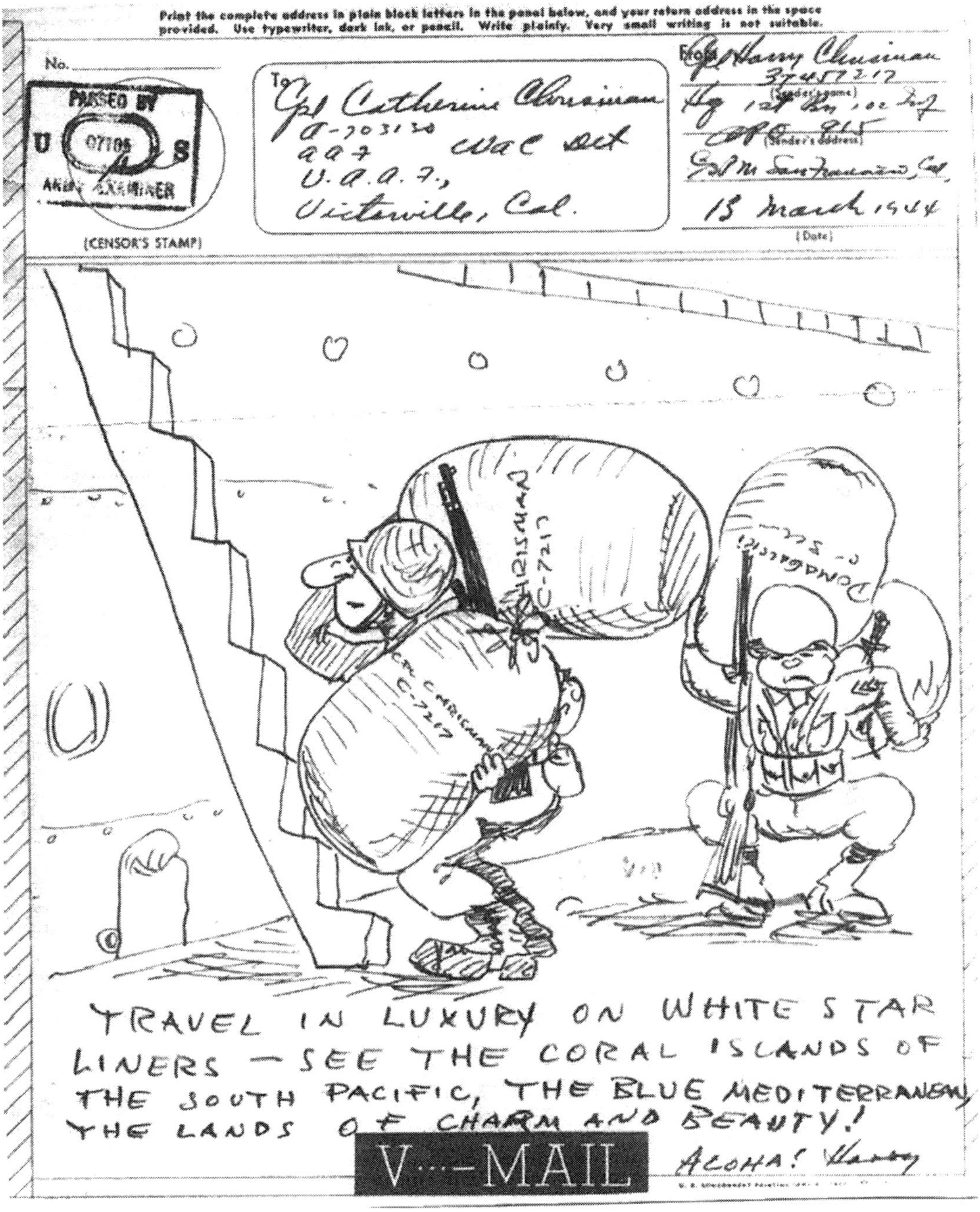
Print the complete address in plain block letters in the panel below, and your return address in the space provided. Use typewriter, dark ink, or pencil. Write plainly. Very small writing is not suitable.

No.

PASSED BY U S ARMY EXAMINER

(CENSOR'S STAMP)

To: Cpl Catherine Chrisman
A-703130 WAC Det
AAF
U.A.A.F.,
Victorville, Cal.

From: Cpl Harry Chrisman
37457217
(Sender's name)
Hq 1st Bn, 102 Inf
APO 915
(Sender's address)
c/o PM San Francisco, Cal.
13 March 1944
(Date)

TRAVEL IN LUXURY ON WHITE STAR LINERS — SEE THE CORAL ISLANDS OF THE SOUTH PACIFIC, THE BLUE MEDITERRANEAN, THE LANDS OF CHARM AND BEAUTY!

ALOHA! Harry

V---MAIL

To Hawaii 3-13-44

Harry sent this V-Mail written and drawn with pencil to see how it worked when reduced. It also "told" Catherine he was in an office doing his "thing." His desk, his maps, his conclusions. Catherine said the word "studying" told her he was making assessments, not doing "clerk" work. She knew how much he really enjoyed using his brain. (S)

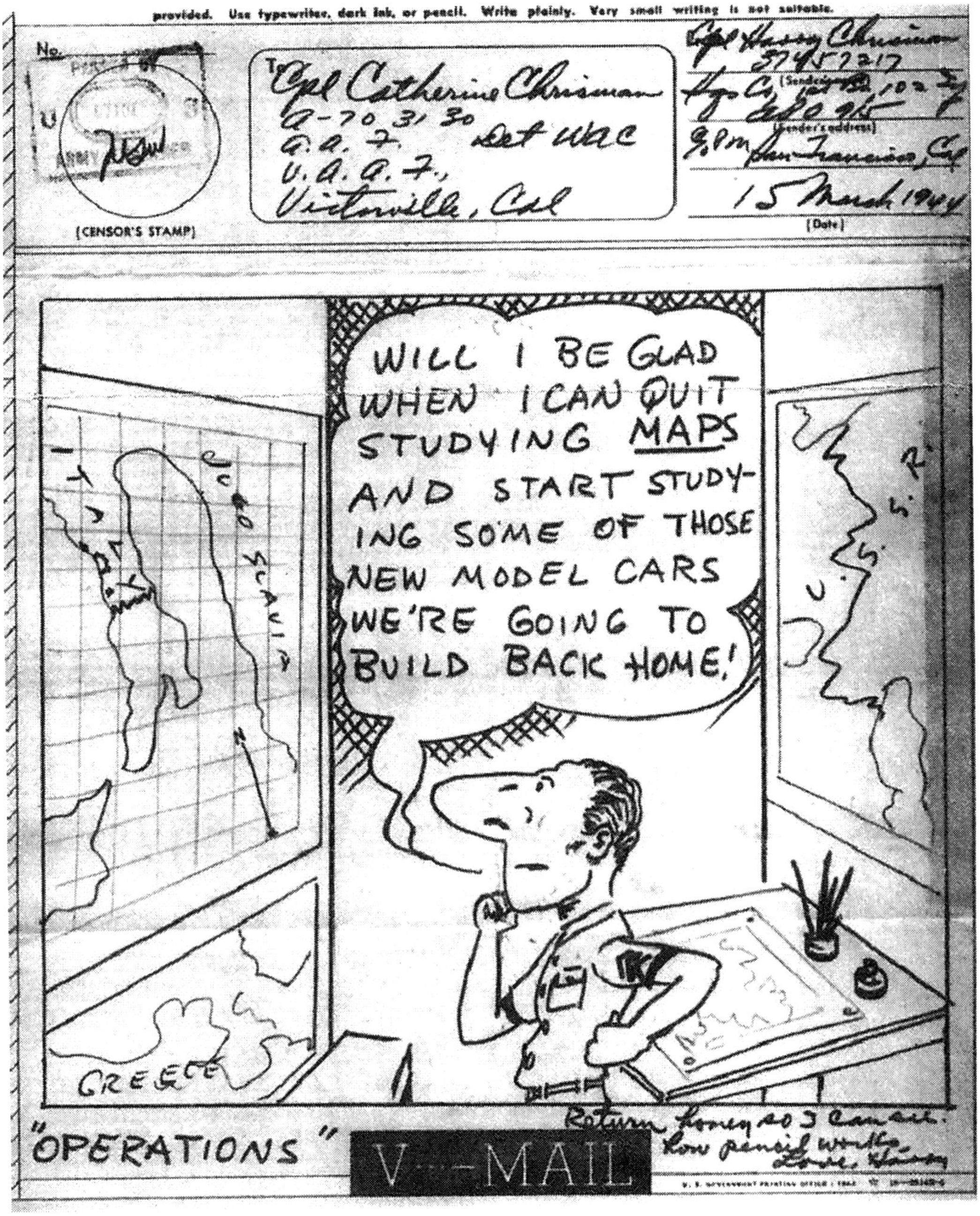
provided. Use typewriter, dark ink, or pencil. Write plainly. Very small writing is not suitable.
No.
(CENSOR'S STAMP)
To Cpl Catherine Chrisman
A-70 31 30
A.A.F. Det WAC
U.A.A.F.,
Victorville, Cal
37457217
(Sender's name)
APO 95
(Sender's address)
San Francisco, Cal
15 March 1944
(Date)
WILL I BE GLAD WHEN I CAN QUIT STUDYING MAPS AND START STUDYING SOME OF THOSE NEW MODEL CARS WE'RE GOING TO BUILD BACK HOME!
GREECE
"OPERATIONS"
V---MAIL

Maps 3-25-44

Harry drew on that wonderful memory of his for this cartoon. He is back on Christmas Island in his tent writing by candlelight. When he had time he often drew several cartoons on the same day. And there was a limit as to what he could draw about his work at the ASPC, so he would draw something from his time on Christmas or perhaps a drawing of one of the Polynesian islands. He loved their beauty. (S)

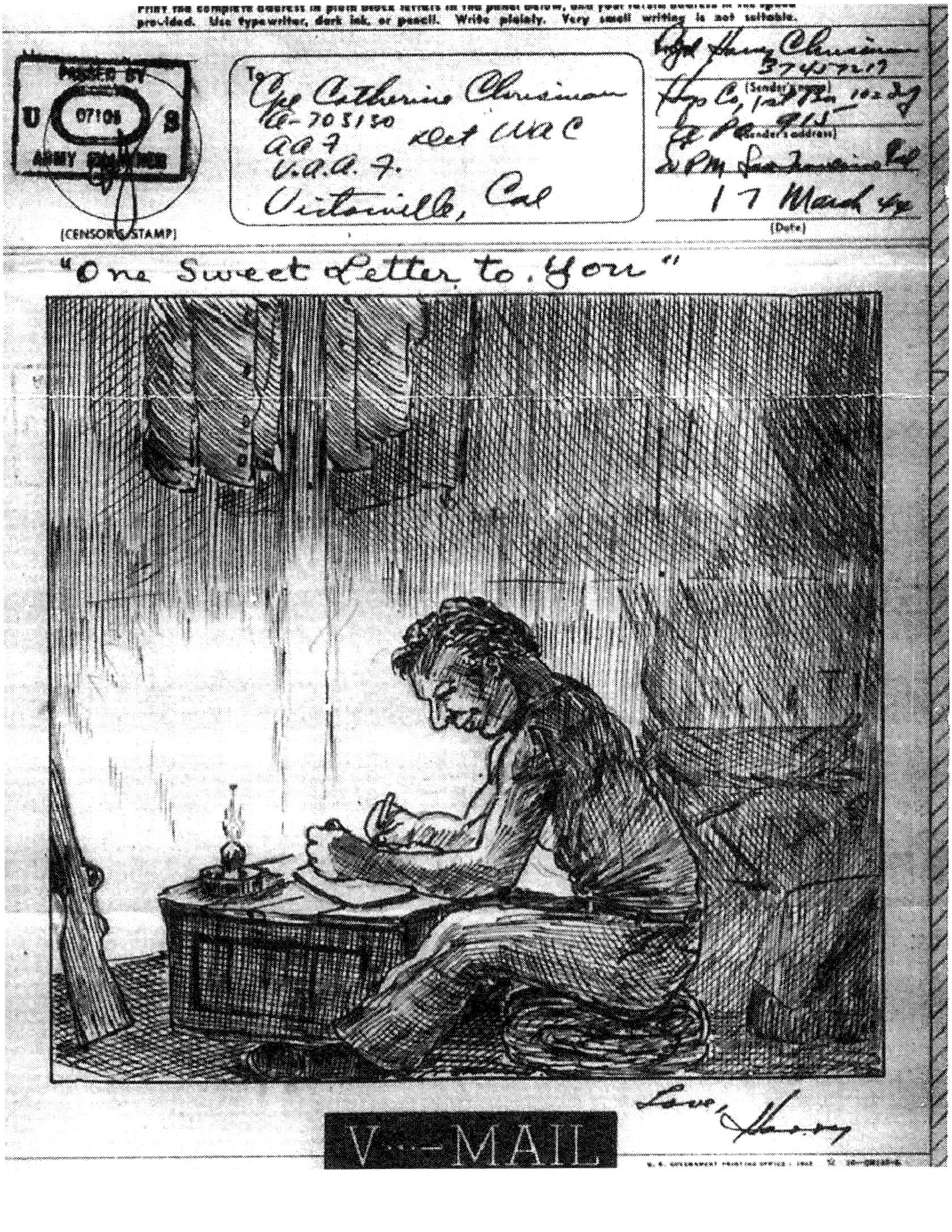
provided. Use typewriter, dark ink, or pencil. Write plainly. Very small writing is not suitable.
PASSED BY
U 07108 S
ARMY EXAMINER
(CENSOR'S STAMP)
To
(Sender's name)
(Sender's address)
17 March 44
(Date)
"One Sweet Letter to You"
V—MAIL

One Sweet Letter 3-17-44

Harry and Catherine never talked much about this except one day as we looked at the V-Mails, he tapped this one with his finger and said, "So difficult," and he raised his head, his eyes seeing beyond and back to the past. The paper points out the difficulty of not thinking! Note the number of days (523) in the lower right-hand corner. I asked Catherine once if she thought the censor smiled as he read this one. "I think he laughed out loud!" she said. We both laughed. (S)

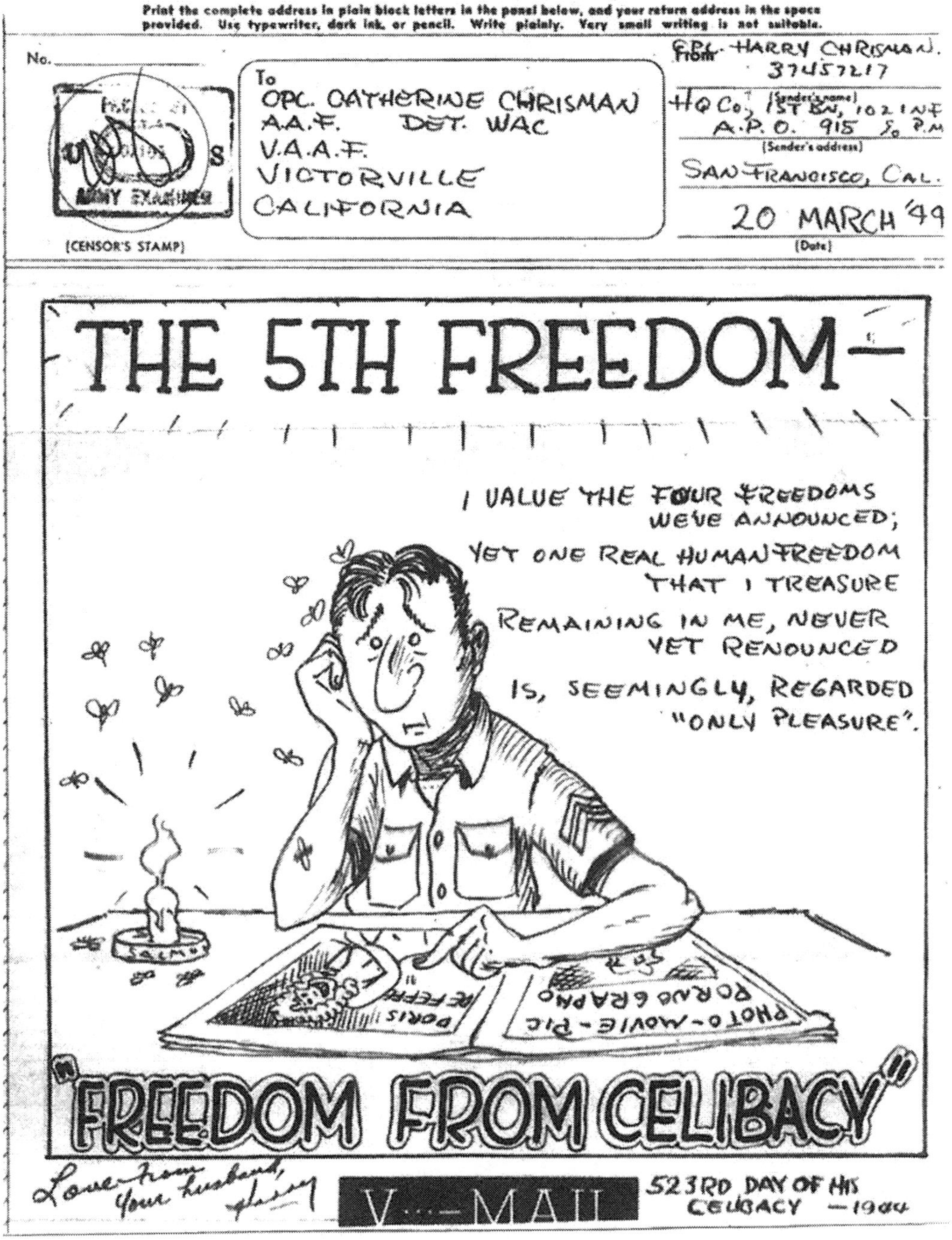
Print the complete address in plain block letters in the panel below, and your return address in the space provided. Use typewriter, dark ink, or pencil. Write plainly. Very small writing is not suitable.
No.
ARMY EXAMINER
(CENSOR'S STAMP)
To
CPL. CATHERINE CHRISMAN
A.A.F. DET. WAC
V.A.A.F.
VICTORVILLE
CALIFORNIA
From CPL. HARRY CHRISMAN
37457217
(Sender's name)
HQ Co., 1ST BN, 102 INF
A.P.O. 915 % P.M.
(Sender's address)
SAN FRANCISCO, CAL.
20 MARCH '44
(Date)
THE 5TH FREEDOM—
I VALUE THE FOUR FREEDOMS
WE'VE ANNOUNCED;
YET ONE REAL HUMAN FREEDOM
THAT I TREASURE
REMAINING IN ME, NEVER
YET RENOUNCED
IS, SEEMINGLY, REGARDED
"ONLY PLEASURE".
"FREEDOM FROM CELIBACY"
Love from
your husband,
Harry
V—MAIL
523RD DAY OF HIS
CELIBACY —1944

Fifth Freedom 3-20-44

Harry never met an instrument with keys he could not play, or at least attempt to play. Once again, he's back on the island playing and singing away. (S)

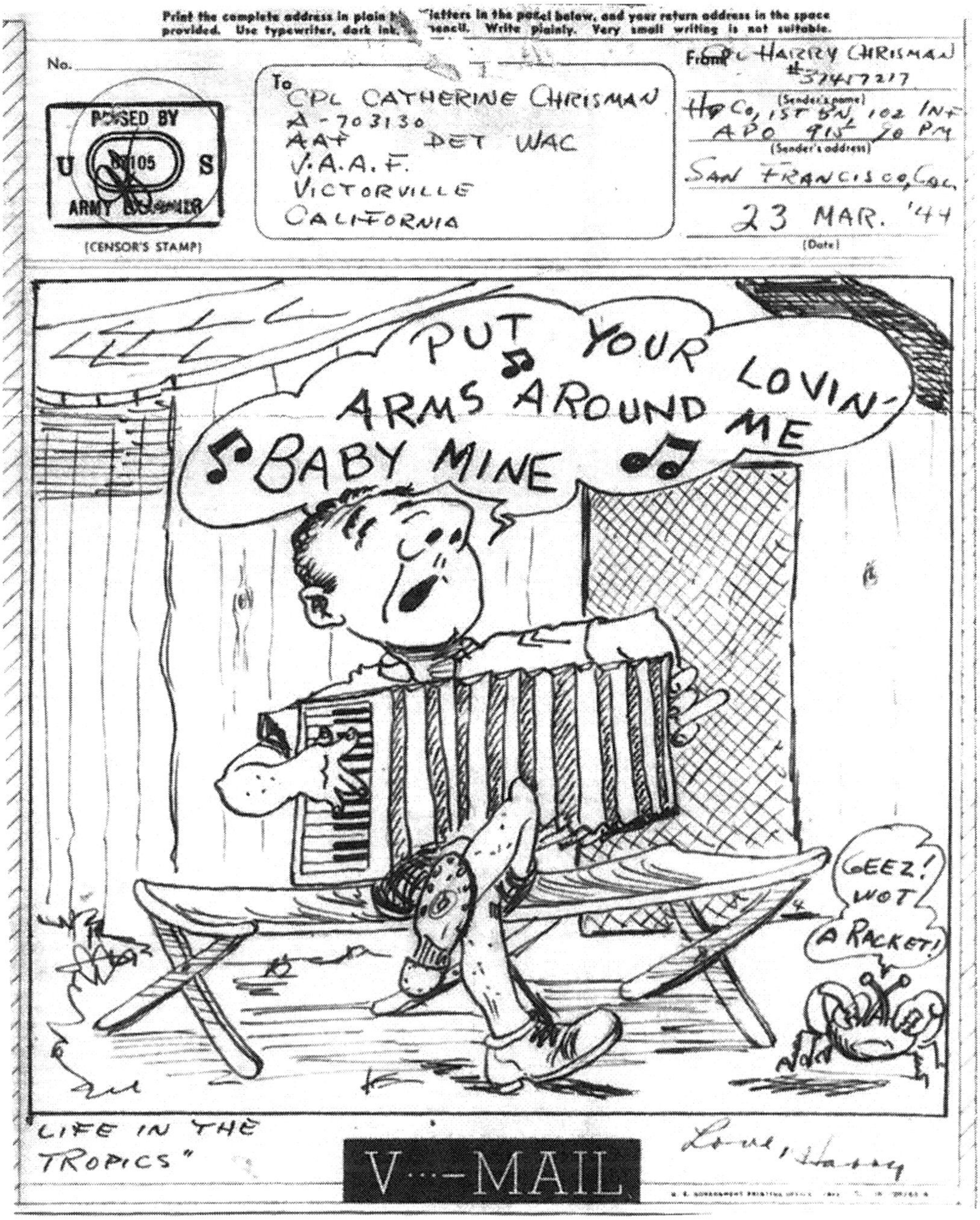

Print the complete address in plain block letters in the panel below, and your return address in the space provided. Use typewriter, dark ink, or pencil. Write plainly. Very small writing is not suitable.
No.
To CPL CATHERINE CHRISMAN
A-703130
AAF DET WAC
V.A.A.F.
VICTORVILLE
CALIFORNIA
From CPL HARRY CHRISMAN
#37417217
(Sender's name)
HQ Co, 1ST BN, 102 INF
APO 915 % PM
(Sender's address)
SAN FRANCISCO, CAL.
23 MAR. '44
(Date)
(CENSOR'S STAMP)
U S
ARMY
PUT YOUR LOVIN' ARMS AROUND ME BABY MINE
GEEZ! WOT A RACKET!
"LIFE IN THE TROPICS"
Love, Harry
V-MAIL

The Squealer 3-23-44

Harry often made fun of the Army regs—what was scheduled was done, never mind the common sense of the order or lack thereof. And if the agenda was interrupted it was not abandoned, but continued at a later time, at the convenience of the assigned officer. Thus, war weary troops on Christmas Island there for a bit of R & R got the lecture. We laughed about the remarks surely made after dismissal! I am sure there were some Harry would not repeat to me. (S)

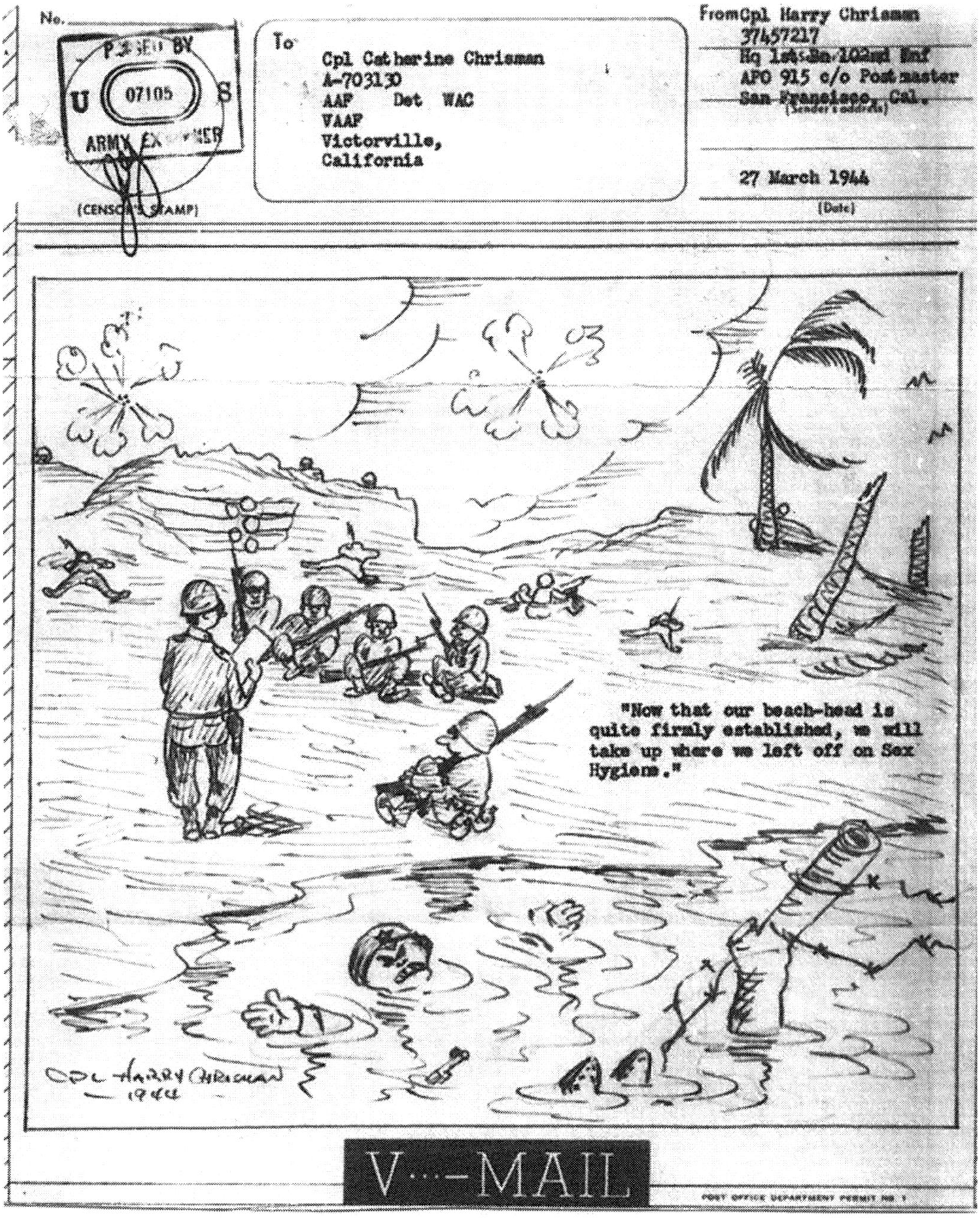
No.
U
07105
S
To
Cpl Catherine Chrisman
A-703130
AAF Det WAC
VAAF
Victorville,
California
From Cpl Harry Chrisman
37457217
APO 915 c/o Postmaster
27 March 1944
(Date)
"Now that our beach-head is quite firmly established, we will take up where we left off on Sex Hygiene."
CPL HARRY CHRISMAN
1944
V-MAIL

Sex Hygiene 3-27-44

Rose Aisenberg was Catherine's best friend both during and after the War. We were privileged to meet her after Harry died. Rose made us promise to send Catherine back east for a visit, which we did. In this V-Mail, "Pest house" refers to isolation in the infirmary; Rose apparently had a bad case of the flu. "Gangplank knees" was perhaps referring to climbing the ladders so often to fix aerial radios. Harry couldn't remember exactly! (S)

Print the complete address in plain block letters in the panel below, and your return address in the space provided. Use typewriter, dark ink, or pencil. Write plainly. Very small writing is not suitable.

No.

U.S. ARMY EXAMINER

(CENSOR'S STAMP)

CPL CATHERINE CHRISMAN
A-703130
AAF DET WAC
V.A.A.F.,
VICTORVILLE,
CAL.

Cpl Harry E. Chrisman
37457217
Co "H" 151st Inf
(Sender's name)
APO #38 % Pm
San Francisco, Cal
(Sender's address)
18 April 44
(Date)

"KNOCKED OUT"

QUIET
CPL
AISENBERG

Oahu, T.H.

Hello My Wild but not Irish Rose!

Gee! Was I sorry to hear from my sweet Catherine that you, of all people, had made the "rest house". That is bad and I want you to get out of there quick — there's a wah on, you know. Maybe it's just a bad case of "Gangplank Knees" eh? Hope its nothing worse.

Don't know where you are so will send this via my wife. Now I know where she thought up the idea of a New England furlough or vacation for us. You're from New England!! You're the responsible one!

Best luck, Rose and get well quick. Your Doosey and Cupids extend their love & hopes!

Yours,

Harry

V---MAIL

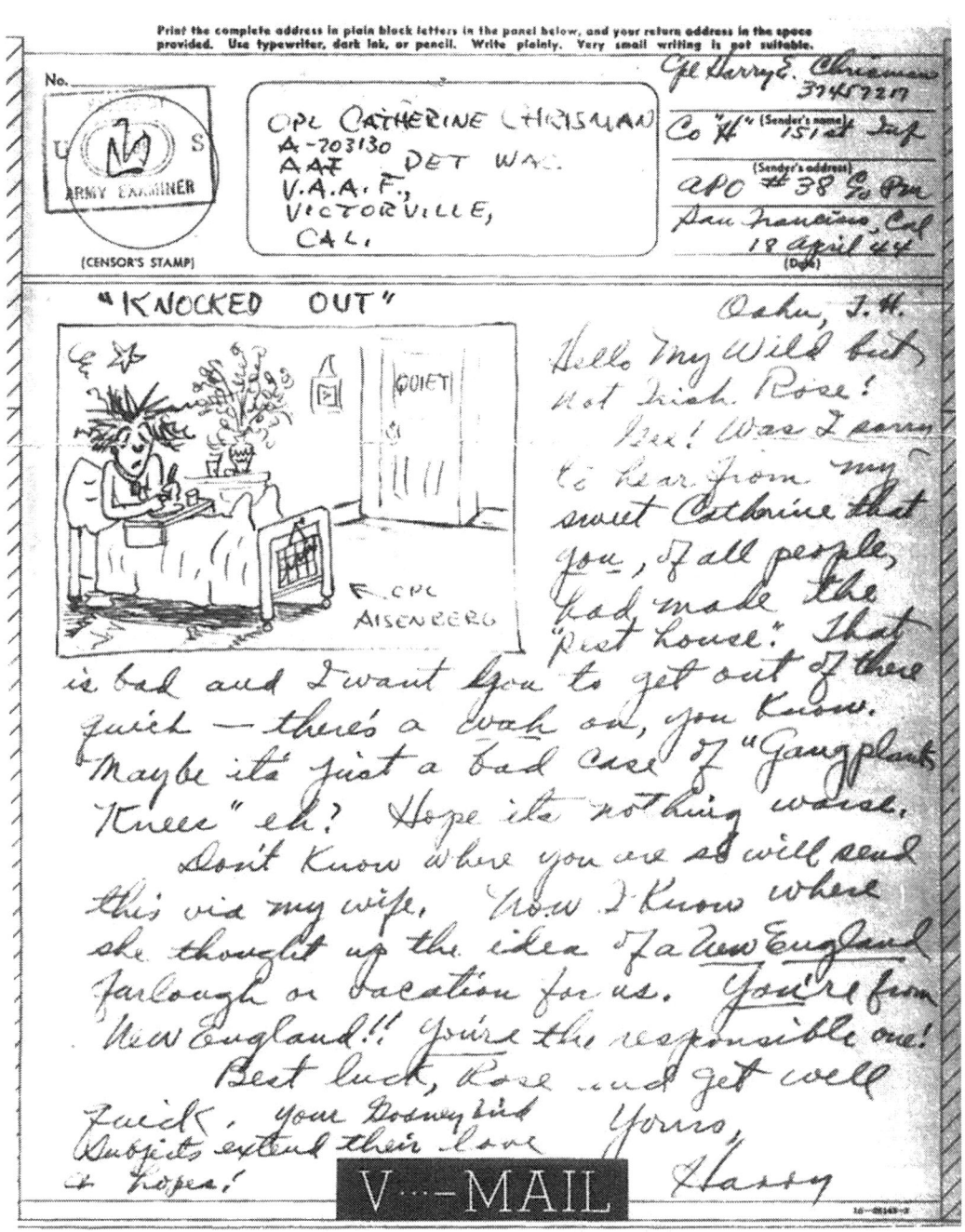

Letter to Rose 4-18-44

They missed each other so much and I think Harry often felt like they were one person. Many of his poems reflect that feeling and Catherine felt it, too. She was quite complacent to allow Harry to take the lead in all things. He often said they were like an old horse team—the horse on the left as the lead, the mare on the right, following the horse's gait. Harry loved describing life as an Old West metaphor. (S)

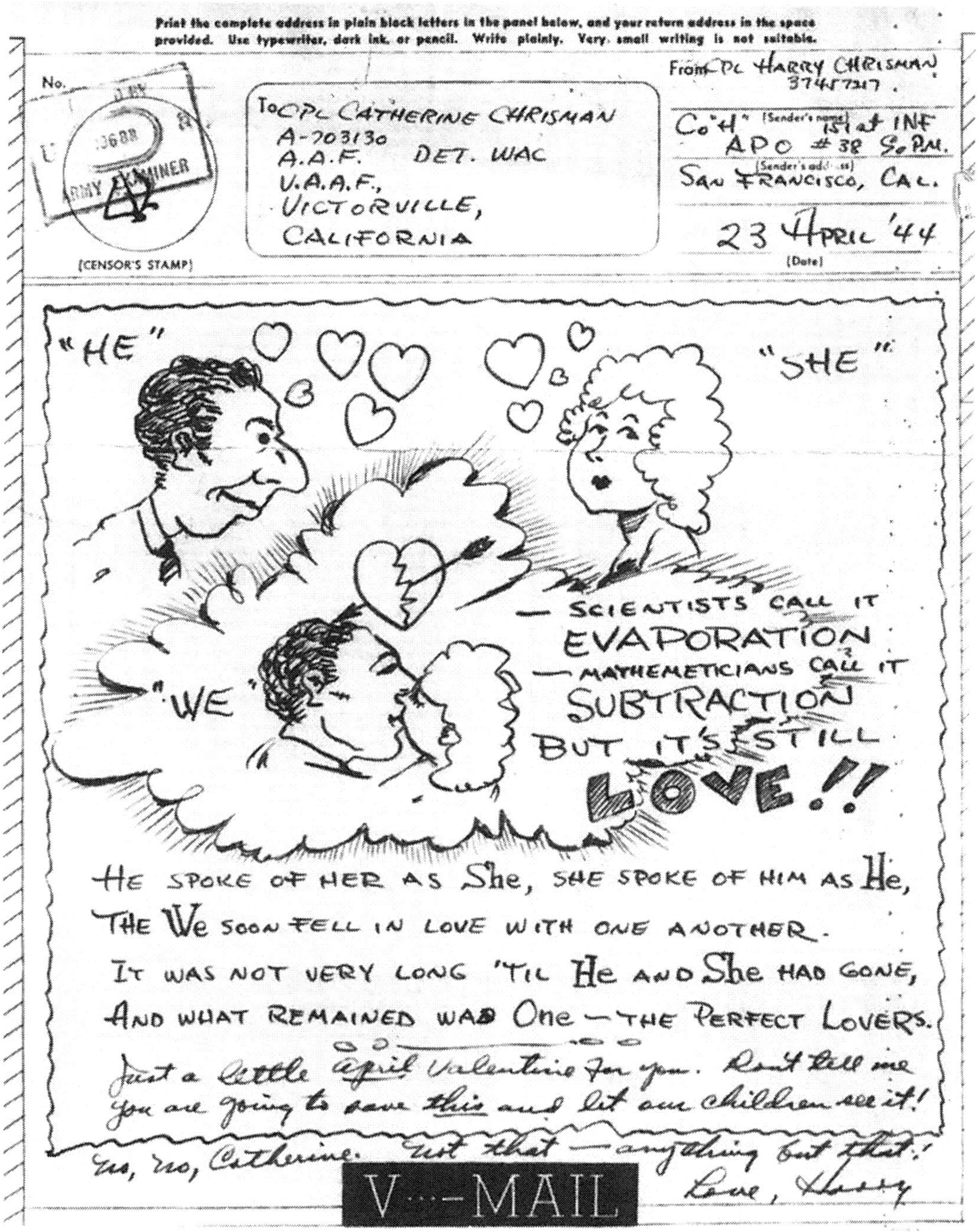

Print the complete address in plain block letters in the panel below, and your return address in the space provided. Use typewriter, dark ink, or pencil. Write plainly. Very small writing is not suitable.

No.

ARMY EXAMINER

(CENSOR'S STAMP)

To CPL CATHERINE CHRISMAN
A-703130
A.A.F. DET. WAC
V.A.A.F.,
VICTORVILLE,
CALIFORNIA

From PC HARRY CHRISMAN
37457217
(Sender's name)
Co "H" 151st INF
APO #38 % P.M.
(Sender's address)
SAN FRANCISCO, CAL.

23 APRIL '44
(Date)

"HE"

"SHE"

"WE"

— SCIENTISTS CALL IT
EVAPORATION
— MATHEMETICIANS CALL IT
SUBTRACTION
BUT IT'S STILL
LOVE!!

HE SPOKE OF HER AS She, SHE SPOKE OF HIM AS He,
THE We SOON FELL IN LOVE WITH ONE ANOTHER.
IT WAS NOT VERY LONG 'TIL He AND She HAD GONE,
AND WHAT REMAINED WAS One — THE PERFECT LOVERS.

Just a little April Valentine for you. Don't tell me you are going to save this and let our children see it! No, no, Catherine. Not that — anything but that!

Love, Harry

V—MAIL

He-She 4-23-44

This was posted on the Hysteria Haven bulletin board and every WAC on base came to see it, including the officers. There were many discussions as to what could be carried in that "Purse Packer" besides unanswered mail! (S)

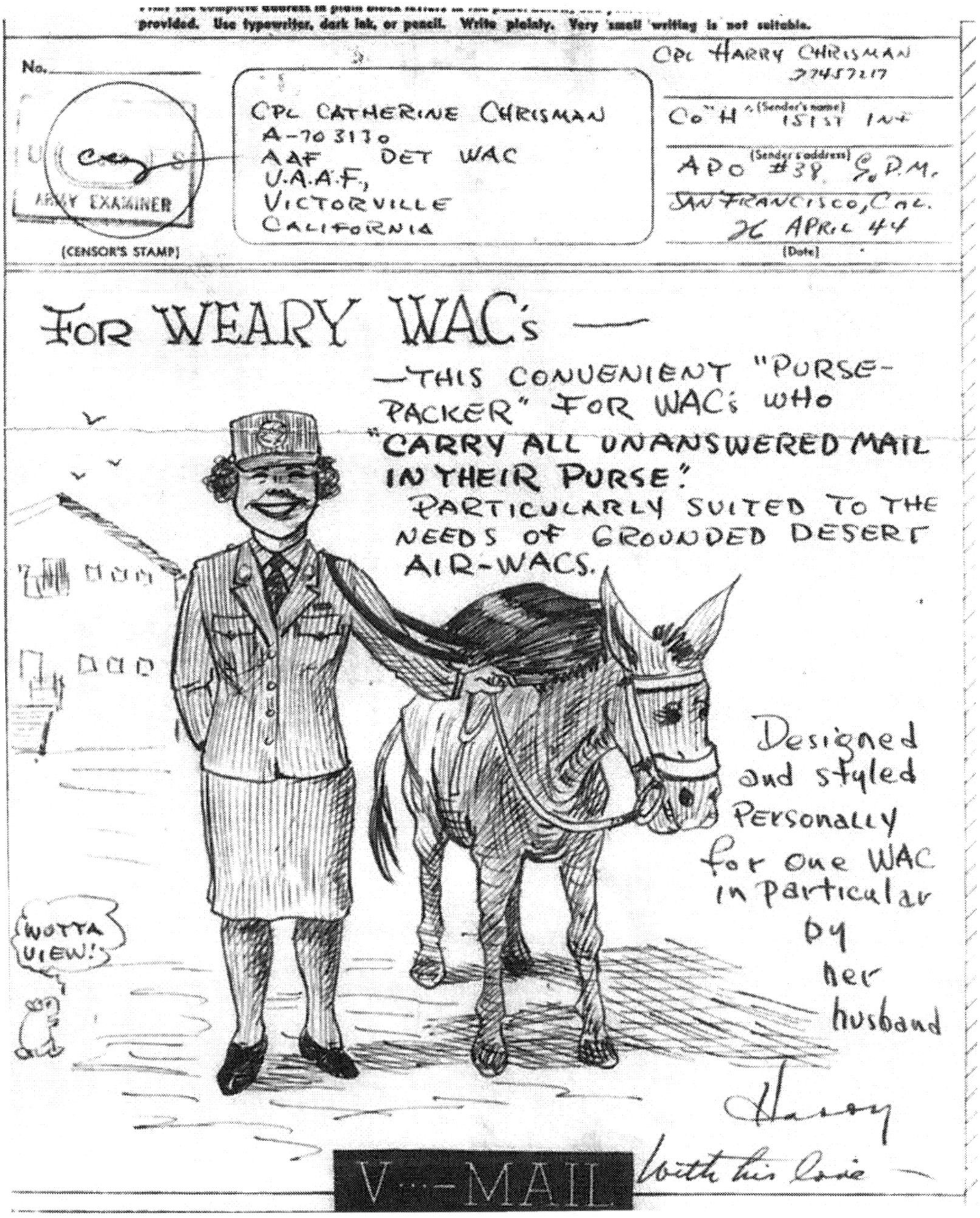
provided. Use typewriter, dark ink, or pencil. Write plainly. Very small writing is not suitable.
No.
ARMY EXAMINER
(CENSOR'S STAMP)
CPL CATHERINE CHRISMAN
A-703130
AAF DET WAC
U.A.A.F.,
VICTORVILLE
CALIFORNIA
CPL HARRY CHRISMAN
37457217
(Sender's name)
Co "H" 151ST INF
(Sender's address)
APO #38 C/o P.M.
SAN FRANCISCO, CAL.
26 APRIL 44
(Date)
FOR WEARY WAC's —
—THIS CONVENIENT "PURSE-PACKER" FOR WAC's WHO "CARRY ALL UNANSWERED MAIL IN THEIR PURSE."
PARTICULARLY SUITED TO THE NEEDS OF GROUNDED DESERT AIR-WACS.
WOTTA VIEW!
Designed and styled personally for one WAC in particular by her husband
Harry
with his love —
V---MAIL

Mail Mule 4-26-44

This cartoon was in reply to a letter Catherine sent remarking how she and a couple of other WACs were made fun of with the old "WAC-WAC, Quack-Quack." Most Americans appreciated the women in the Corps, but there were those "small" people who made themselves feel superior by the quack remark. (S)

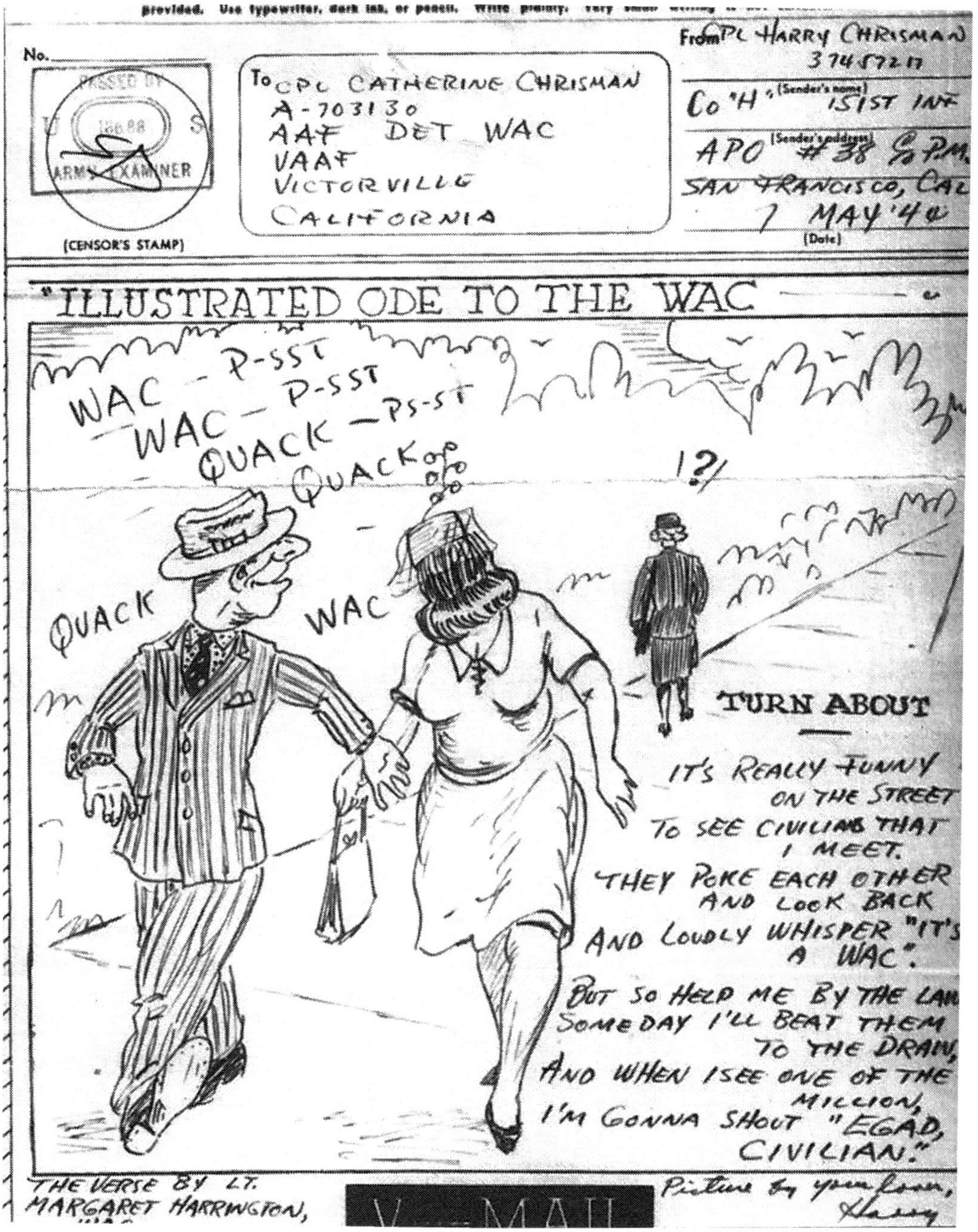
provided. Use typewriter, dark ink, or pencil. Write plainly.
No.
PASSED BY U S ARMY EXAMINER
(CENSOR'S STAMP)
To CPL CATHERINE CHRISMAN
A-703130
AAF DET WAC
VAAF
VICTORVILLE
CALIFORNIA
From CPL HARRY CHRISMAN
37457217
(Sender's name)
Co "H" 151ST INF
(Sender's address)
APO #38 % PM
SAN FRANCISCO, CAL
7 MAY '44
(Date)
"ILLUSTRATED ODE TO THE WAC"
WAC - P-SST
WAC - P-SST
QUACK - PS-ST
QUACK
QUACK
WAC
!?!
TURN ABOUT
IT'S REALLY FUNNY ON THE STREET
TO SEE CIVILIANS THAT I MEET.
THEY POKE EACH OTHER AND LOOK BACK
AND LOUDLY WHISPER "IT'S A WAC".
BUT SO HELP ME BY THE LAW
SOMEDAY I'LL BEAT THEM TO THE DRAW,
AND WHEN I SEE ONE OF THE MILLION,
I'M GONNA SHOUT "EGAD, CIVILIAN!"
THE VERSE BY LT. MARGARET HARRINGTON,
V-MAIL
Picture by your lover, Harry

Ode to the WAC 5-1-44

Harry was between assignments and, although he was now assigned to APSC, he had to wait for quarters, the "Army Way." He had tent space at Schofield Barracks as a temporary home. Catherine knew he was in Hawaii but she didn't get a letter of explanation of his new assignment until late May. (S)

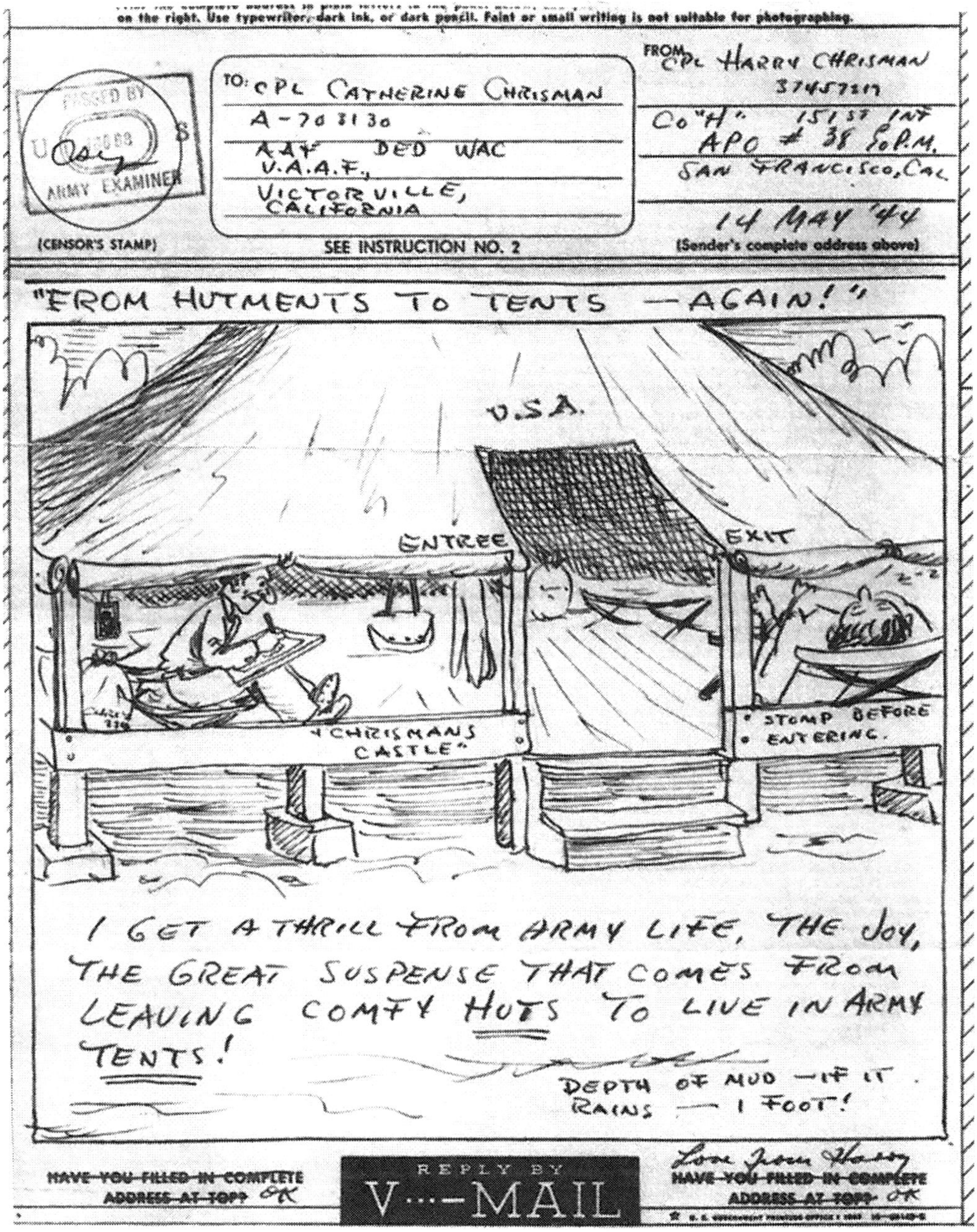
on the right. Use typewriter, dark ink, or dark pencil. Faint or small writing is not suitable for photographing.
PASSED BY
ARMY EXAMINER
(CENSOR'S STAMP)
TO: CPL CATHERINE CHRISMAN
A-708130
AAF DED WAC
V.A.A.F.,
VICTORVILLE,
CALIFORNIA
SEE INSTRUCTION NO. 2
FROM: CPL HARRY CHRISMAN
37457317
CO "H" 151ST INF
APO # 38 P.M.
SAN FRANCISCO, CAL
14 MAY '44
(Sender's complete address above)
"FROM HUTMENTS TO TENTS — AGAIN!"
U.S.A.
ENTREE
EXIT
"CHRISMANS CASTLE"
STOMP BEFORE ENTERING.
I GET A THRILL FROM ARMY LIFE, THE JOY, THE GREAT SUSPENSE THAT COMES FROM LEAVING COMFY HUTS TO LIVE IN ARMY TENTS!
DEPTH OF MUD — IF IT RAINS — 1 FOOT!
Love from Harry
HAVE YOU FILLED IN COMPLETE ADDRESS AT TOP? OK
REPLY BY V-MAIL
HAVE YOU FILLED IN COMPLETE ADDRESS AT TOP? OK

Tents Again 5-4-44

Harry was quick to pick up humor in any situation and he said it was hard not to laugh out loud when he overheard this comment. Catherine said the WACs at Victorville didn't think it was a very kind remark! (S)

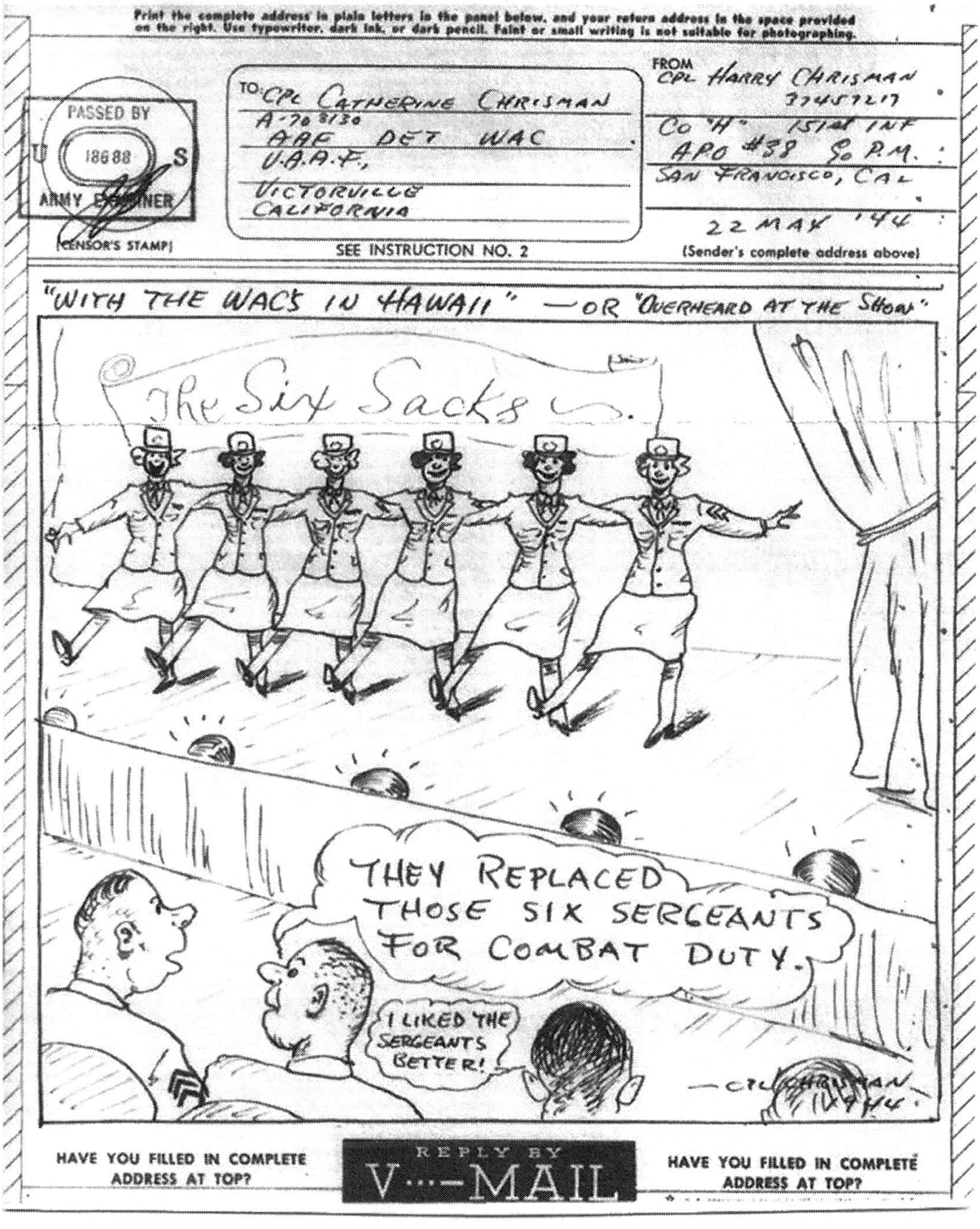

Print the complete address in plain letters in the panel below, and your return address in the space provided on the right. Use typewriter, dark ink, or dark pencil. Faint or small writing is not suitable for photographing.
PASSED BY
U 18688 S
ARMY EXAMINER
(CENSOR'S STAMP)
TO: CPL CATHERINE CHRISMAN
A-708130
AAF DET WAC
V.A.A.F.,
VICTORVILLE
CALIFORNIA
SEE INSTRUCTION NO. 2
FROM
CPL HARRY CHRISMAN
37457217
CO "H" 151ST INF
APO #38 % P.M.
SAN FRANCISCO, CAL
22 MAY '44
(Sender's complete address above)
"WITH THE WAC'S IN HAWAII" — OR "OVERHEARD AT THE SHOW"
The Six Sacks
THEY REPLACED THOSE SIX SERGEANTS FOR COMBAT DUTY.
I LIKED THE SERGEANTS BETTER!
— CPL CHRISMAN
HAVE YOU FILLED IN COMPLETE ADDRESS AT TOP?
REPLY BY V-MAIL
HAVE YOU FILLED IN COMPLETE ADDRESS AT TOP?

With the WACs in Hawaii 5-22-44

Fair-skinned women suffered from the desert sun at Victorville Air Base. Catherine said she used anything to cover her face, particularly her nose. The gals often wore a work hat with a brim they would pull down over their face. Although a sunscreen was invented for soldiers in the Pacific to use, and of course others who might need it, the women often scorned it as it was a most unattractive red. It was called "Red Vet Pet" for red veterinary petrolatum. It had limited effectiveness so many of the women just covered up and pulled that hat down over their faces (S)

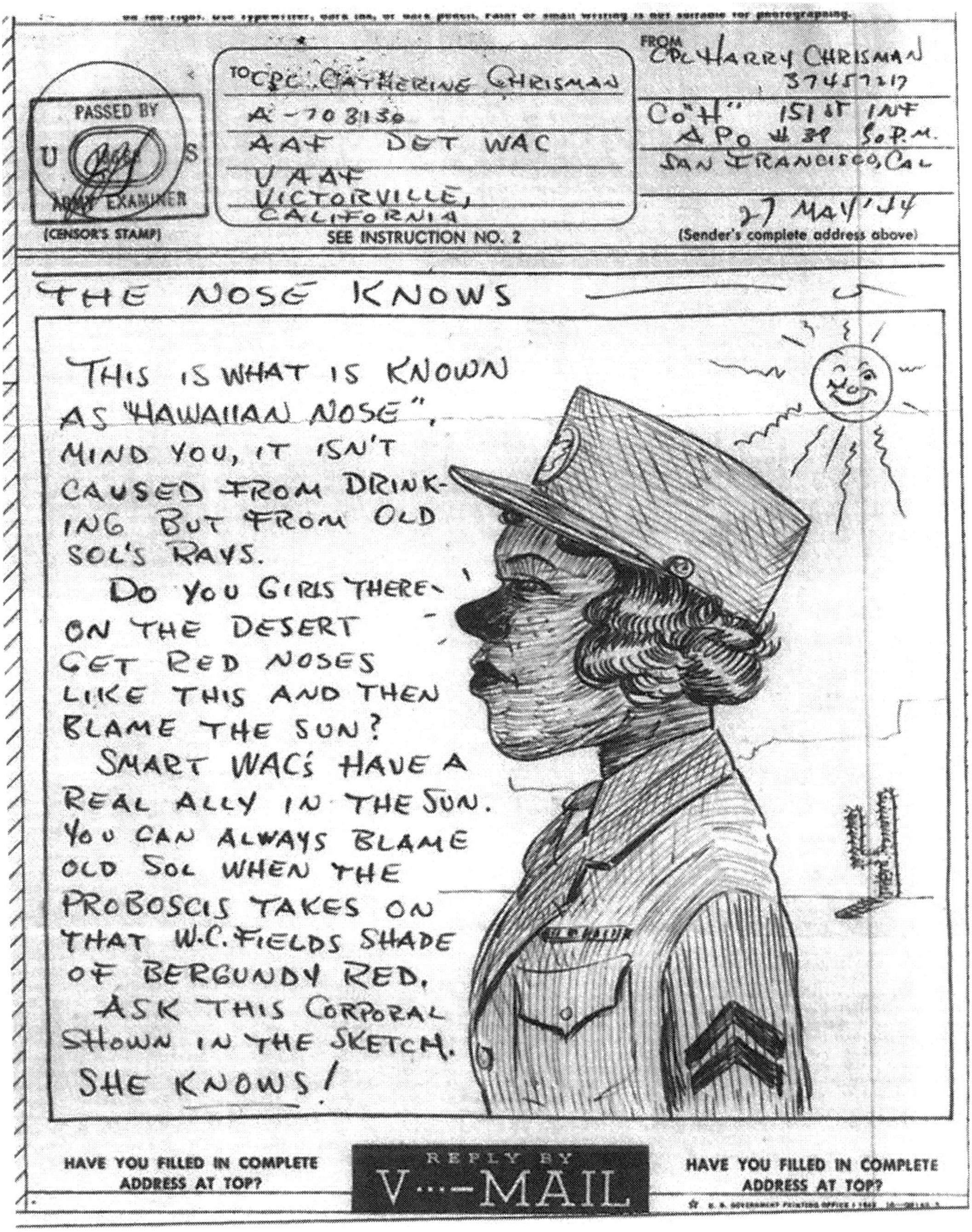
TO CPL. CATHERINE CHRISMAN
A-708130
AAF DET WAC
VAAF
VICTORVILLE,
CALIFORNIA
FROM CPL HARRY CHRISMAN
37457217
CO "H" 151ST INF
APO #39 S.O.P.M.
SAN FRANCISCO, CAL
27 MAY '44
PASSED BY
U S
ARMY EXAMINER
(CENSOR'S STAMP)
SEE INSTRUCTION NO. 2
(Sender's complete address above)
THE NOSE KNOWS
THIS IS WHAT IS KNOWN AS "HAWAIIAN NOSE". MIND YOU, IT ISN'T CAUSED FROM DRINKING BUT FROM OLD SOL'S RAYS.
DO YOU GIRLS THERE ON THE DESERT GET RED NOSES LIKE THIS AND THEN BLAME THE SUN?
SMART WAC'S HAVE A REAL ALLY IN THE SUN. YOU CAN ALWAYS BLAME OLD SOL WHEN THE PROBOSCIS TAKES ON THAT W.C. FIELDS SHADE OF BERGUNDY RED.
ASK THIS CORPORAL SHOWN IN THE SKETCH. SHE KNOWS!
HAVE YOU FILLED IN COMPLETE ADDRESS AT TOP?
REPLY BY
V...—MAIL
HAVE YOU FILLED IN COMPLETE ADDRESS AT TOP?

The Nose Knows 5-27-44

Of all the cartoons Harry sent to Catherine this one received the most accolades. The WACs in Hysteria Haven, plus others who regularly checked the bulletin board, would loudly comment, "Yes!," "Amen!," "No kidding!" etc. (S)

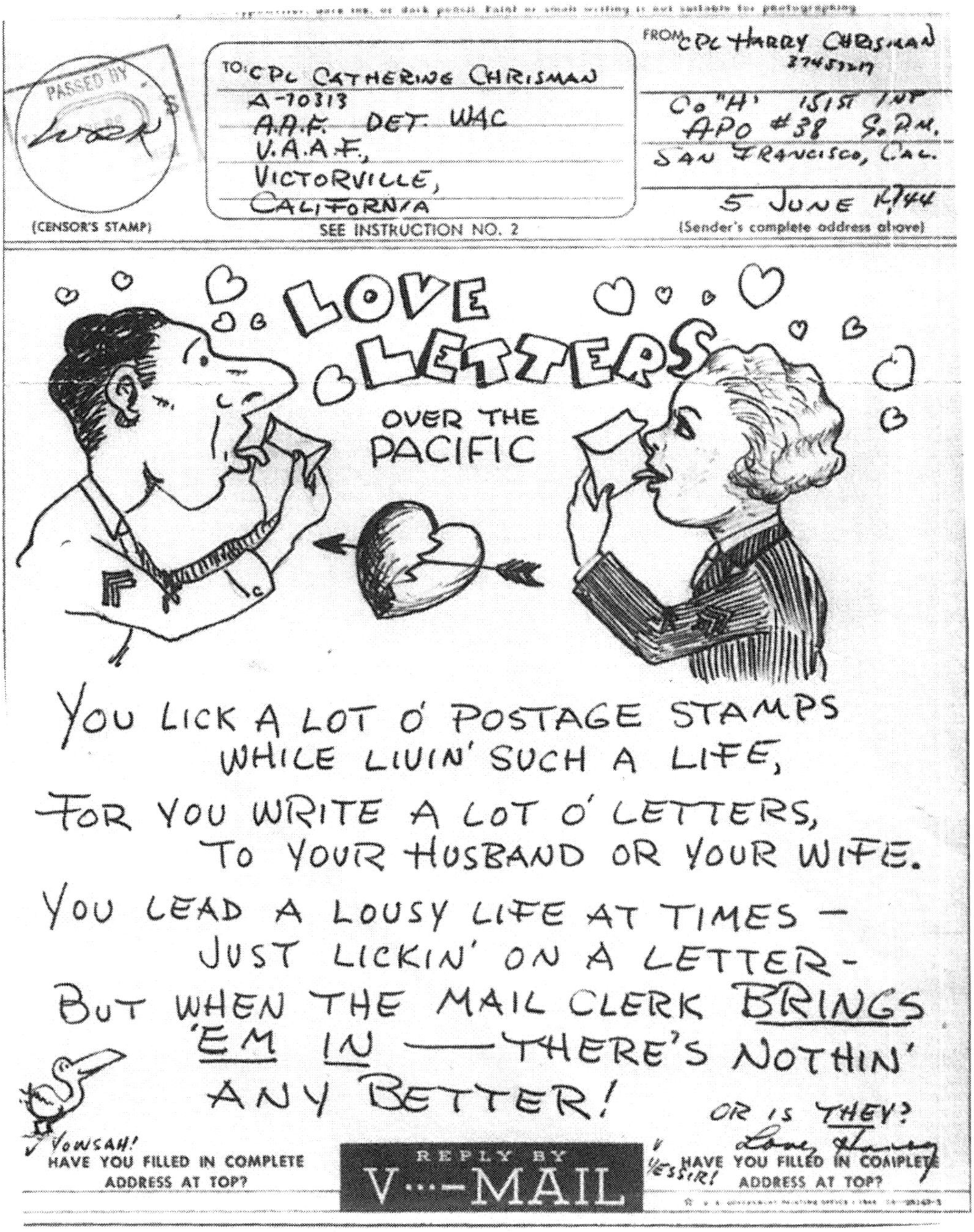
TO: CPL CATHERINE CHRISMAN
A-10313
A.A.F. DET. WAC
V.A.A.F.,
VICTORVILLE,
CALIFORNIA
FROM CPL HARRY CHRISMAN
37453217
Co "H" 151ST INF
APO #38 % P.M.
SAN FRANCISCO, CAL.
5 JUNE 1944
PASSED BY
(CENSOR'S STAMP)
SEE INSTRUCTION NO. 2
(Sender's complete address above)
LOVE LETTERS
OVER THE PACIFIC
YOU LICK A LOT O' POSTAGE STAMPS
WHILE LIVIN' SUCH A LIFE,
FOR YOU WRITE A LOT O' LETTERS,
TO YOUR HUSBAND OR YOUR WIFE.
YOU LEAD A LOUSY LIFE AT TIMES —
JUST LICKIN' ON A LETTER -
BUT WHEN THE MAIL CLERK BRINGS
'EM IN — THERE'S NOTHIN'
ANY BETTER!
OR IS THEY?
YOWSAH!
HAVE YOU FILLED IN COMPLETE
ADDRESS AT TOP?
REPLY BY
V...—MAIL
YESSIR!
HAVE YOU FILLED IN COMPLETE
ADDRESS AT TOP?

Love Over the Pacific 6-5-44

Harry and Catherine loved to read any book about ideas. Both seldom read fiction, preferring non-fiction. We would often have invigorating discussions about books such as The World as Will and Idea *by Arthur Schopenhauer (1819), which holds that all nature, including man, is the expression of an insatiable will to life; that the truest understanding of the world comes through art... Harry also could quote from Immanuel Kant's major work,* The Critique of Pure Reason *(1781). I didn't always understand, but Catherine did! (S)*

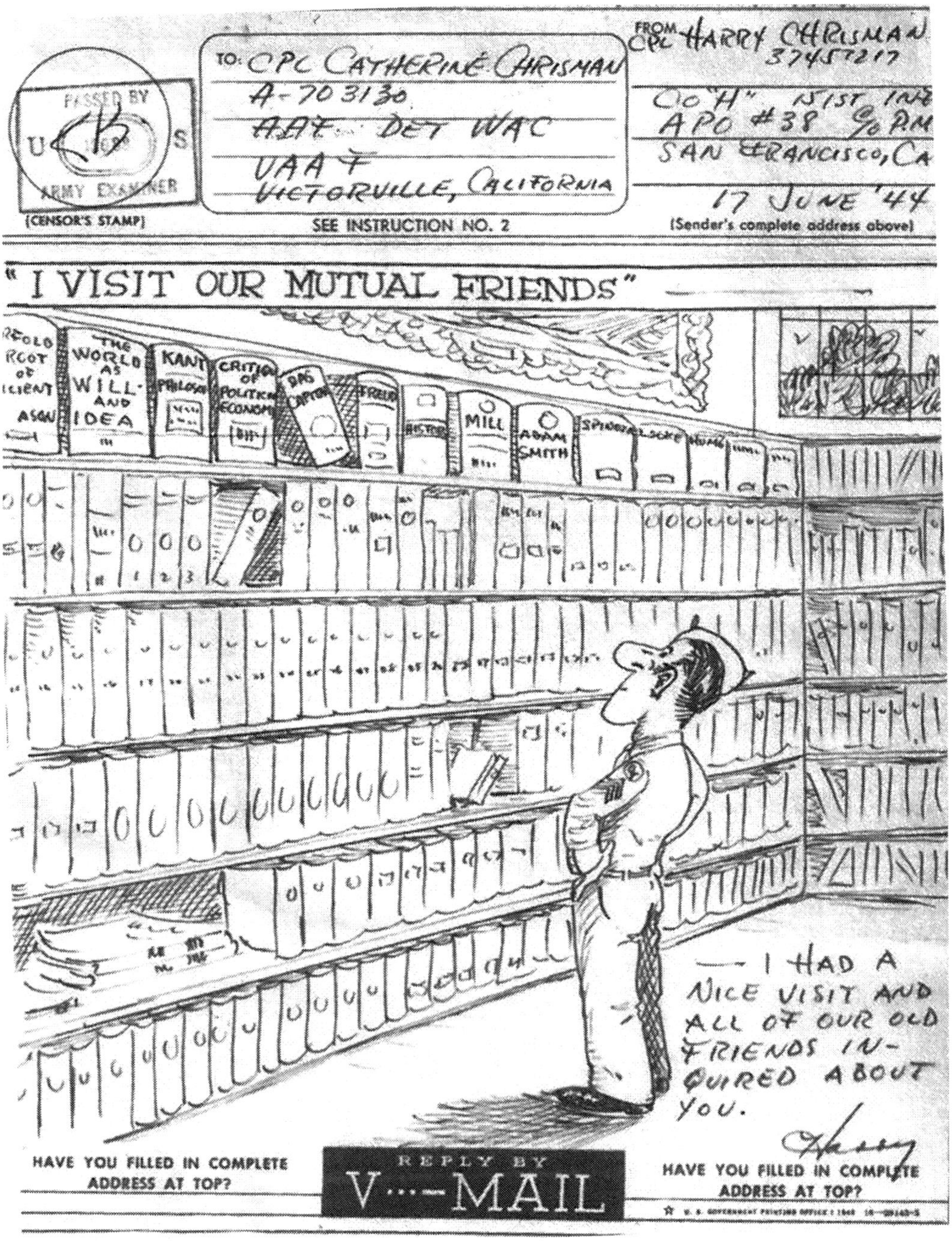
FROM CPL HARRY CHRISMAN
37457217
TO: CPL CATHERINE CHRISMAN
A-703130
AAF DET WAC
VAAF
VICTORVILLE, CALIFORNIA
PASSED BY
U S
ARMY EXAMINER
(CENSOR'S STAMP)
SEE INSTRUCTION NO. 2
C/o "H" 151ST INF
APO #38 % PM
SAN FRANCISCO, CA
17 JUNE '44
(Sender's complete address above)
"I VISIT OUR MUTUAL FRIENDS" —
THE WORLD AS WILL AND IDEA
KANT
DAS KAPITAL
FREUD
MILL
ADAM SMITH
— I HAD A NICE VISIT AND ALL OF OUR OLD FRIENDS INQUIRED ABOUT YOU.
Harry
HAVE YOU FILLED IN COMPLETE ADDRESS AT TOP?
REPLY BY
V---MAIL
HAVE YOU FILLED IN COMPLETE ADDRESS AT TOP?

Old Friends 6-17-44

Harry was fascinated by the Hawaiian language. I think his ability to hear a song or music only once and remember it was a real gift and a foreign language was just a song in his head. He would often play one of his ukuleles and sing a Hawaiian song in Hawaiian. I asked him about the translation and he laughed and said I wouldn't know if he was telling the truth or not. He was right.

"Ua Mau ke Ea o ka 'Āina i ka Pono" is a well-known Hawaiian phrase which was adopted as the motto of the state of Hawaii. As such, it is commonly translated as "The life of the land is perpetuated in righteousness".

Shortly after this V-Mail, Harry was granted a furlough, the first and only one he had during those three and a half years. He corrected the blot when he came home. (S)

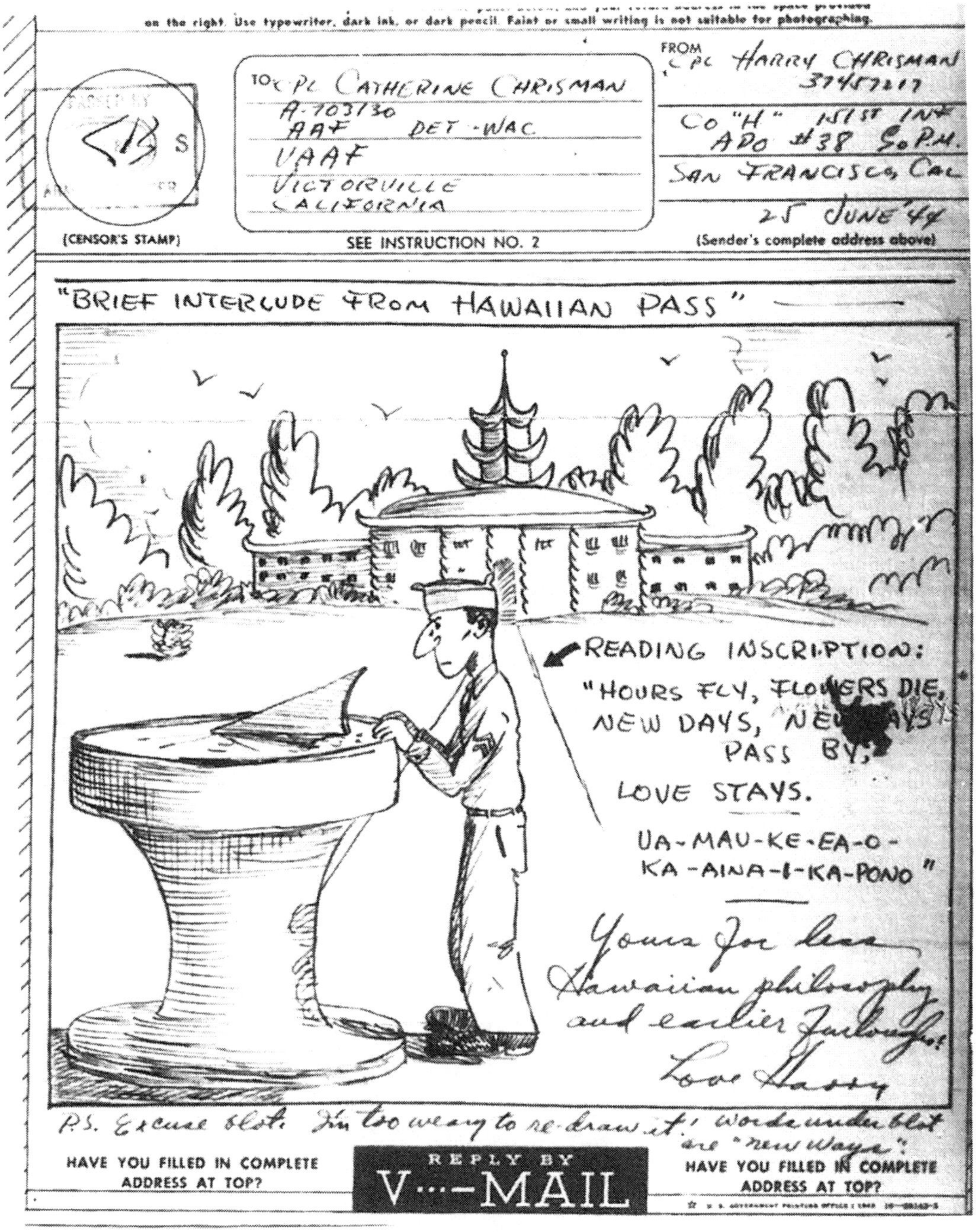
on the right. Use typewriter, dark ink, or dark pencil. Faint or small writing is not suitable for photographing.
TO CPL CATHERINE CHRISMAN
A-703130
AAF DET-WAC
VAAF
VICTORVILLE
CALIFORNIA
FROM CPL HARRY CHRISMAN
37457217
CO "H" 151ST INF
APO #38 % P.M.
SAN FRANCISCO, CAL
25 JUNE '44
(CENSOR'S STAMP)
SEE INSTRUCTION NO. 2
(Sender's complete address above)
"BRIEF INTERLUDE FROM HAWAIIAN PASS"
READING INSCRIPTION:
"HOURS FLY, FLOWERS DIE,
NEW DAYS, NE AYS
PASS BY,
LOVE STAYS.
UA-MAU-KE-EA-O-
KA-AINA-I-KA-PONO"
Yours for less
Hawaiian philosophy
and earlier furloughs!
Love Harry
P.S. Excuse blot. I'm too weary to re-draw it. Words under blot are "new ways".
HAVE YOU FILLED IN COMPLETE ADDRESS AT TOP?
REPLY BY V···– MAIL
HAVE YOU FILLED IN COMPLETE ADDRESS AT TOP?

Sundial 6-25-44

Every G.I. who got letters was the envy of those who did not. Harry would often get six or seven at a time. He would sometimes read his out loud to others as both his mother and Catherine wrote interesting letters. He smiled once while reminiscing and said the fellows complained that he left out "the good" parts of Catherine's. As far as I know she never sent him a V-Mail and Harry destroyed most of her letters as he just didn't have room for them. She did likewise after his death. (S)

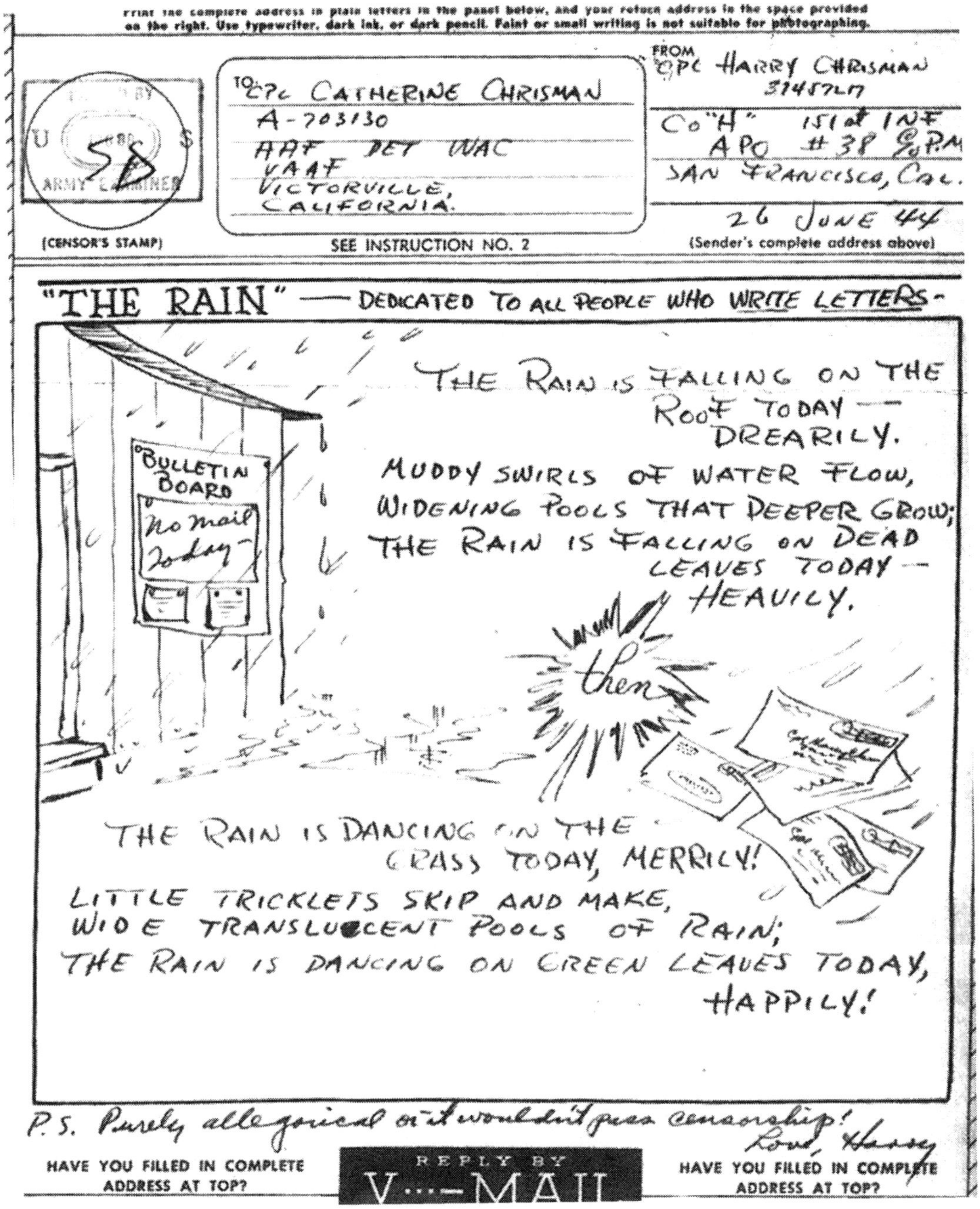

Print the complete address in plain letters in the panel below, and your return address in the space provided on the right. Use typewriter, dark ink, or dark pencil. Faint or small writing is not suitable for photographing.

TO: CPL CATHERINE CHRISMAN
A-703130
AAF DET WAC
VAAF
VICTORVILLE,
CALIFORNIA.

(CENSOR'S STAMP)

SEE INSTRUCTION NO. 2

FROM CPL HARRY CHRISMAN
37457417
CO "H" 151st INF
APO #38 % P.M.
SAN FRANCISCO, CAL.

26 JUNE 44

(Sender's complete address above)

"THE RAIN" — DEDICATED TO ALL PEOPLE WHO WRITE LETTERS —

BULLETIN BOARD
No mail Today—
then

THE RAIN IS FALLING ON THE ROOF TODAY — DREARILY.
MUDDY SWIRLS OF WATER FLOW,
WIDENING POOLS THAT DEEPER GROW;
THE RAIN IS FALLING ON DEAD LEAVES TODAY — HEAVILY.

THE RAIN IS DANCING ON THE GRASS TODAY, MERRILY!
LITTLE TRICKLETS SKIP AND MAKE,
WIDE TRANSLUCENT POOLS OF RAIN;
THE RAIN IS DANCING ON GREEN LEAVES TODAY, HAPPILY!

P.S. Purely allegorical or it wouldn't pass censorship!
Love, Harry

HAVE YOU FILLED IN COMPLETE ADDRESS AT TOP?

REPLY BY V···—MAIL

HAVE YOU FILLED IN COMPLETE ADDRESS AT TOP?

The Rain 6-26-44

Harry's new job at the Army Port and Service Command was right up his alley! He loved it and the soldiers in his classes enjoyed his teaching. He was smart, funny, and entertaining. He drew this for Catherine after a particularly good session! (S)

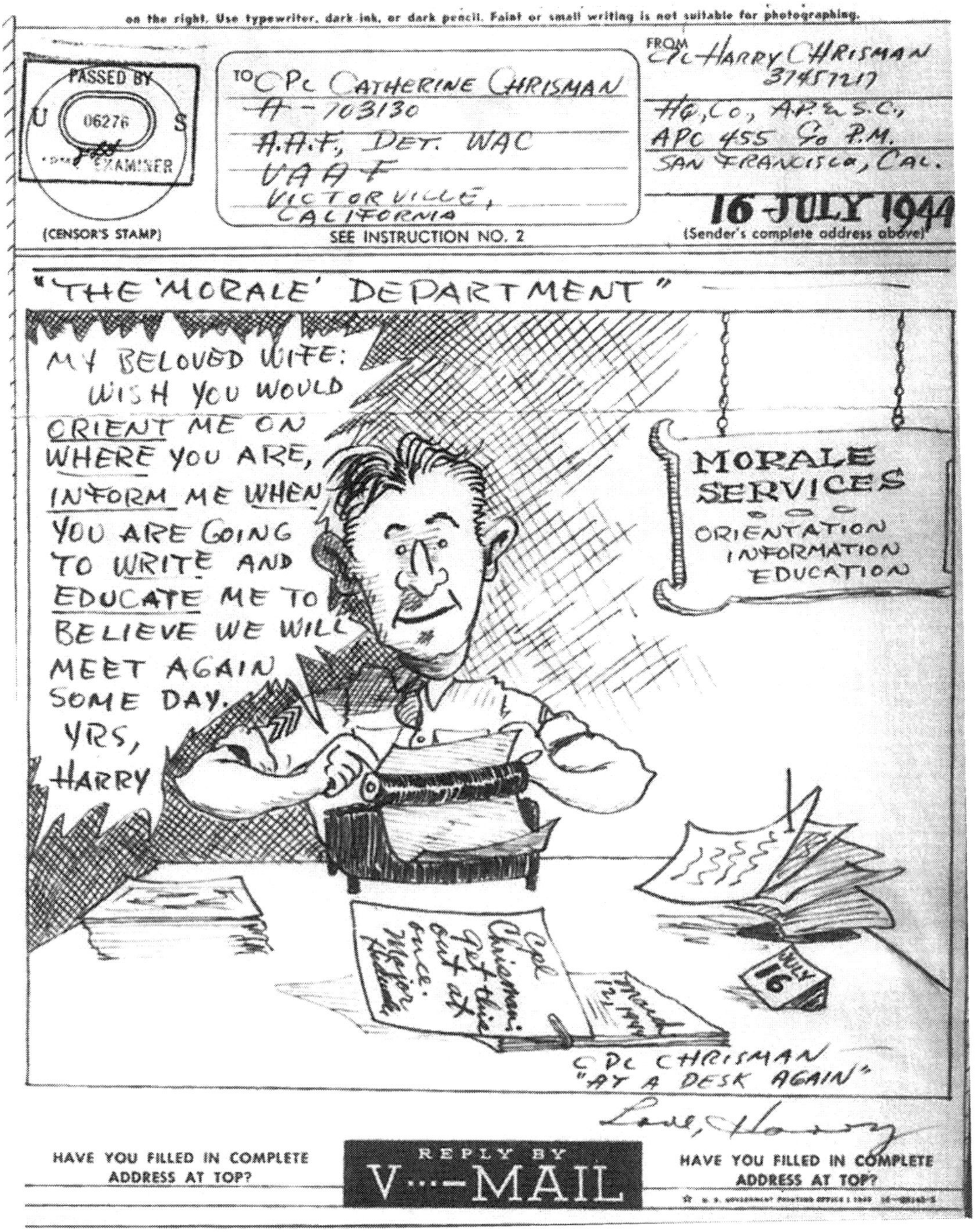
on the right. Use typewriter, dark ink, or dark pencil. Faint or small writing is not suitable for photographing.
PASSED BY
U 06276 S
EXAMINER
(CENSOR'S STAMP)
TO CPL CATHERINE CHRISMAN
A-703130
A.A.F. DET. WAC
VAAF
VICTORVILLE,
CALIFORNIA
SEE INSTRUCTION NO. 2
FROM CPL HARRY CHRISMAN
37457217
HQ. CO. AP. & S.C.
APO 455 C/O P.M.
SAN FRANCISCO, CAL.
16 JULY 1944
(Sender's complete address above)
"THE 'MORALE' DEPARTMENT"
MY BELOVED WIFE: WISH YOU WOULD ORIENT ME ON WHERE YOU ARE, INFORM ME WHEN YOU ARE GOING TO WRITE AND EDUCATE ME TO BELIEVE WE WILL MEET AGAIN SOME DAY. YRS, HARRY
MORALE SERVICES
ORIENTATION
INFORMATION
EDUCATION
JULY 16
CPL CHRISMAN "AT A DESK AGAIN"
Love, Harry
HAVE YOU FILLED IN COMPLETE ADDRESS AT TOP?
REPLY BY V-MAIL
HAVE YOU FILLED IN COMPLETE ADDRESS AT TOP?

Morale 7-16-44

Many non-military personnel worked at the APSC. Harry said it was refreshing to look at feminine pulchritude rather than gooney birds! (S)

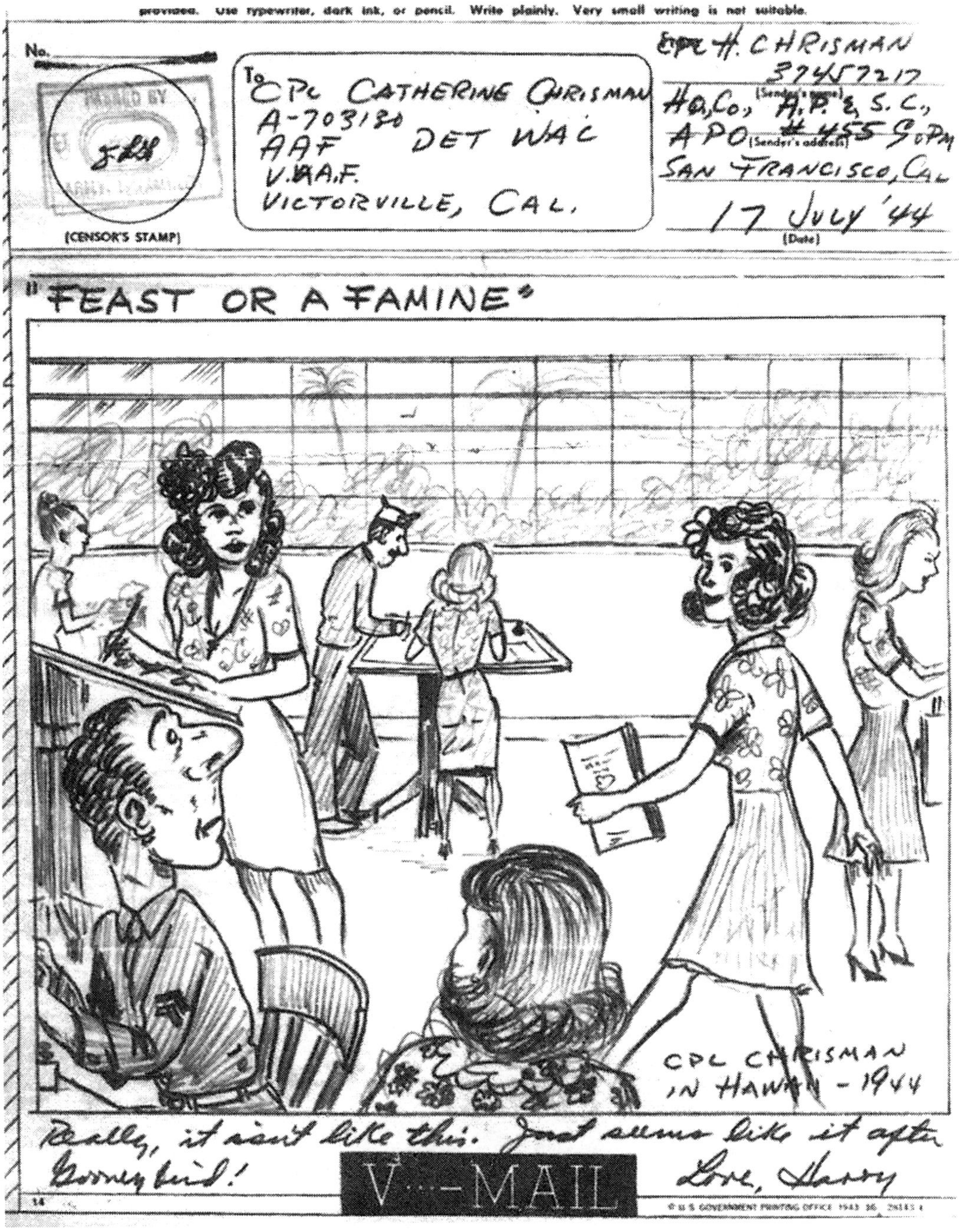
provided. Use typewriter, dark ink, or pencil. Write plainly. Very small writing is not suitable.
No.
To CPL CATHERINE CHRISMAN
A-703180
AAF DET WAC
V.A.A.F.
VICTORVILLE, CAL.
CPL H. CHRISMAN
37457217
(Sender's name)
HQ, Co., A.P. & S.C.,
APO #455 % PM
(Sender's address)
SAN FRANCISCO, CAL
17 JULY '44
(Date)
(CENSOR'S STAMP)
"FEAST OR A FAMINE"
CPL CHRISMAN IN HAWAII - 1944
Really, it ain't like this. Just seems like it after Gooneybird!
Love, Harry
V---MAIL
U.S. GOVERNMENT PRINTING OFFICE 1943

Feast or Famine 7-17-44

Harry was busy learning his new job so only a few V-Mails were sent in June and July 1944. He was amused at the soldiers who tied to date the local females. By that time many of the women on the island, both native and non-native, had experienced the sorrow of trusting a man in uniform. (S)

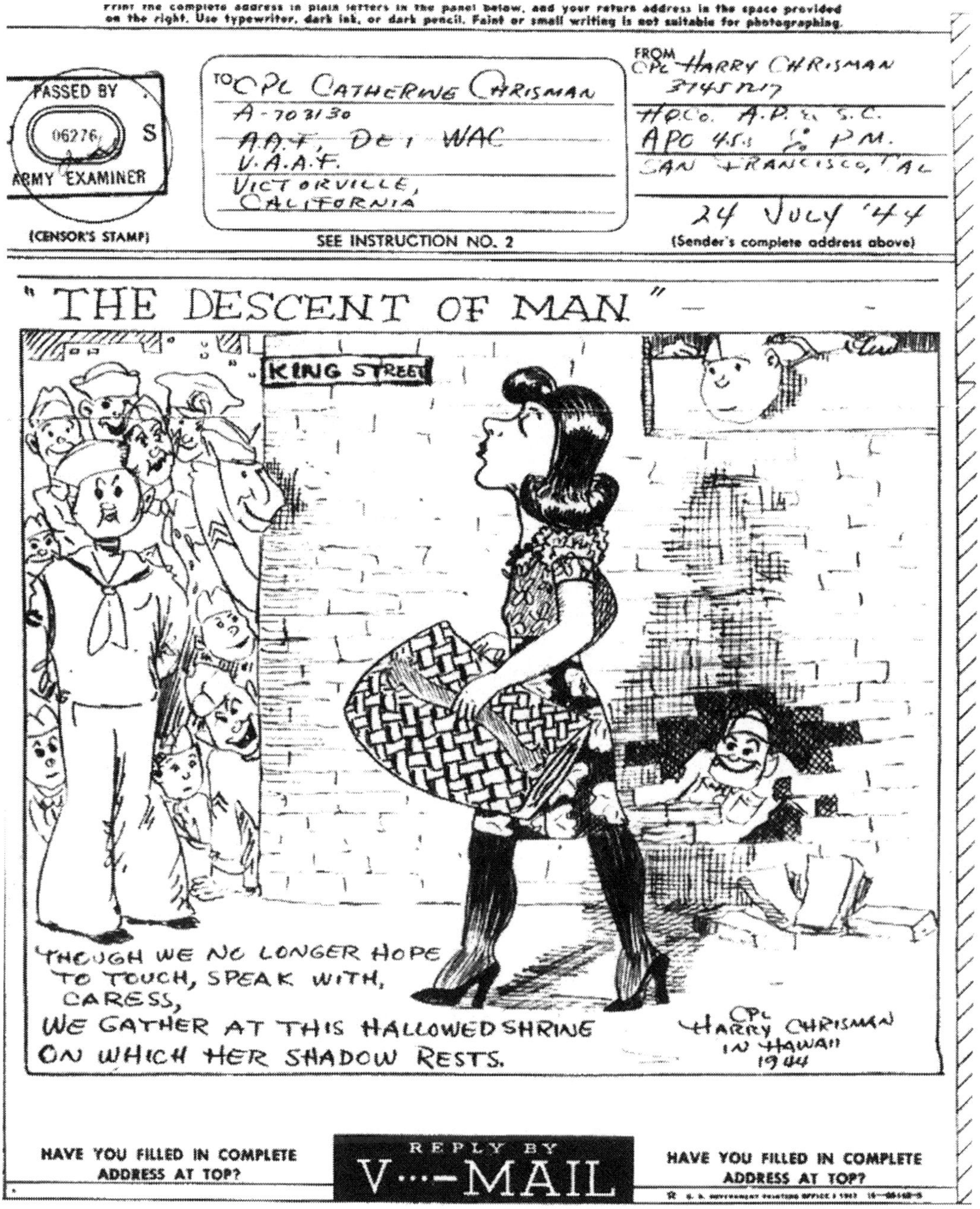
Print the complete address in plain letters in the panel below, and your return address in the space provided on the right. Use typewriter, dark ink, or dark pencil. Faint or small writing is not suitable for photographing.
PASSED BY
06276
S
ARMY EXAMINER
(CENSOR'S STAMP)
TO CPL CATHERINE CHRISMAN
A-703130
A.A.F. DET WAC
V.A.A.F.
VICTORVILLE,
CALIFORNIA
SEE INSTRUCTION NO. 2
FROM CPL HARRY CHRISMAN
HQ. Co. A.P. & S.C.
SAN FRANCISCO, CAL
24 JULY '44
(Sender's complete address above)
"THE DESCENT OF MAN" —
KING STREET
THOUGH WE NO LONGER HOPE TO TOUCH, SPEAK WITH, CARESS,
WE GATHER AT THIS HALLOWED SHRINE ON WHICH HER SHADOW RESTS.
CPL HARRY CHRISMAN IN HAWAII 1944
HAVE YOU FILLED IN COMPLETE ADDRESS AT TOP?
REPLY BY V—MAIL
HAVE YOU FILLED IN COMPLETE ADDRESS AT TOP?

Descent of Man 7-24-44

Harry longed for a furlough but he did not get one until July of 1945. The rule that a WAC could spend her husband's furlough with him was duly embraced and Harry and Catherine spent a lovely time at their favorite lake in Nebraska, Lake Minatare. The picture Harry drew for the WACs still in Victorville is in the appendix of this book. This V-Mail was sent 11 months before he was granted a furlough. (S)

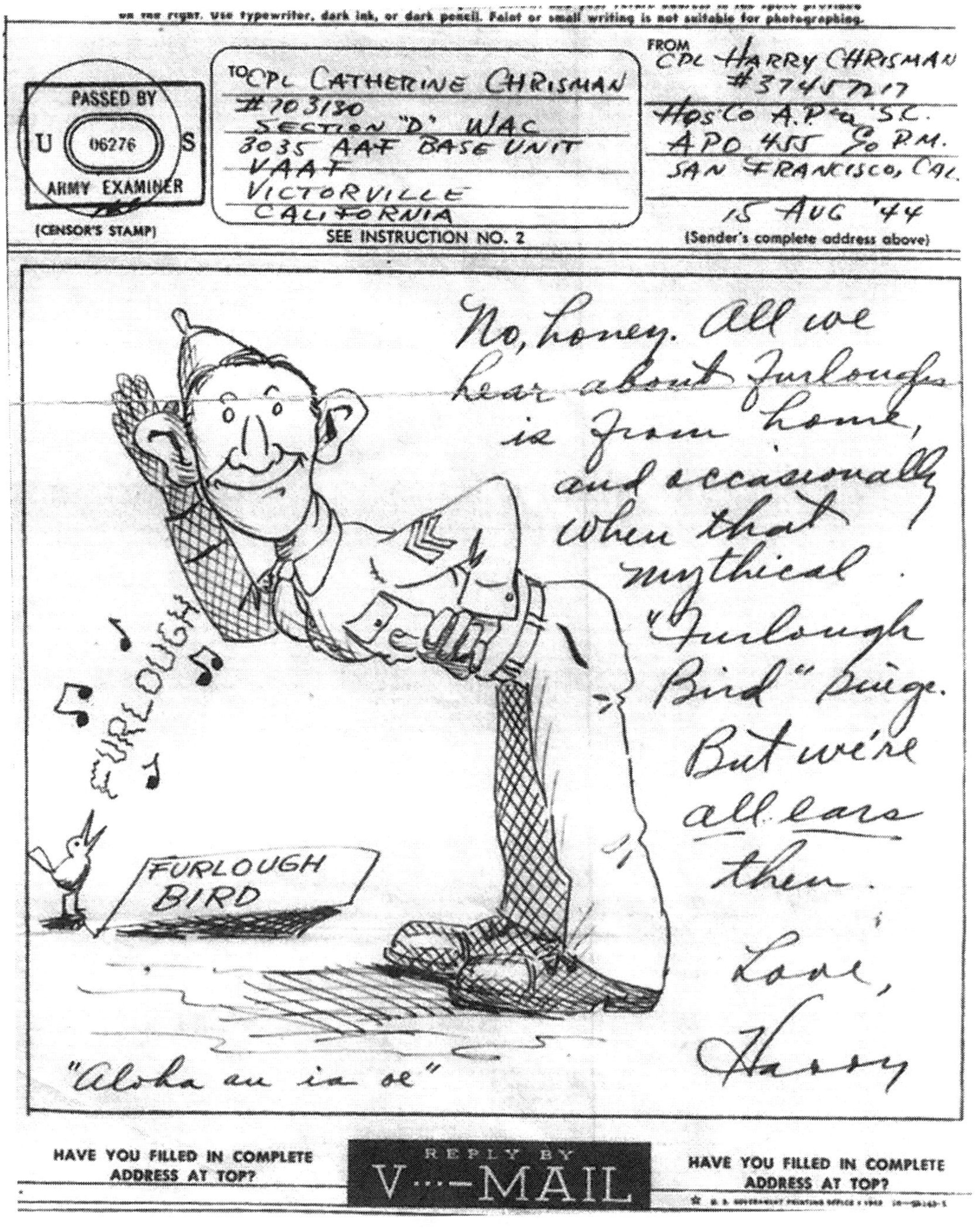

on the right. Use typewriter, dark ink, or dark pencil. Faint or small writing is not suitable for photographing.

PASSED BY
U 06276 S
ARMY EXAMINER
(CENSOR'S STAMP)

TO CPL CATHERINE CHRISMAN
#703130
SECTION "D" WAC
3035 AAF BASE UNIT
VAAF
VICTORVILLE
CALIFORNIA

SEE INSTRUCTION NO. 2

FROM CPL HARRY CHRISMAN
#37457217
HQS CO A.P.O.'S.C.
APO 455 % P.M.
SAN FRANCISCO, CAL.
15 AUG '44

(Sender's complete address above)

No, honey. All we hear about furloughs is from home, and occasionally when that mythical "Furlough Bird" sings. But we're all ears then.

Love,
Harry

FURLOUGH
FURLOUGH BIRD
"Aloha au ia oe"

HAVE YOU FILLED IN COMPLETE ADDRESS AT TOP?

REPLY BY V---MAIL

HAVE YOU FILLED IN COMPLETE ADDRESS AT TOP?

Furlough Bird 8-15-44

Catherine knew boredom was the bane of every enlisted soldier, especially those who were support troops. Harry really wanted to see action, but Catherine was relieved he was playing a ukulele rather than a bazooka. Oh, how she missed Harry's singing. Whenever I was around him he "sang" his work. He never heard a song he couldn't play or sing after listening to it just once! (S)

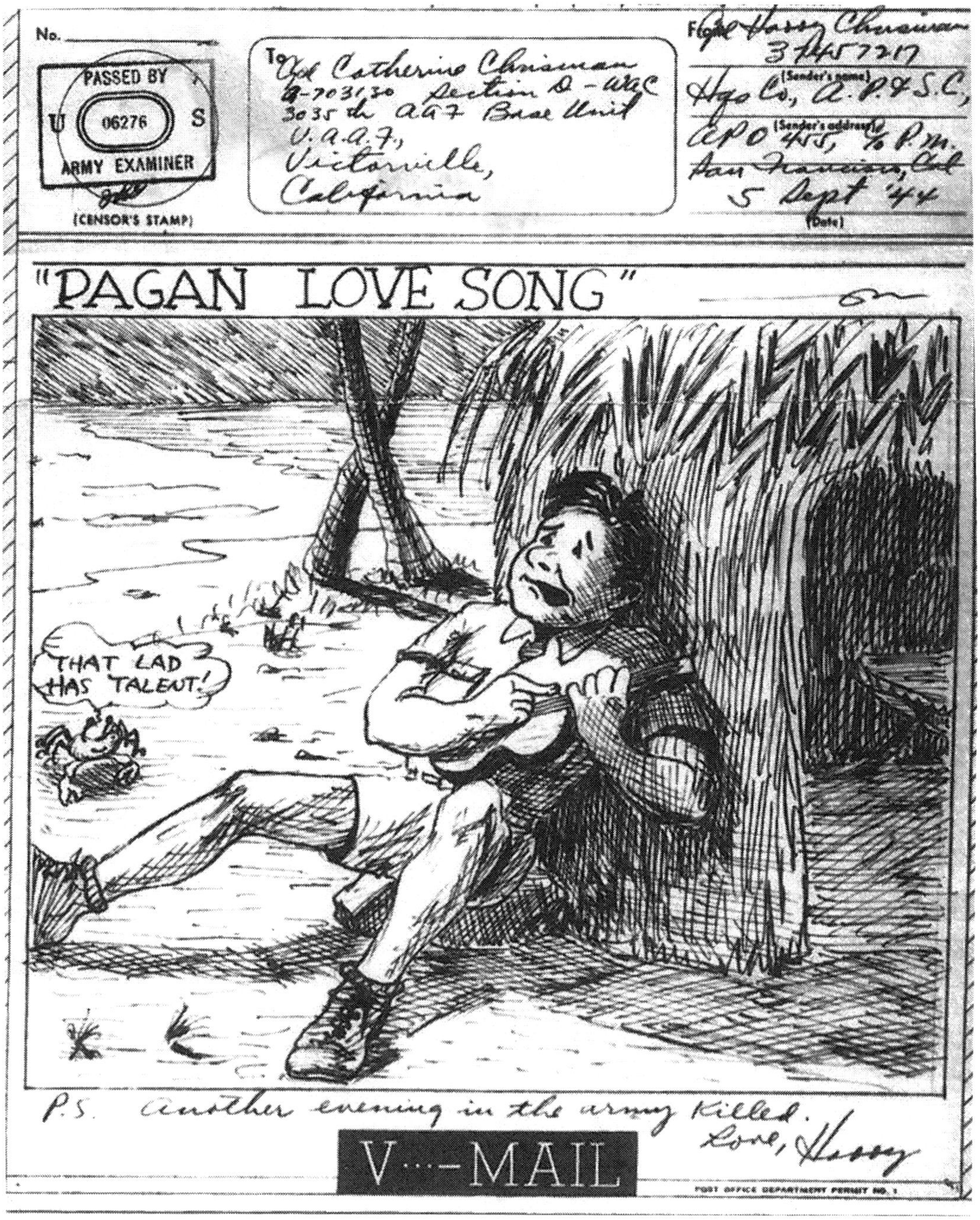
No.
PASSED BY
U 06276 S
ARMY EXAMINER
(CENSOR'S STAMP)
To
Victorville,
California
From
(Sender's name)
(Sender's address)
5 Sept '44
(Date)
"PAGAN LOVE SONG"
THAT LAD HAS TALENT!
P.S. Another evening in the army killed.
Love, Harry
V---MAIL
POST OFFICE DEPARTMENT PERMIT NO. 1

Pagan Love Song 9-5-44

Harry's sense of humor did not always set well with Catherine, but this kind of V-Mail was certainly a change from the usual, no pun intended! (S)

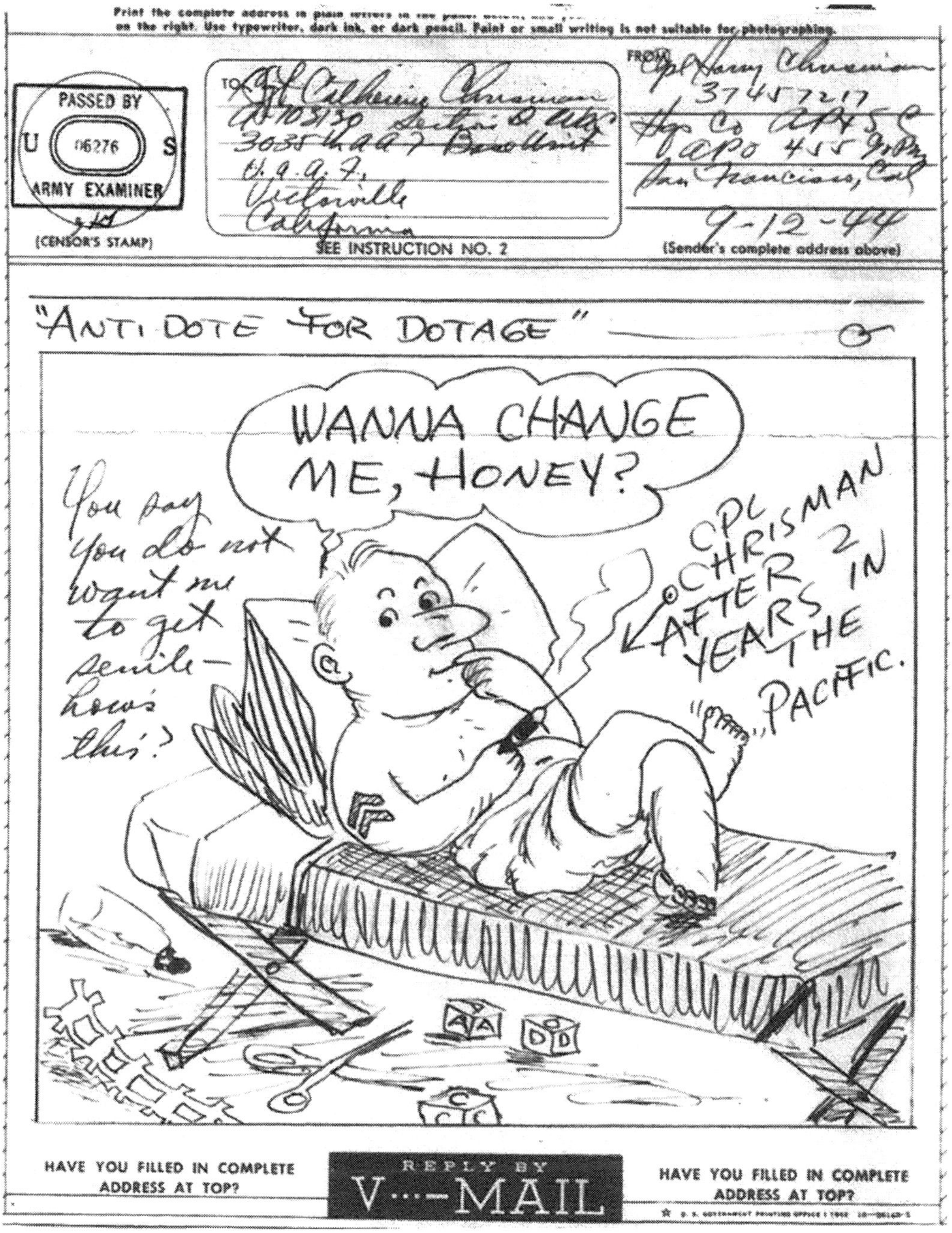
on the right. Use typewriter, dark ink, or dark pencil. Faint or small writing is not suitable for photographing.
PASSED BY
U 06276 S
ARMY EXAMINER
(CENSOR'S STAMP)
TO
Victorville
California
SEE INSTRUCTION NO. 2
FROM
Cpl Harry Chrisman
37457217
San Francisco, Cal
9-12-44
(Sender's complete address above)
"ANTI-DOTE FOR DOTAGE"
WANNA CHANGE ME, HONEY?
You say you do not want me to get senile—hows this?
CPL CHRISMAN AFTER 2 YEARS IN THE PACIFIC.
HAVE YOU FILLED IN COMPLETE ADDRESS AT TOP?
REPLY BY V···–MAIL
HAVE YOU FILLED IN COMPLETE ADDRESS AT TOP?

Dotage 9-12-44

Catherine got her sergeant stripes before Harry, a promotion he had trouble accepting gracefully, and he grumbled and griped about it with acerbic wit. His sister, Stell, tried to make Catherine feel better by congratulating her promotion. Catherine appreciated Stell's support but she was sure Harry would get his deserving third stripe soon. He eventually did but I think it always grated him a bit. His male chauvinism showed through at times. But, surprisingly enough, he accepted my admonishments. It makes me smile to remember them.

This is the last V-Mail he drew with Effie, the Gooney Bird, on it. But not the last one he drew using memories of Christmas Island. (S)

P. S. "Dog in the manger" = An attempt to belittle another's accomplishment.

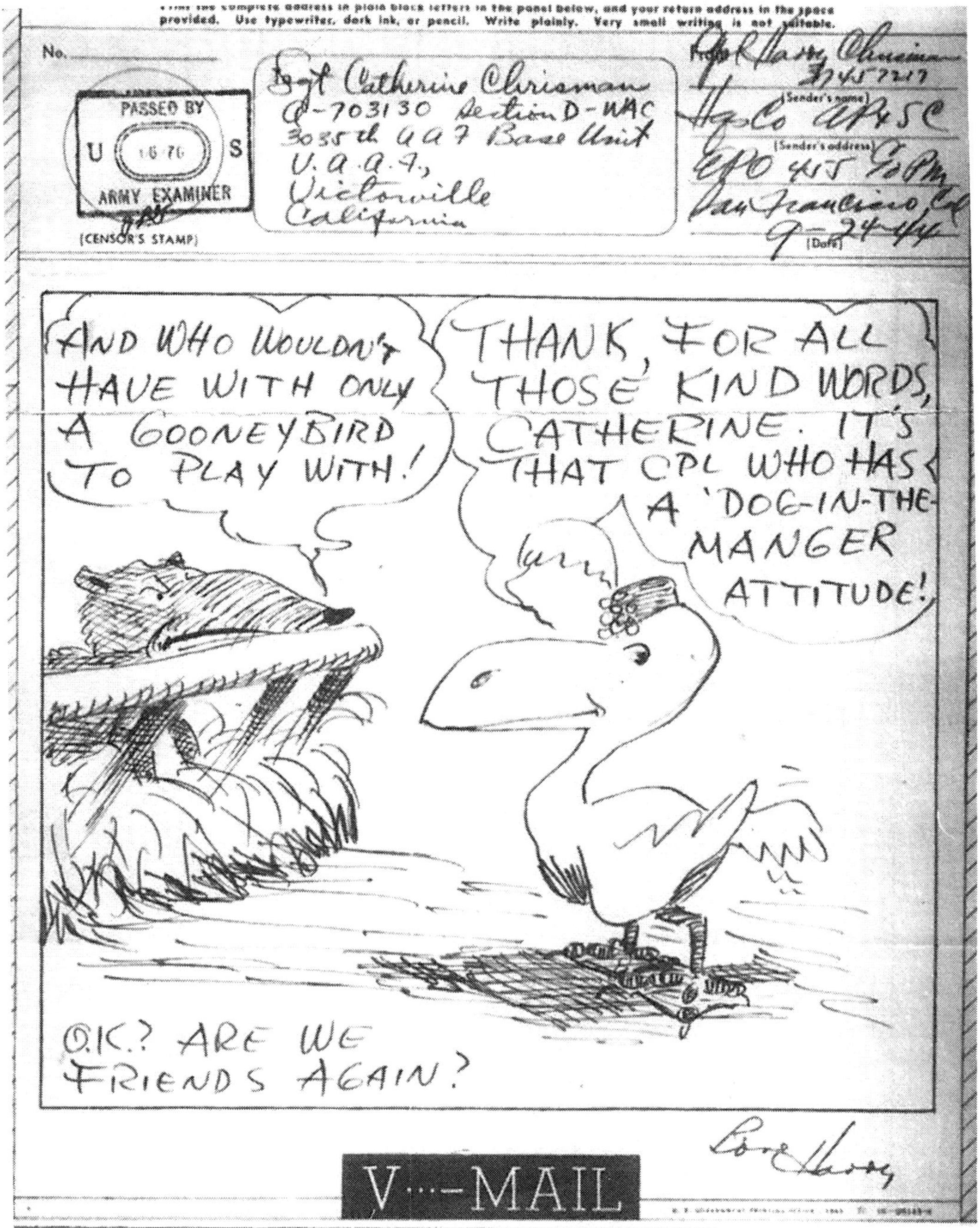
provided. Use typewriter, dark ink, or pencil. Write plainly. Very small writing is not suitable.
No.
PASSED BY
U S
ARMY EXAMINER
(CENSOR'S STAMP)
Sgt Catherine Chrisman
A-703130 Section D-WAC
3035th AAF Base Unit
V.A.A.F.,
Victorville
California
(Sender's name)
(Sender's address)
San Francisco, Cal
9-24-44
(Date)
AND WHO WOULDN'T HAVE WITH ONLY A GOONEYBIRD TO PLAY WITH!
THANK, FOR ALL THOSE KIND WORDS, CATHERINE. IT'S THAT CPL WHO HAS A 'DOG-IN-THE-MANGER ATTITUDE!
O.K.? ARE WE FRIENDS AGAIN?
Love Harry
V—MAIL

Dog in the Manger 9-24-44

Cathy called me in Honolulu from her Base in California. The call was a failure, because of electrical static. But the phone company got its pay nevertheless. (H)

Catherine's sister, Bernice, told Catherine that there was a special rate for Army personnel on a call to Honolulu since restrictions had been lifted. For $12 she could call Harry and that would be Catherine's birthday present. Well, that was just too good to pass up so Catherine called. As Harry writes, static was so bad they could barely hear each other and then it was, "Hello...Hello...Who is this?...Is this Harry?"

Well they kept screaming at each other for some time and finally Catherine hung up. The operator called her and said she heard Catherine tell Harry that it was only $12 for the call. "But, Madam, that's just for the first three minutes. You talked much longer. The cost is now $47." It took Catherine two months to pay Bernice the $35 extra! (S)

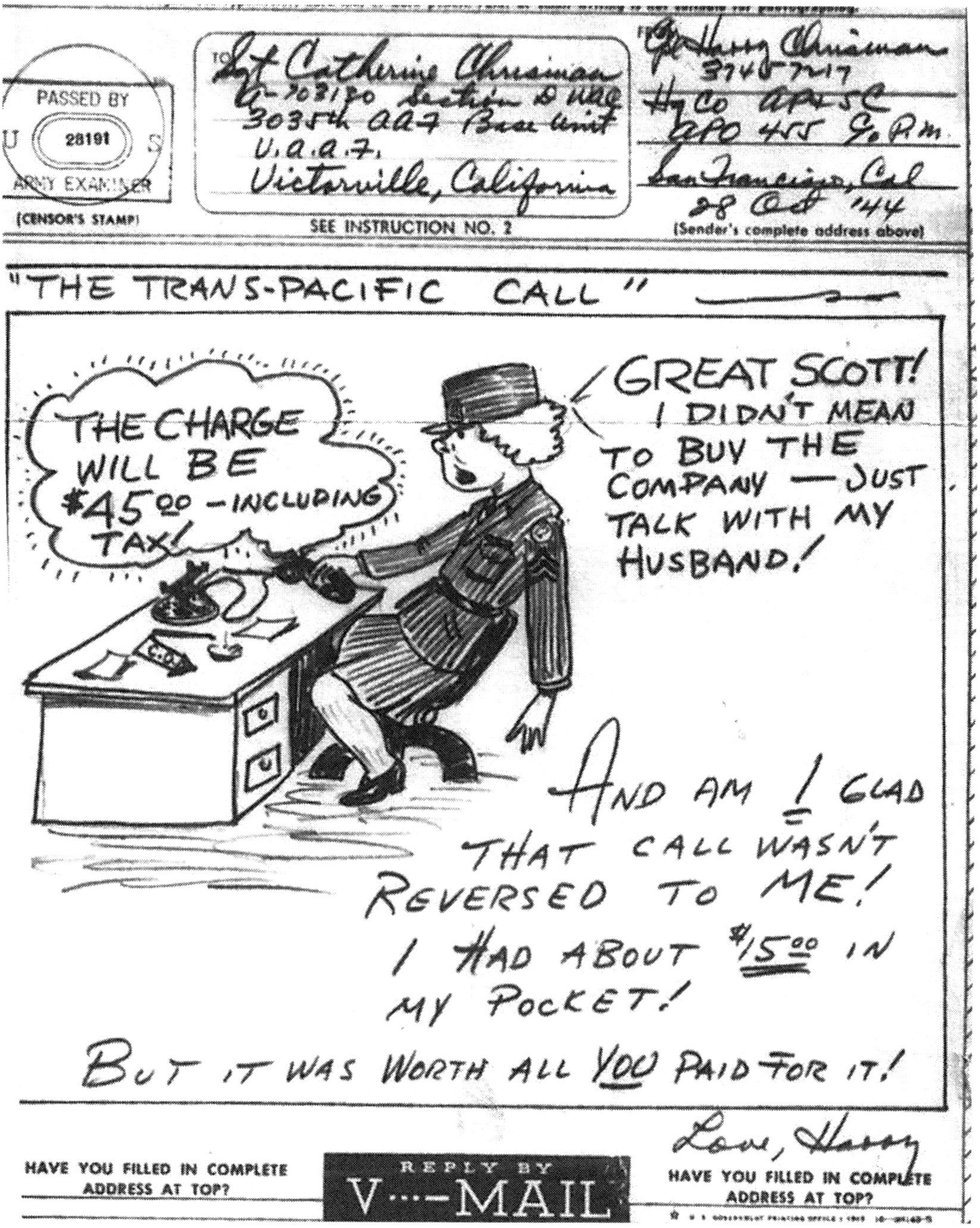
PASSED BY
U 28191 S
ARMY EXAMINER
(CENSOR'S STAMP)
To Sgt Catherine Chrisman
3035th AAF Base Unit
Victorville, California
SEE INSTRUCTION NO. 2
28 Oct '44
(Sender's complete address above)
"THE TRANS-PACIFIC CALL"
THE CHARGE WILL BE $45.00 - INCLUDING TAX!
GREAT SCOTT! I DIDN'T MEAN TO BUY THE COMPANY — JUST TALK WITH MY HUSBAND!
AND AM I GLAD THAT CALL WASN'T REVERSED TO ME! I HAD ABOUT $15.00 IN MY POCKET!
BUT IT WAS WORTH ALL YOU PAID FOR IT!
Love, Harry
HAVE YOU FILLED IN COMPLETE ADDRESS AT TOP?
REPLY BY V---MAIL
HAVE YOU FILLED IN COMPLETE ADDRESS AT TOP?

Phone Call 10-28-44

Oh, how Harry longed for a furlough, not only to see Catherine, but also his mother and other relatives. He particularly appreciated his mother who really kept the family together after his father could no longer work the homestead close to Broken Bow, Nebraska. Eugene Chrisman suffered from rheumatoid arthritis and for several years Harry's mother took care of his father and the four children. Eventually his father was well enough to buy the livery stable in Scottsbluff, Nebraska, move the family there and raise mules for the Army. Berna Hunter Chrisman wrote many magazine articles, wrote to many lonely soldiers during WWII, and published her memoir, "When You And I Were Young, Nebraska!" (S)

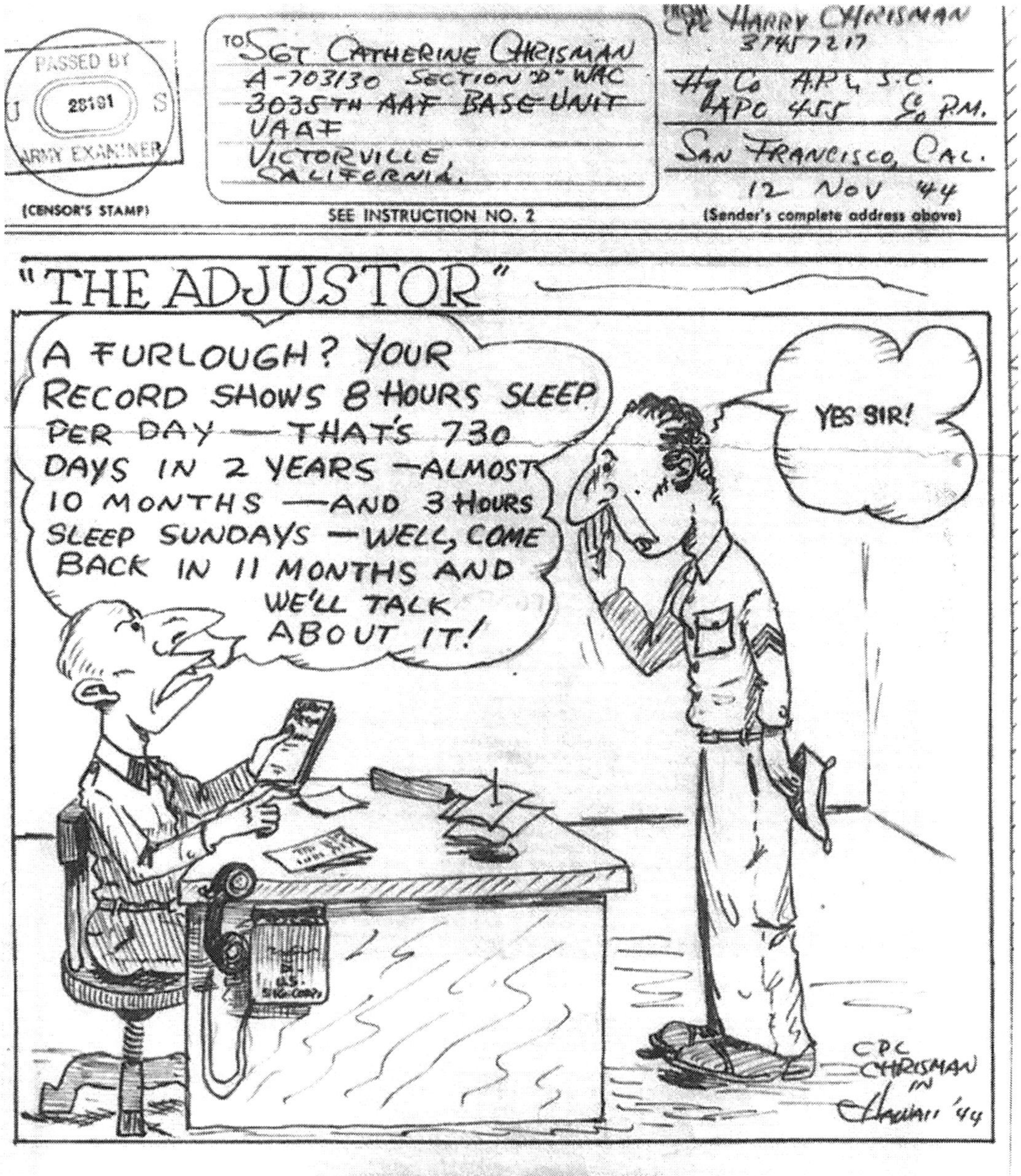
PASSED BY
28181
U S
ARMY EXAMINER
(CENSOR'S STAMP)
TO SGT CATHERINE CHRISMAN
A-703130 SECTION "D" WAC
3035TH AAF BASE UNIT
VAAF
VICTORVILLE,
CALIFORNIA.
SEE INSTRUCTION NO. 2
FROM CPL HARRY CHRISMAN
37457217
Hq Co ARG S.C.
APO 455 % P.M.
SAN FRANCISCO, CAL.
12 NOV 44
(Sender's complete address above)
"THE ADJUSTOR"
A FURLOUGH? YOUR RECORD SHOWS 8 HOURS SLEEP PER DAY — THAT'S 730 DAYS IN 2 YEARS — ALMOST 10 MONTHS — AND 3 HOURS SLEEP SUNDAYS — WELL, COME BACK IN 11 MONTHS AND WE'LL TALK ABOUT IT!
YES SIR!
CPL CHRISMAN IN Hawaii '44
HAVE YOU FILLED IN COMPLETE ADDRESS AT TOP?
REPLY BY V...-MAIL
HAVE YOU FILLED IN COMPLETE ADDRESS AT TOP?
18

The Adjustor 11-12-44

It began to be "unfunny" when an old Major Hilliger, a Special Service "dropout," a Harvard man and a resident of Honolulu who lived in a fine home with his family, gave a lecture on how good celibacy was for the rest of us! (H)

This was Harry's way of griping. The two V-Mails he sent Catherine that day pointed out how inane and unfair some of the Army policies were. It would be seven months before he was granted a furlough. (S)

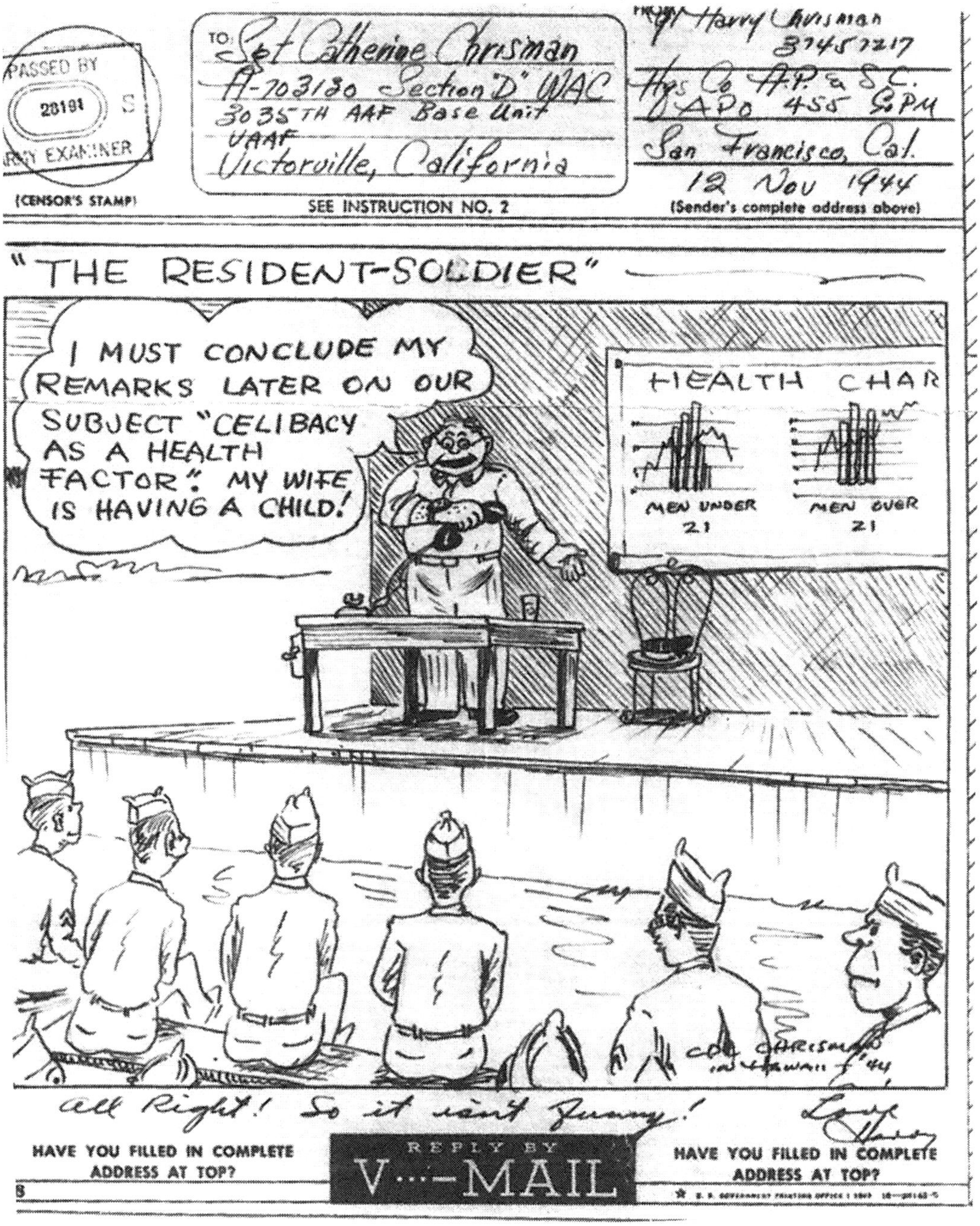
PASSED BY
20191
ARMY EXAMINER
(CENSOR'S STAMP)
TO: Sgt Catherine Chrisman
A-703130 Section "D" WAC
3035TH AAF Base Unit
VAAF
Victorville, California
SEE INSTRUCTION NO. 2
FROM: Pvt Harry Chrisman
37457217
Hqs Co A.P. & S.C.
APO 455 SPM
San Francisco, Cal.
12 Nov 1944
(Sender's complete address above)
"THE RESIDENT-SOLDIER"
I MUST CONCLUDE MY REMARKS LATER ON OUR SUBJECT "CELIBACY AS A HEALTH FACTOR". MY WIFE IS HAVING A CHILD!
HEALTH CHAR
MEN UNDER 21
MEN OVER 21
All Right! So it isn't funny!
Love Harry
HAVE YOU FILLED IN COMPLETE ADDRESS AT TOP?
REPLY BY V-MAIL
HAVE YOU FILLED IN COMPLETE ADDRESS AT TOP?

Resident Soldier 11-12-44

Just another way for Harry to tell Catherine how much her letter writing meant to him. This V-Mail would have been sent on to his mother. She kept everything he wrote to her and the V-Mails also sent to Catherine or other family members. (S)

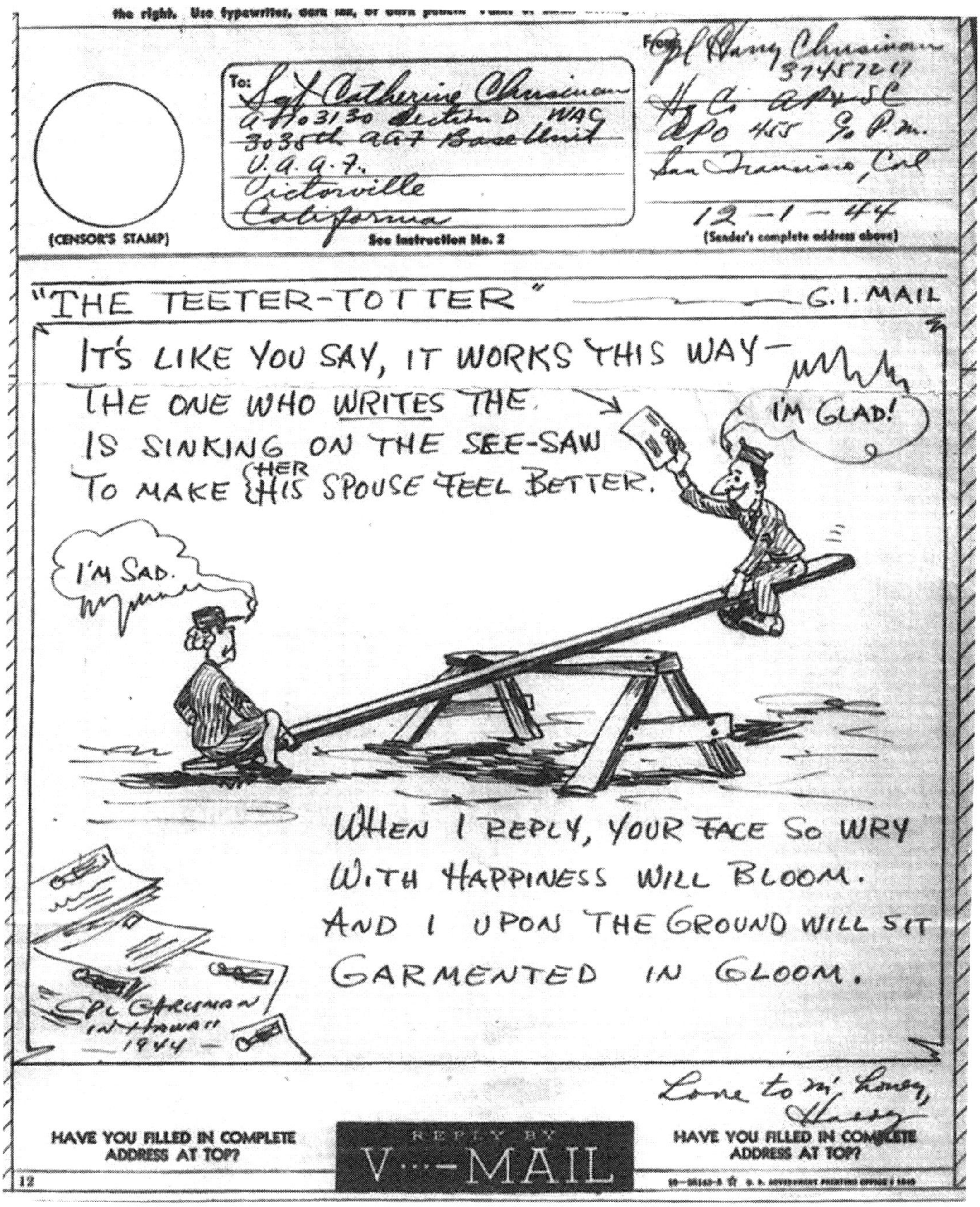
To: Sgt Catherine Chrisman
Victorville
California
(CENSOR'S STAMP)
See Instruction No. 2
12-1-44
(Sender's complete address above)
"THE TEETER-TOTTER" G.I. MAIL
IT'S LIKE YOU SAY, IT WORKS THIS WAY—
THE ONE WHO WRITES THE
IS SINKING ON THE SEE-SAW
TO MAKE {HER HIS SPOUSE FEEL BETTER.
I'M GLAD!
I'M SAD.
WHEN I REPLY, YOUR FACE SO WRY
WITH HAPPINESS WILL BLOOM.
AND I UPON THE GROUND WILL SIT
GARMENTED IN GLOOM.
Cpl Chrisman in Hawaii 1944
Love to m' Honey,
Harry
HAVE YOU FILLED IN COMPLETE ADDRESS AT TOP?
REPLY BY V···—MAIL
HAVE YOU FILLED IN COMPLETE ADDRESS AT TOP?
12

Teeter-Totter 12-1-44

Harry often found it difficult to draw cartoons about his work at the APSC because he was mainly teaching classes, so he described his day in long letters. This V-Mail takes him back to his time on Christmas Island. It was something to draw, a pastime which gave him great pleasure. (S)

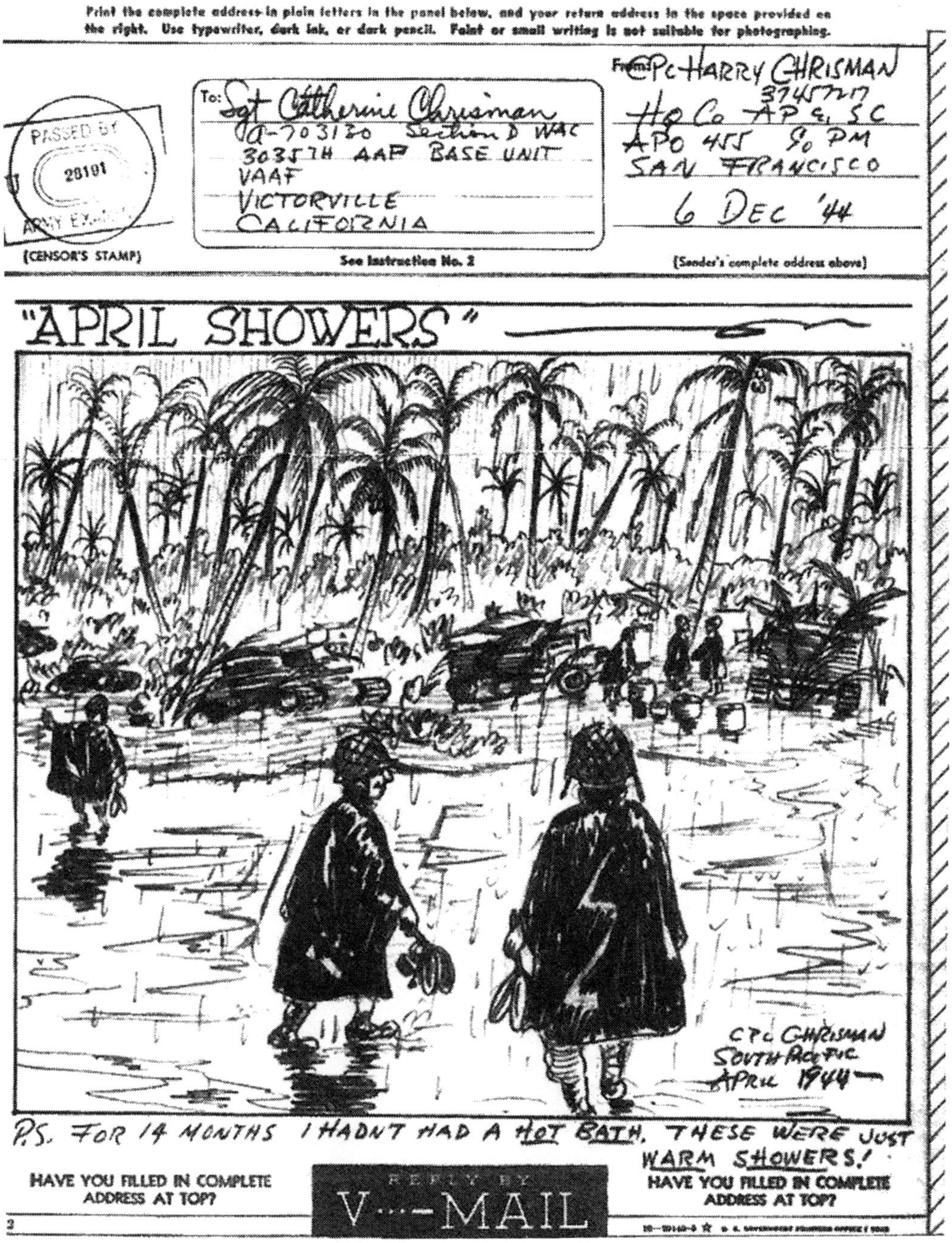
Print the complete address in plain letters in the panel below, and your return address in the space provided on the right. Use typewriter, dark ink, or dark pencil. Faint or small writing is not suitable for photographing.
PASSED BY 28101 ARMY EXAMINER
(CENSOR'S STAMP)
To: Sgt Catherine Chrisman
A-703130 Section D WAC
3035TH AAF BASE UNIT
VAAF
VICTORVILLE
CALIFORNIA
See Instruction No. 2
From: CPL HARRY CHRISMAN
37457217
HQ CO AP & SC
APO 455 % PM
SAN FRANCISCO
6 DEC '44
(Sender's complete address above)
"APRIL SHOWERS"
CPL CHRISMAN
SOUTH PACIFIC
APRIL 1944
P.S. FOR 14 MONTHS I HADN'T HAD A HOT BATH. THESE WERE JUST WARM SHOWERS!
HAVE YOU FILLED IN COMPLETE ADDRESS AT TOP?
REPLY BY V---MAIL
HAVE YOU FILLED IN COMPLETE ADDRESS AT TOP?

April Showers 12-6-44

Harry told me this cartoon came from a trip he made to the harbor for something or other. He said he could tell this load of soldiers had just come off ship and were probably headed for some R & R at Schofield Barracks. He was surprised there was no hooting and hollering from the men, just soft gasps. (S)

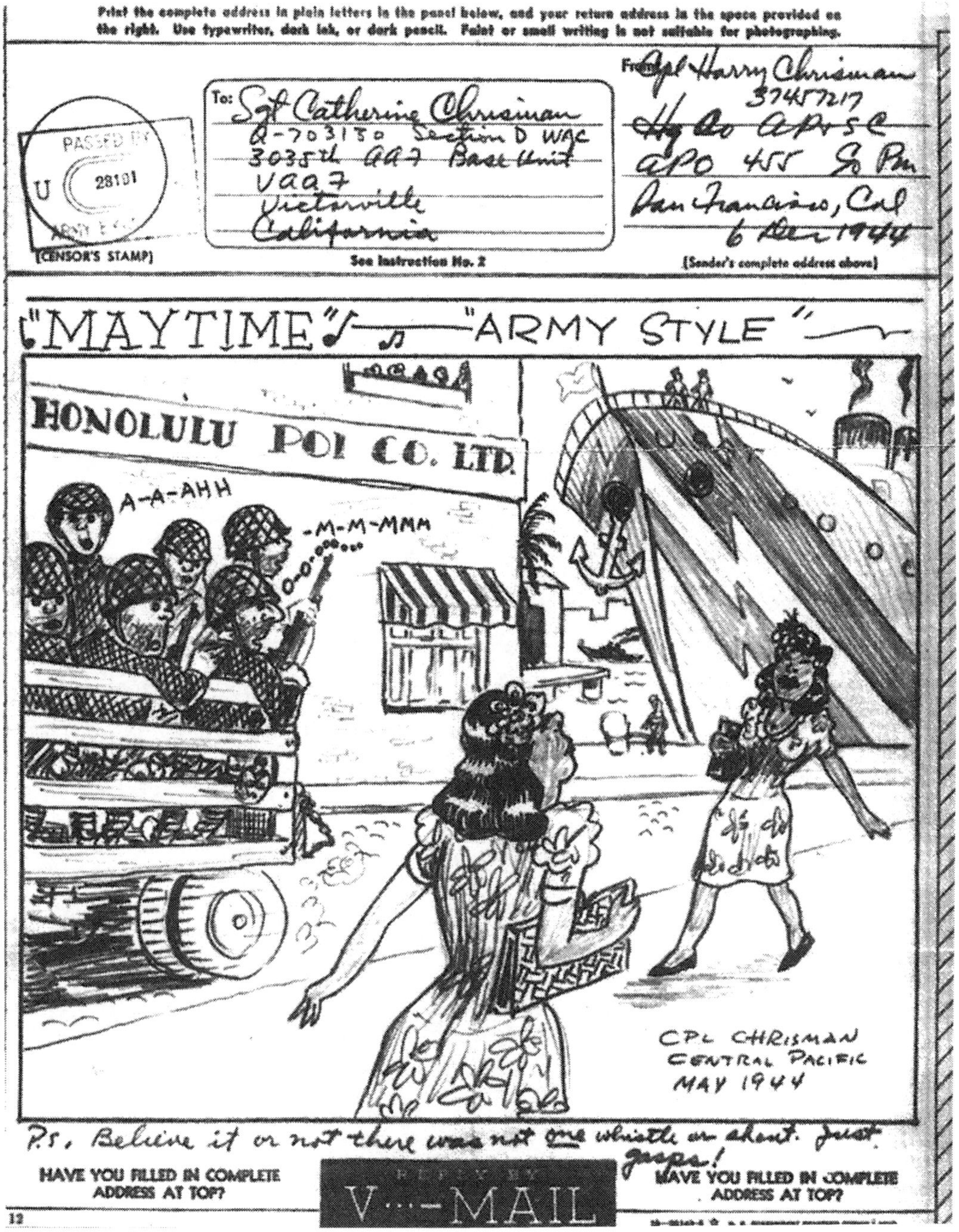
Print the complete address in plain letters in the panel below, and your return address in the space provided on the right. Use typewriter, dark ink, or dark pencil. Faint or small writing is not suitable for photographing.
To: Sgt Catherine Chrisman
Q-703150 Section D WAC
3035th AAF Base Unit
VAAF
Victorville
California
PASSED BY
U 28101
ARMY EXAM
(CENSOR'S STAMP)
See Instruction No. 2
From: Cpl Harry Chrisman
37457217
Hq Co APrSC
APO 455 % Pm
San Francisco, Cal
6 Dec 1944
(Sender's complete address above)
"MAYTIME" — "ARMY STYLE"
HONOLULU POI CO. LTD.
A-A-AHH
-M-M-MMM
CPL CHRISMAN
CENTRAL PACIFIC
MAY 1944
P.S. Believe it or not there was not one whistle or shout. Just gasps!
HAVE YOU FILLED IN COMPLETE ADDRESS AT TOP?
V...—MAIL
HAVE YOU FILLED IN COMPLETE ADDRESS AT TOP?

Maytime 12-6-44

How we envied those civilian war workers their lovely (and colorful) clothes. (H)

Harry loved color and the emotions it caused within the human species. I think it was a part of his philosophy of life. Note the date he put in the upper right hand corner of the letter: 12-10-45. Wishful thinking? Because on that date, he was home, along with Catherine, both out of the Army, in Nebraska. He seldom made a mistake like this and I wonder the censor did not catch it. Perhaps it really didn't matter what date was written on the address line. But in the lower right corner he writes. "Chrisman In Hawaii 1944." (S)

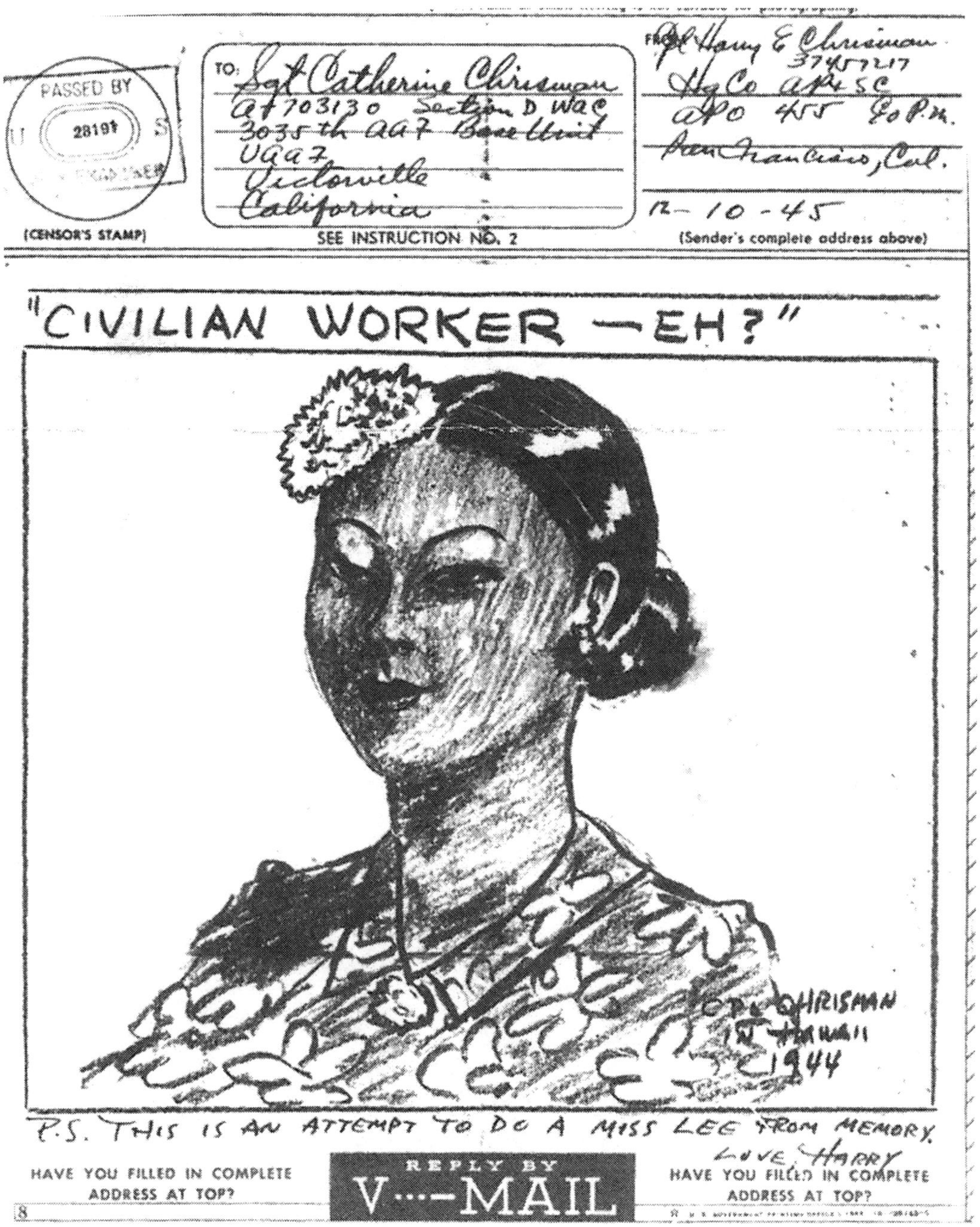
PASSED BY
28191
(CENSOR'S STAMP)
TO: Sgt Catherine Chrisman
Victorville
California
SEE INSTRUCTION NO. 2
San Francisco, Cal.
12-10-45
(Sender's complete address above)
"CIVILIAN WORKER —EH?"
CPL CHRISMAN
1944
P.S. THIS IS AN ATTEMPT TO DO A MISS LEE FROM MEMORY.
LOVE, HARRY
HAVE YOU FILLED IN COMPLETE ADDRESS AT TOP?
REPLY BY
V---MAIL
HAVE YOU FILLED IN COMPLETE ADDRESS AT TOP?

Civilian Worker 12-10-44

How pleased Catherine was to get this V-Mail. She knew from his letters he was happy doing his work, but also enjoying his off hours. He could paint, read, and play the piano! (S)

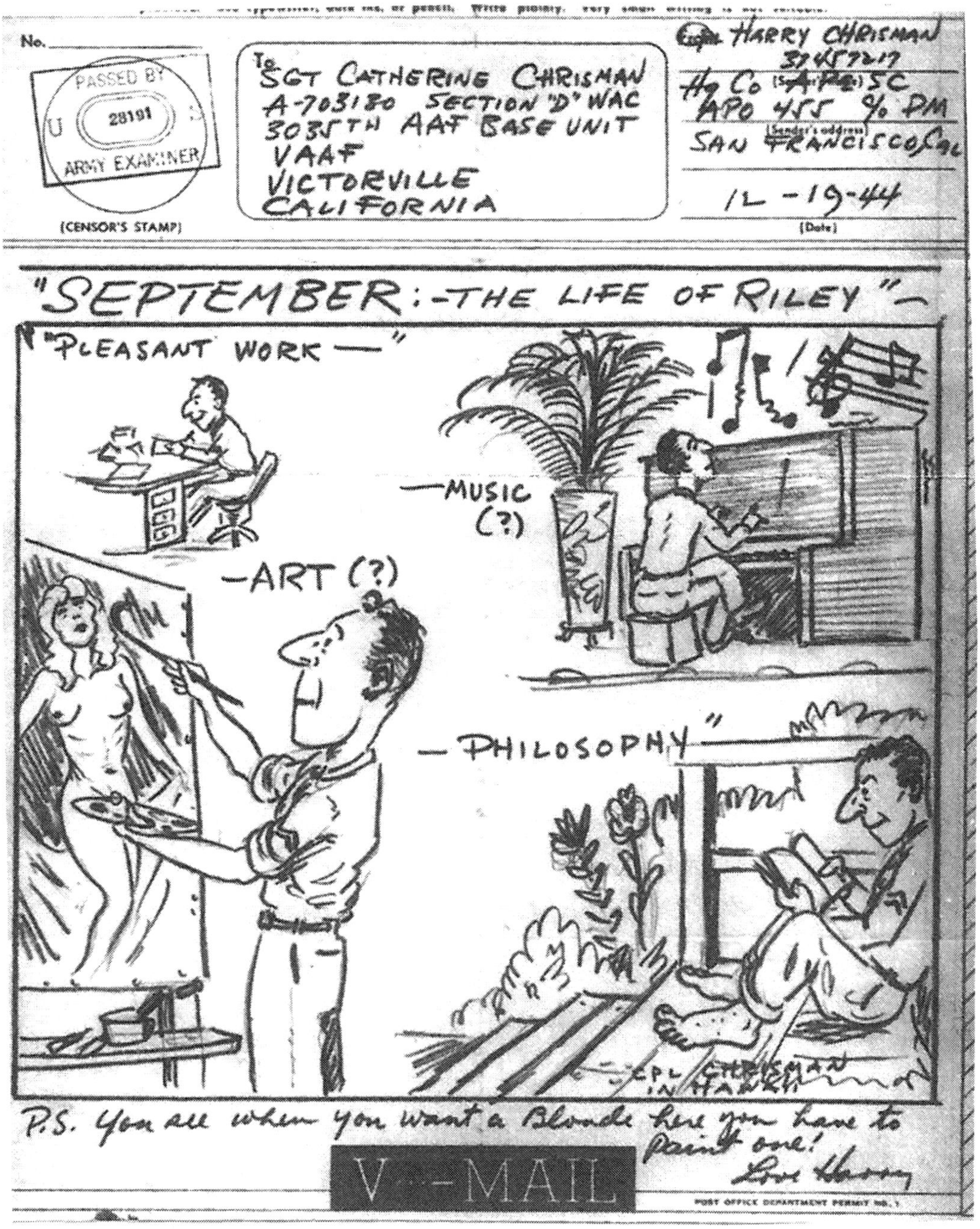
No.
PASSED BY
28191
ARMY EXAMINER
(CENSOR'S STAMP)
To. SGT CATHERINE CHRISMAN
A-703180 SECTION "D" WAC
3035TH AAF BASE UNIT
VAAF
VICTORVILLE
CALIFORNIA
HARRY CHRISMAN
APO 455 % PM
(Sender's address)
SAN FRANCISCO, Cal
12-19-44
(Date)
"SEPTEMBER:-THE LIFE OF RILEY"—
"PLEASANT WORK —"
—MUSIC (?)
—ART (?)
—PHILOSOPHY"
CPL CHRISMAN
P.S. You all when you want a Blonde here you have to paint one!
Love Harry
V-MAIL

Life of Riley 12-19-44

Although Catherine was writing everyday, the letters were not getting through. Harry said he though maybe transports were being used further north in the Pacific as the war was being fought on the islands there. "I guess the arena had moved," he said. "But, boy, I hadn't got mail for a couple of weeks and I usually got more than anyone on the island. We still got mail, but not me and I knew she was writing everyday. Why on earth did I send her this one?" Hindsight is so good! (S)

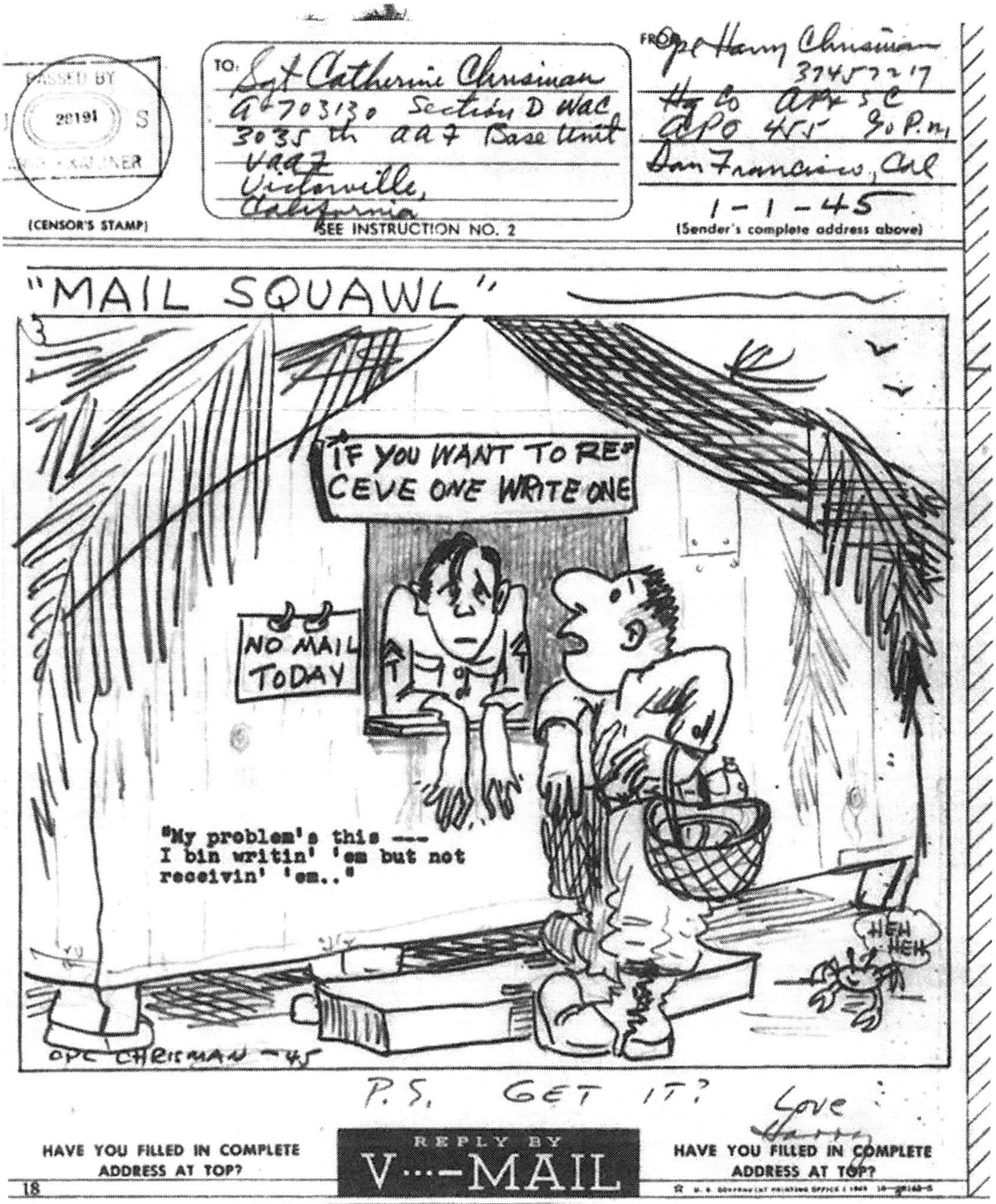
PASSED BY
20191
(CENSOR'S STAMP)
TO: Sgt Catherine Chrisman
A-703130 Section D WAC
3035 th AAF Base Unit
VAAF
Victorville,
California
SEE INSTRUCTION NO. 2
FROM Cpl Harry Chrisman
37457217
Hq Co APO 5C
APO 455 % P.M.
San Francisco, Cal
1-1-45
(Sender's complete address above)
"MAIL SQUAWL"
IF YOU WANT TO RE- CEVE ONE WRITE ONE
NO MAIL TODAY
"My problem's this ---
I bin writin' 'em but not
receivin' 'em.."
HEH HEH
CPL CHRISMAN -45
P.S. GET IT?
Love
Harry
HAVE YOU FILLED IN COMPLETE ADDRESS AT TOP?
REPLY BY
V---MAIL
HAVE YOU FILLED IN COMPLETE ADDRESS AT TOP?
18

Mail Squawl 1-1-45

Mrs. McAdams was a good sort and ran the small Rec Hall at APSC. (H)

The recreation hall was a great place for Harry and several of the soldiers he worked with to spend an evening. They were much like Harry, happily married, but lonely, so they enjoyed "shooting the bull" over a glass or two of beer. Most were older men and not interested in the sights and sounds of Honolulu. Harry remembered Mrs. McAdams, so she must have been a nice lady and one who ran a clean rec center, otherwise he would not have remembered her name. (S)

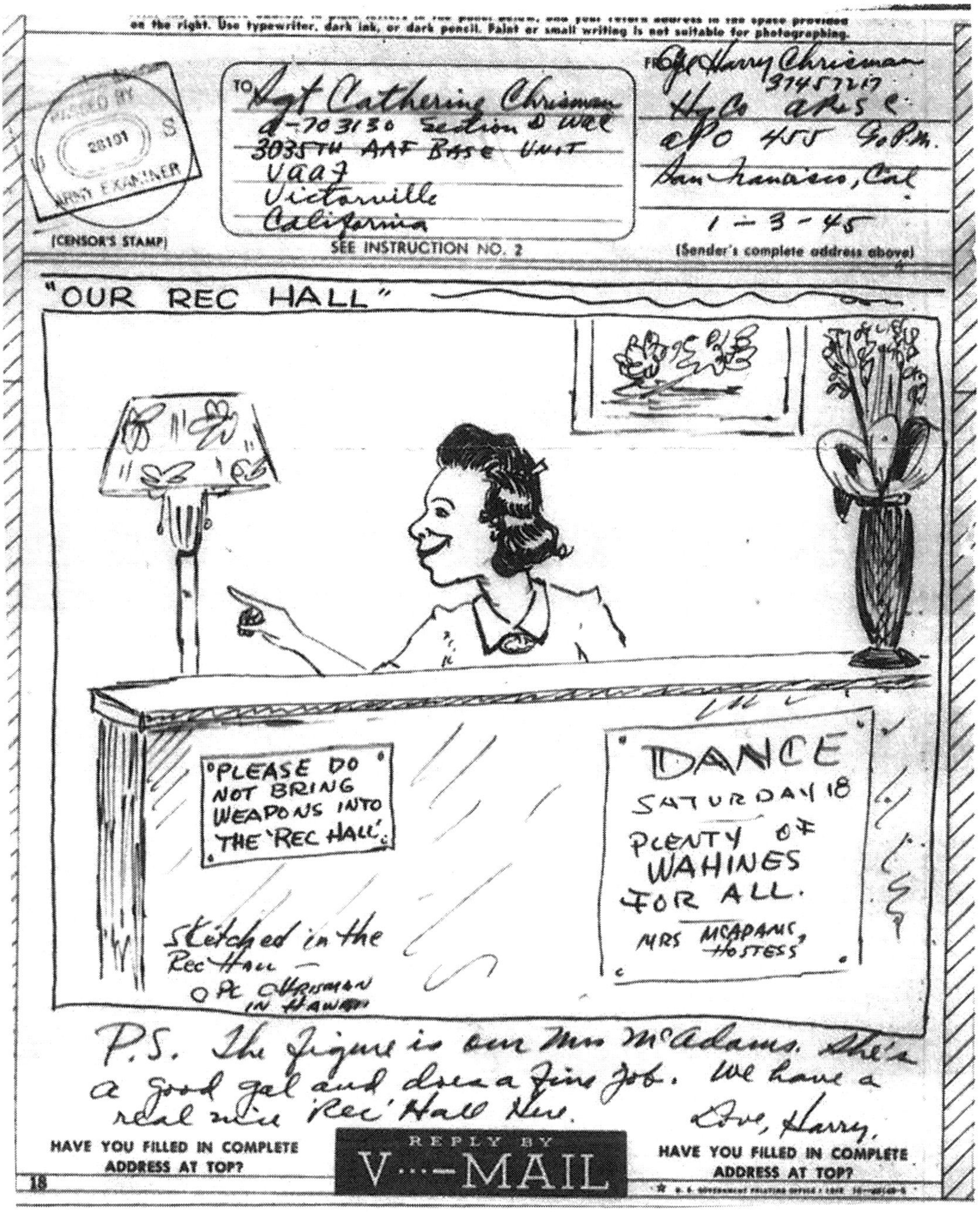
on the right. Use typewriter, dark ink, or dark pencil. Faint or small writing is not suitable for photographing.

PASSED BY 28191 ARMY EXAMINER S

(CENSOR'S STAMP)

TO Sgt Catherine Chrisman
A-703130 Section D WAC
3035th AAF Base Unit
VAAF
Victorville
California

SEE INSTRUCTION NO. 2

FROM Cpl Harry Chrisman
37457217
Hq Co APSC
APO 455 % P.M.
San Francisco, Cal
1-3-45

(Sender's complete address above)

"OUR REC HALL"
"PLEASE DO NOT BRING WEAPONS INTO THE 'REC HALL'."
DANCE
SATURDAY 18
PLENTY OF WAHINES FOR ALL.
MRS MCADAMS, HOSTESS
Sketched in the Rec Hall – Cpl Chrisman in Hawaii

P.S. The figure is our Mrs McAdams. She's a good gal and does a fine job. We have a real nice 'Rec' Hall here.

Love, Harry.

HAVE YOU FILLED IN COMPLETE ADDRESS AT TOP?

REPLY BY V---MAIL

HAVE YOU FILLED IN COMPLETE ADDRESS AT TOP?

18

Rec Hall 1-3-45

This was Pops—a 32-year-old squad leader in my Heavy Weapons platoon when I was with H Co. on Oahu in jungle training camp. Pop was a good soldier. He once asked me to not tell the squad members I was 37, for it might make him appear "too young" to be their leader. (H)

Harry was a bit sensitive about his age because most of his fellow soldiers were in their twenties. Usually only the COs were older than he was. But he was still there doing the job the Army wanted him to do and always giving 110% as did Catherine. It was an ethic prevalent in both families, thus a given for both Harry and Catherine. (S)

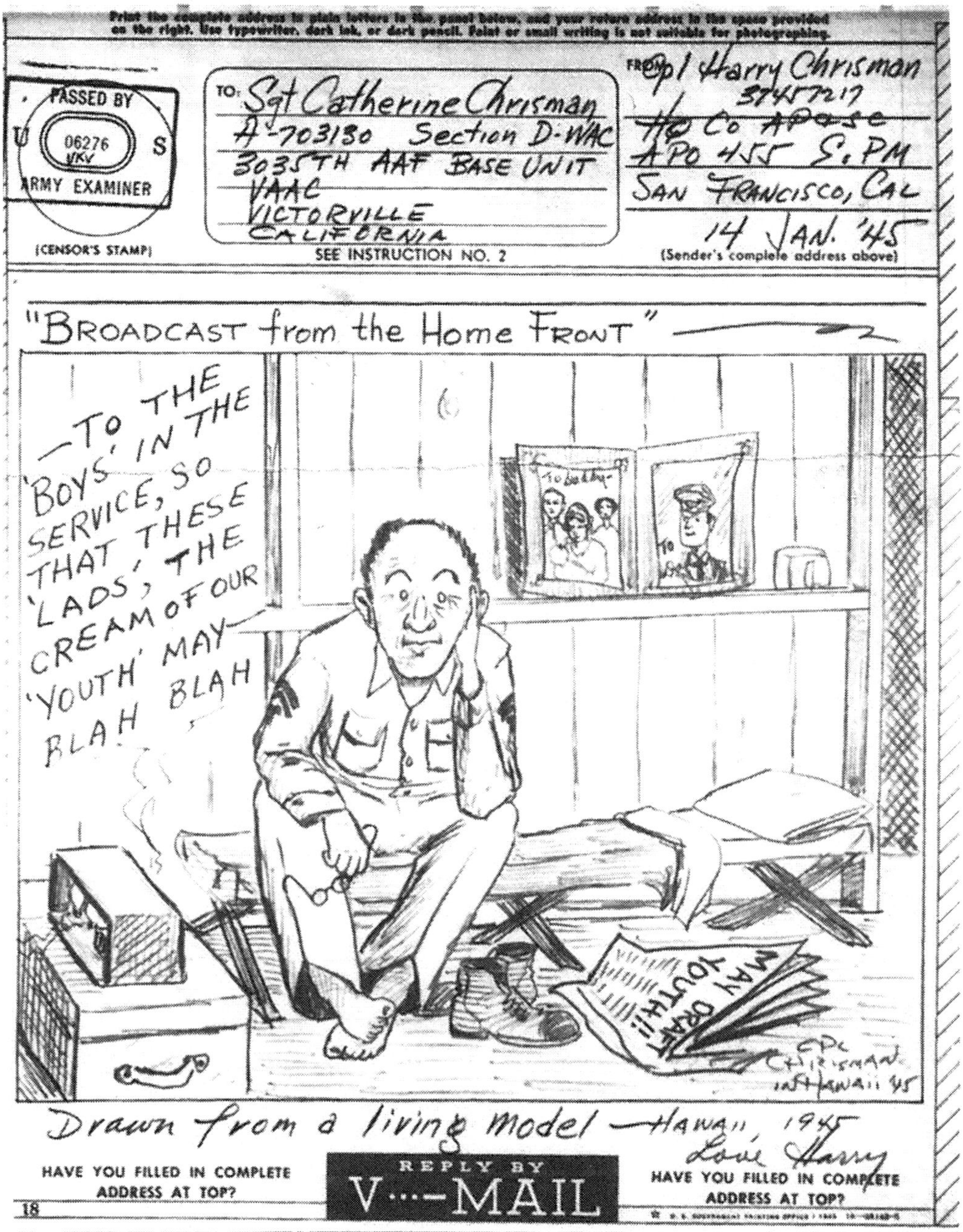
Print the complete address in plain letters in the panel below, and your return address in the space provided on the right. Use typewriter, dark ink, or dark pencil. Faint or small writing is not suitable for photographing.
PASSED BY
U 06276 S
ARMY EXAMINER
(CENSOR'S STAMP)
TO: Sgt Catherine Chrisman
A-703130 Section D-WAC
3035TH AAF BASE UNIT
VAAC
VICTORVILLE
CALIFORNIA
SEE INSTRUCTION NO. 2
FROM Cpl Harry Chrisman
37457217
APO 455 % PM
SAN FRANCISCO, CAL
14 JAN. '45
(Sender's complete address above)
"BROADCAST from the Home FRONT"
—TO THE 'BOYS' IN THE SERVICE, SO THAT THESE 'LADS', THE CREAM OF OUR 'YOUTH' MAY— BLAH BLAH
MAY OUR YOUTH!!
CPL CHRISMAN
Drawn from a living model — Hawaii, 1945
Love Harry
HAVE YOU FILLED IN COMPLETE ADDRESS AT TOP?
REPLY BY V···—MAIL
HAVE YOU FILLED IN COMPLETE ADDRESS AT TOP?
18

Pops on Oahu 1-14-45

As usual Harry dealt with disappointment with humor, but there was an underlying barb to his poetry. The typing is difficult to read so the Manifesto goes as follows:

To me my wife no longer is a Being, or a Fact,
She's just a Serial Number—and a member of the WAC.
No longer do I think of her as being "Catherine,"
She's just an automaton, who was once my village Queen.

No longer can I visualize her golden, nut-brown tresses,
She's a figure who is tailored now in uniforms, not dresses.
Upon her head I see a crown, a monstrous millinery
Creation, fashioned up, no doubt, by Brass Hat villainy.

I see our future life as one in which, when 'tis resumed
I'll polish up her brogans when she retires to Her room,
And when the first cock's crowing and she wakens as from sleep
'Twill be by blowing bugles—and at night I'll stand retreat.

She'll have me doing K. P.—and my passes stopped at night,
I may get "company punishment" if my conduct isn't right;
She'll run our home on G.I. lines, my future sure looks black,
A corporal that is married to a Sergeant of the WAC.

But on one matter I'll refuse to be intimidated
Nor brass, nor man, nor God can change the Order as 'tis stated,
When we resume our married life (Let's pray that it's soon, brother),
I'll be the father of our child—the Sergeant'll be the mother!

Oooh, it still stung for Catherine to make sergeant before Harry! He was made acting sergeant several times, the last time when he was sent to the States to help with discharging all those G.I.s. Catherine was kind in her book writing that Harry received that third stripe soon after she did. She did not, however, explain that it was a temporary assignment. However, every WAC in Hysteria Haven loved the poem! (S)

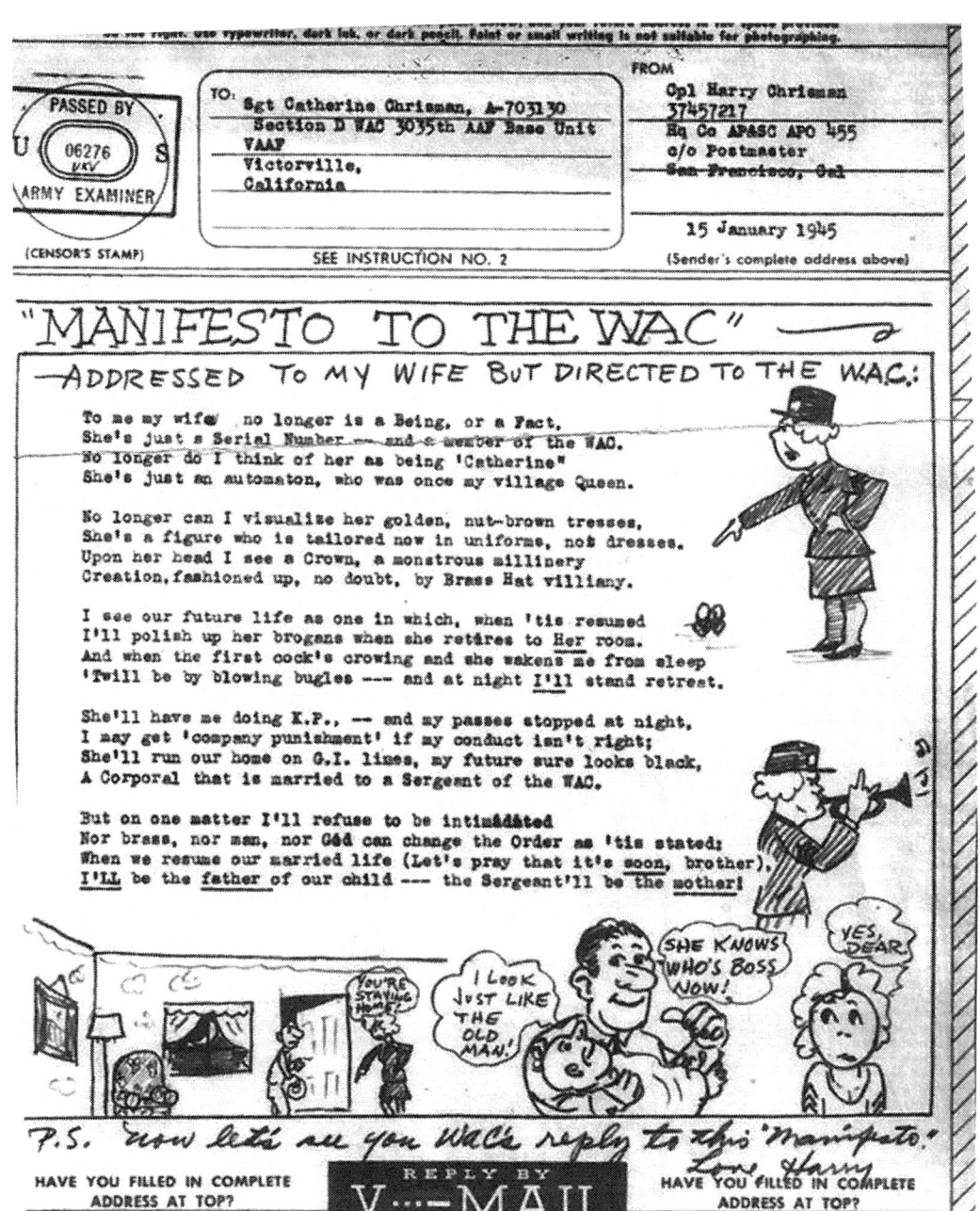

Manifesto to the WAC 1-15-45

Many civilian girls from the States came to Hawaii to work in the 1940s. Several worked in offices of APSC. They were inclined to treat enlisted men like pariahs, and usually married the officers. I got along well with them, for I had no interest in dating them. (H)

I don't think it hurt that Harry had Catherine's picture on his desk and other soldiers were always asking him about his wife! He was a good-looking guy, but taken and not worth the bother to entice! (S)

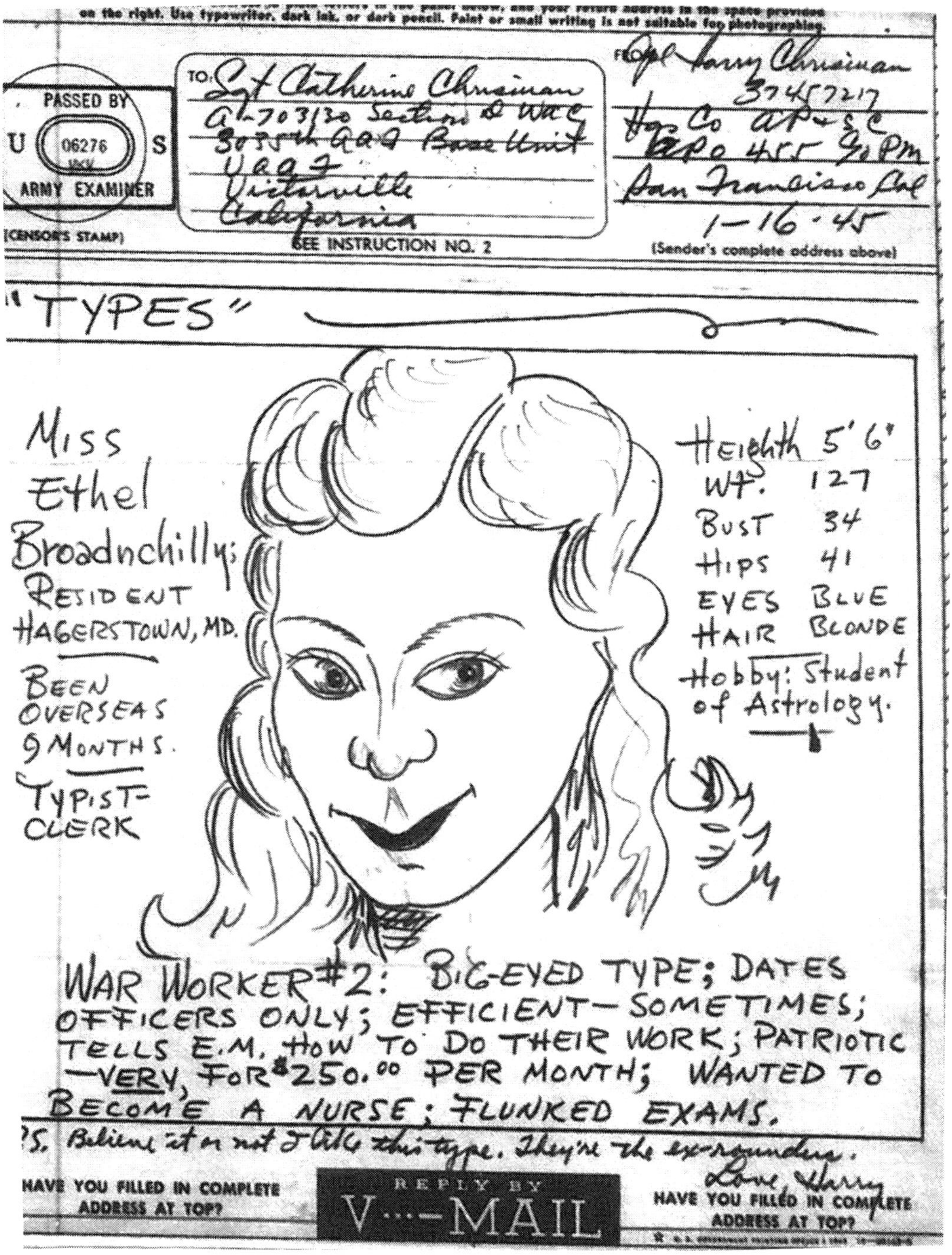
on the right. Use typewriter, dark ink, or dark pencil. Faint or small writing is not suitable for photographing.
PASSED BY
U 06276 S
ARMY EXAMINER
(CENSOR'S STAMP)
TO: Sgt Catherine Chrisman
Victorville
California
SEE INSTRUCTION NO. 2
FROM:
37457217
San Francisco Cal
1-16-45
(Sender's complete address above)
"TYPES"
Miss Ethel Broadnchilly;
RESIDENT HAGERSTOWN, MD.
BEEN OVERSEAS 9 MONTHS.
TYPIST-CLERK
Heighth 5'6"
WT. 127
BUST 34
HIPS 41
EYES BLUE
HAIR BLONDE
Hobby: Student of Astrology.
WAR WORKER #2: BIG-EYED TYPE; DATES OFFICERS ONLY; EFFICIENT—SOMETIMES; TELLS E.M. HOW TO DO THEIR WORK; PATRIOTIC—VERY, FOR $250.00 PER MONTH; WANTED TO BECOME A NURSE; FLUNKED EXAMS.
P.S. Believe it or not I like this type.
Love, Harry
HAVE YOU FILLED IN COMPLETE ADDRESS AT TOP?
REPLY BY V···—MAIL
HAVE YOU FILLED IN COMPLETE ADDRESS AT TOP?

Types 1-16-45

How Harry would have loved to have Catherine be his secretary, a position which was not at all possible. But it would have fulfilled her dream of working overseas. He was still embarrassed, as he should have been, with the snit-fit he threw when she told him she wanted to apply for overseas duty. He did not honor the promise they made to each other. (S)

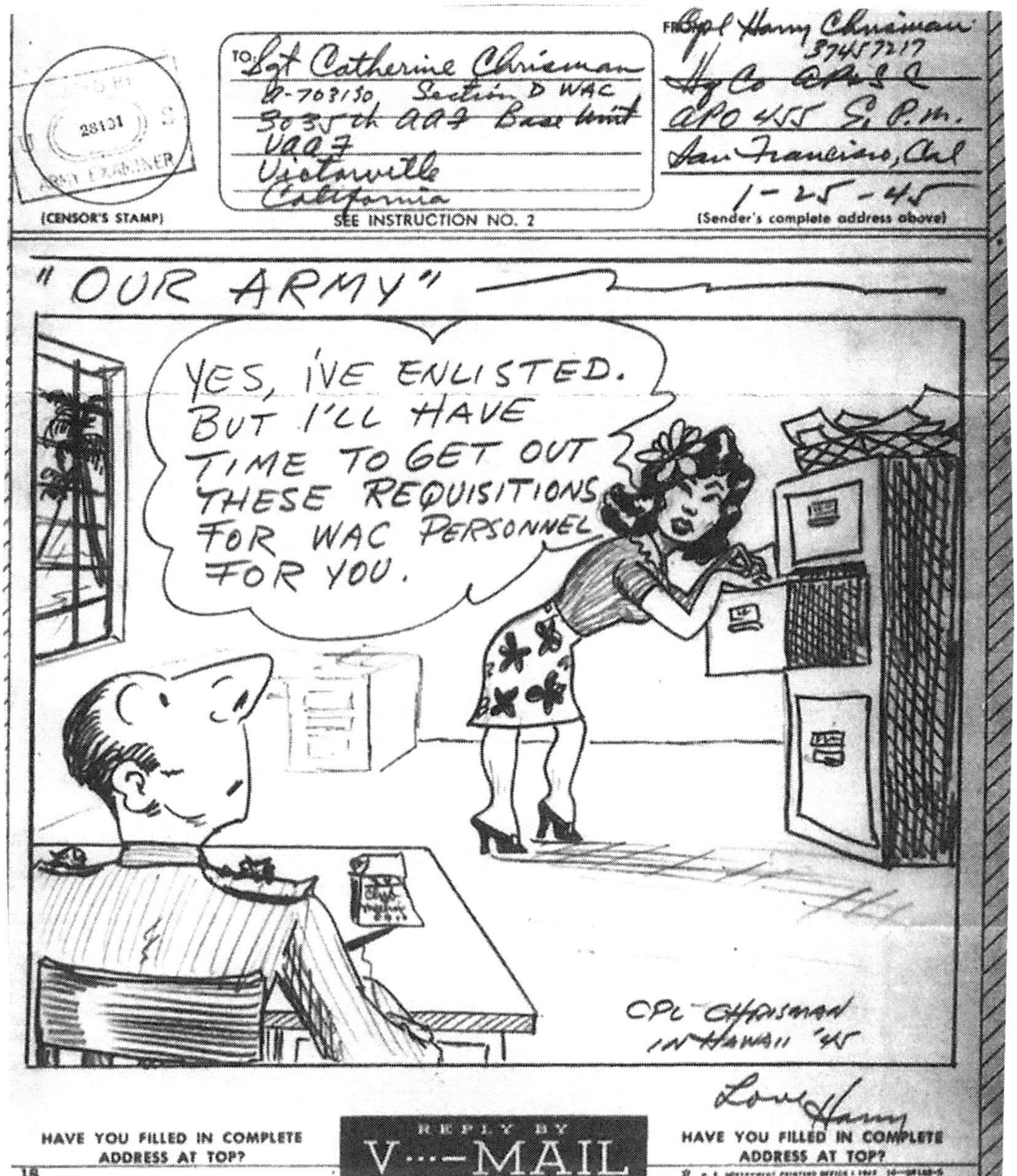
TO: Sgt Catherine Chrisman
Section D WAC
Victorville
California
(CENSOR'S STAMP)
SEE INSTRUCTION NO. 2
1-25-45
(Sender's complete address above)
"OUR ARMY"
YES, I'VE ENLISTED. BUT I'LL HAVE TIME TO GET OUT THESE REQUISITIONS FOR WAC PERSONNEL FOR YOU.
CPL CHRISMAN IN HAWAII '45
Love Harry
HAVE YOU FILLED IN COMPLETE ADDRESS AT TOP?
REPLY BY V---MAIL
HAVE YOU FILLED IN COMPLETE ADDRESS AT TOP?

Our Army 1-25-45

Catherine and her WAC friends got a big kick out of this V-Mail. She knew the women who worked with him were really young women, most of them native Hawaiians, who were well educated, etc. They rather adopted Harry who was funny and enjoyable to work with and for. Many a nice cake or piece of pineapple ended up on his desk at the APSC! (S)

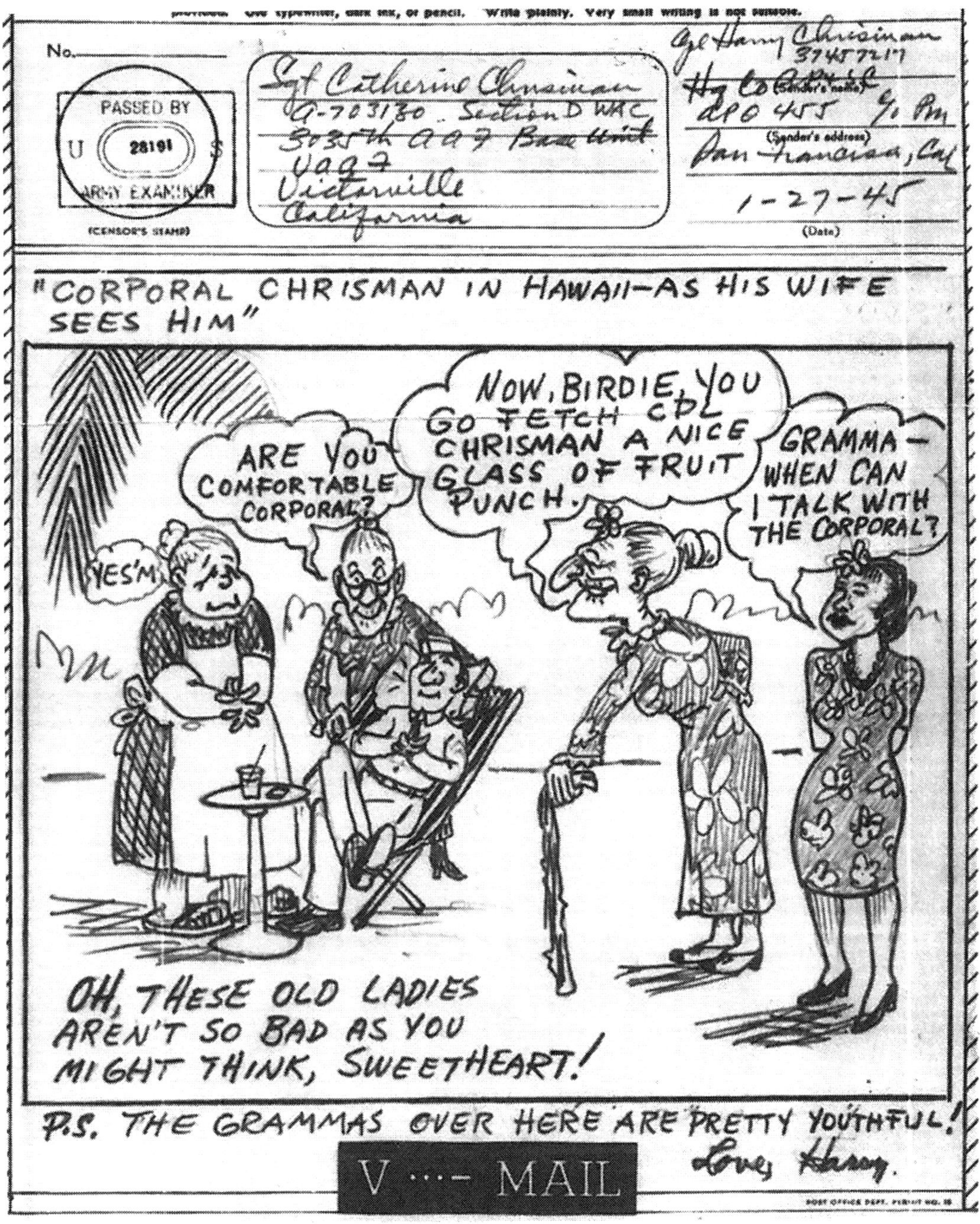
No.
PASSED BY
U 28191 S
ARMY EXAMINER
(CENSOR'S STAMP)
Sgt Catherine Chrisman
A-703180 Section D WAC
Victorville
California
(Sender's name)
APO 455
(Sender's address)
San Francisco, Cal
1-27-45
(Date)
"CORPORAL CHRISMAN IN HAWAII—AS HIS WIFE SEES HIM"
ARE YOU COMFORTABLE CORPORAL?
YES'M
NOW, BIRDIE, YOU GO FETCH CPL CHRISMAN A NICE GLASS OF FRUIT PUNCH.
GRAMMA—WHEN CAN I TALK WITH THE CORPORAL?
OH, THESE OLD LADIES AREN'T SO BAD AS YOU MIGHT THINK, SWEETHEART!
P.S. THE GRAMMAS OVER HERE ARE PRETTY YOUTHFUL!
Love, Harry
V ···– MAIL

Grandmas 1-27-45

Always dreaming. There was no way while at APSC for Harry to earn another stripe. The war was drawing to an end and he told me he thought his commanding officer didn't want another sergeant on his staff because it would increase his budget. Harry had just celebrated his 39th birthday. He was born in 1906.

The line below the bar reads, "For Christ's sake don't get a rocker before we go on furlough! It would be too, too embarrassing!!" Their furlough was coming up in July, the first time they would have seen each other since October of 1942. (S)

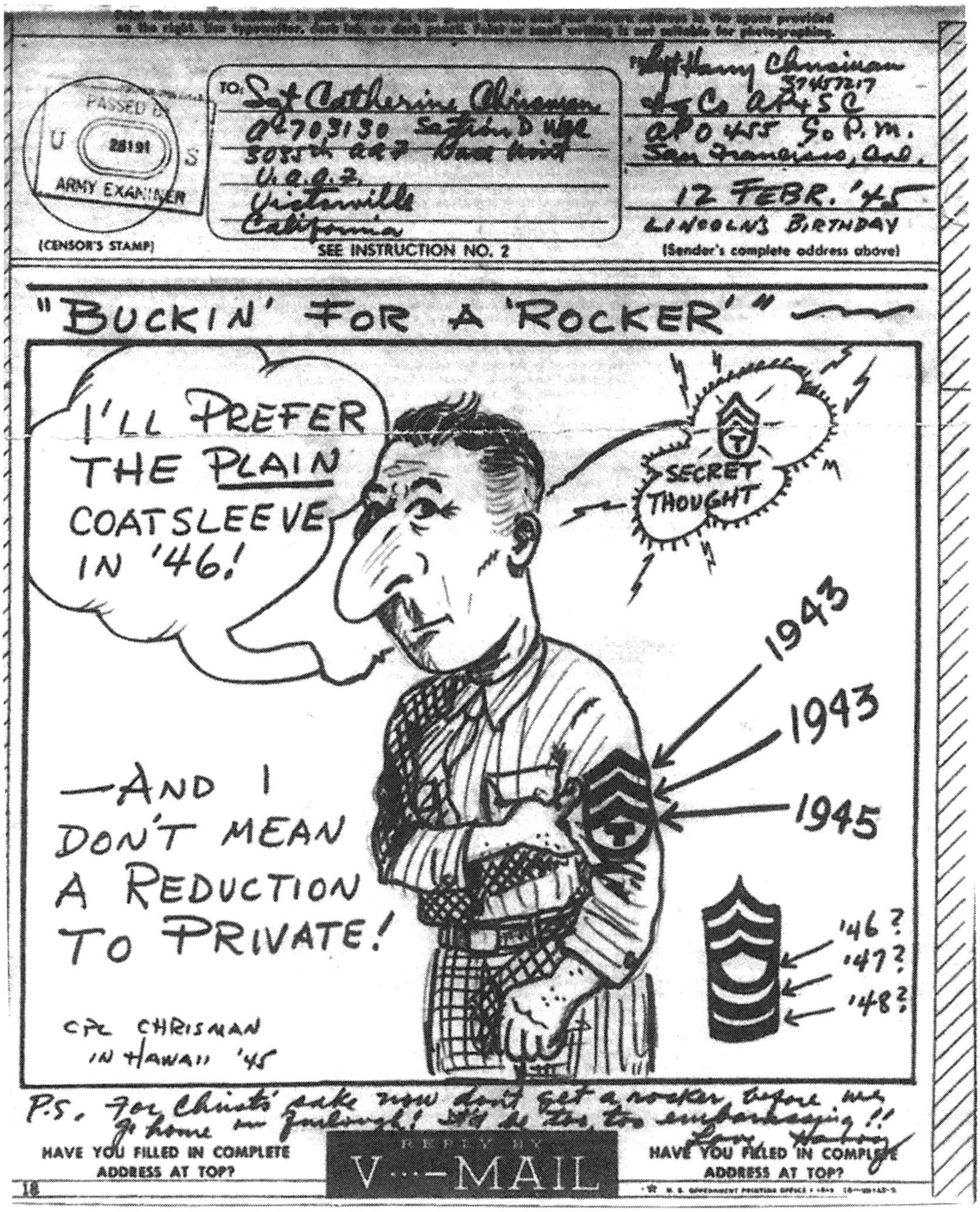
PASSED BY
U.S. ARMY EXAMINER
28191
(CENSOR'S STAMP)
TO:
SEE INSTRUCTION NO. 2
12 FEBR. '45
LINCOLN'S BIRTHDAY
(Sender's complete address above)
"BUCKIN' FOR A 'ROCKER'"
I'LL PREFER THE PLAIN COATSLEEVE IN '46!
SECRET THOUGHT
1943
1943
1945
—AND I DON'T MEAN A REDUCTION TO PRIVATE!
'46?
'47?
'48?
CPL CHRISMAN IN HAWAII '45
HAVE YOU FILLED IN COMPLETE ADDRESS AT TOP?
REPLY BY
V···—MAIL
HAVE YOU FILLED IN COMPLETE ADDRESS AT TOP?
18

Buckin' for a Rocker 2-12-45

Catherine wrote to Harry that she visited her sister, Bernice, and did a bit of shopping for their furlough. In her book, "My War," Catherine tells how she met Harry at a train station, a string of improbable circumstances. (S)

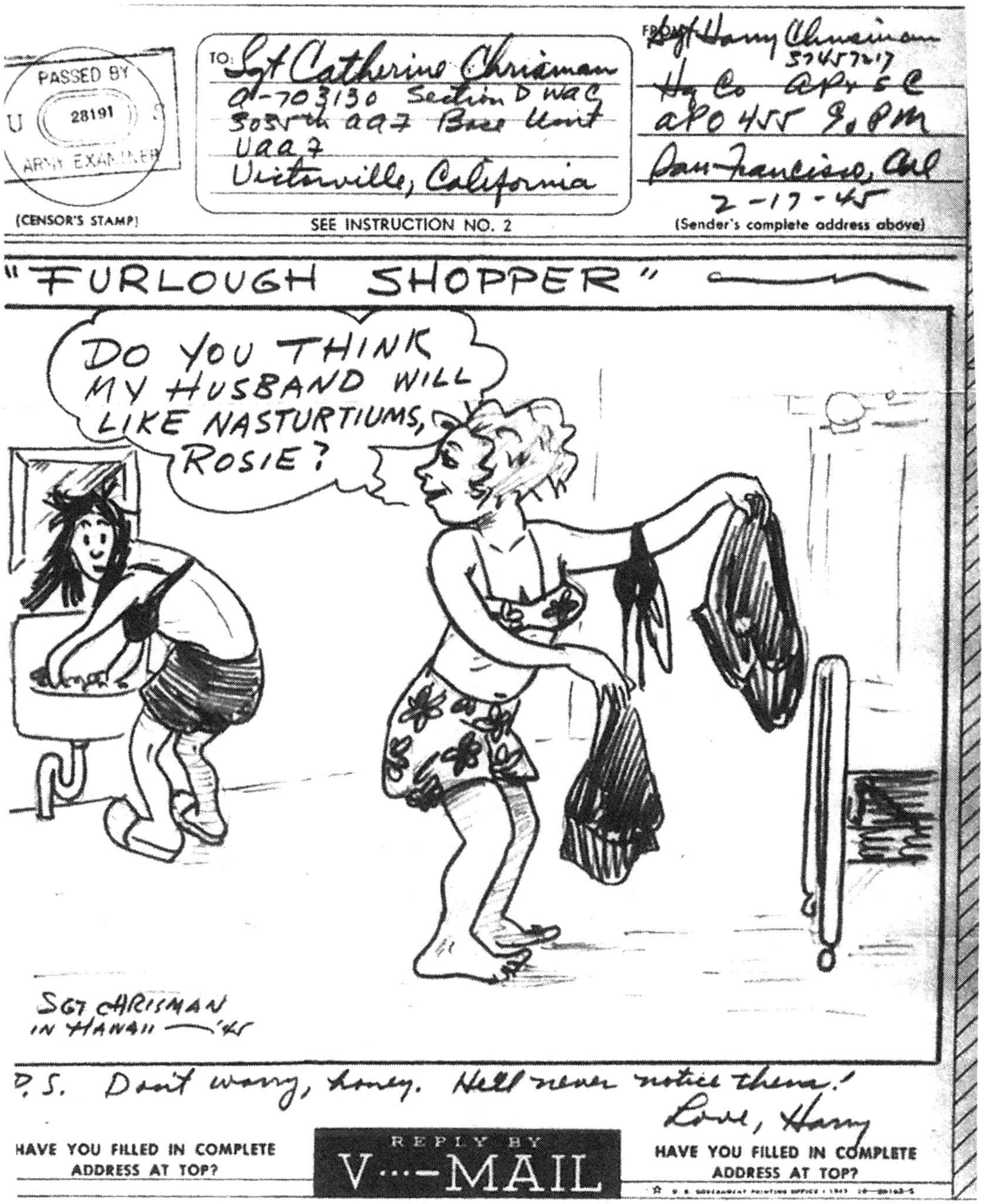
PASSED BY
U.S.
28191
ARMY EXAMINER
(CENSOR'S STAMP)
TO: Sgt Catherine Chrisman
Victorville, California
SEE INSTRUCTION NO. 2
FROM: Sgt Harry Chrisman
San Francisco, Cal
2-17-45
(Sender's complete address above)
"FURLOUGH SHOPPER"
DO YOU THINK MY HUSBAND WILL LIKE NASTURTIUMS, ROSIE?
SGT CHRISMAN IN HAWAII — '45
P.S. Don't worry, honey. He'll never notice them!
Love, Harry
HAVE YOU FILLED IN COMPLETE ADDRESS AT TOP?
REPLY BY V---MAIL
HAVE YOU FILLED IN COMPLETE ADDRESS AT TOP?

Furlough Shopper 2-17-45

Harry really wanted to send all the letters home he received from Catherine and family members, but it proved too costly, so he had to choose carefully the ones he sent. He loved the fact that he got so many from Catherine. She wrote everyday, but admitted that sometimes they were short, and she often put two or three letters on one sheet of paper, especially since she didn't have time some days to write very much. (S)

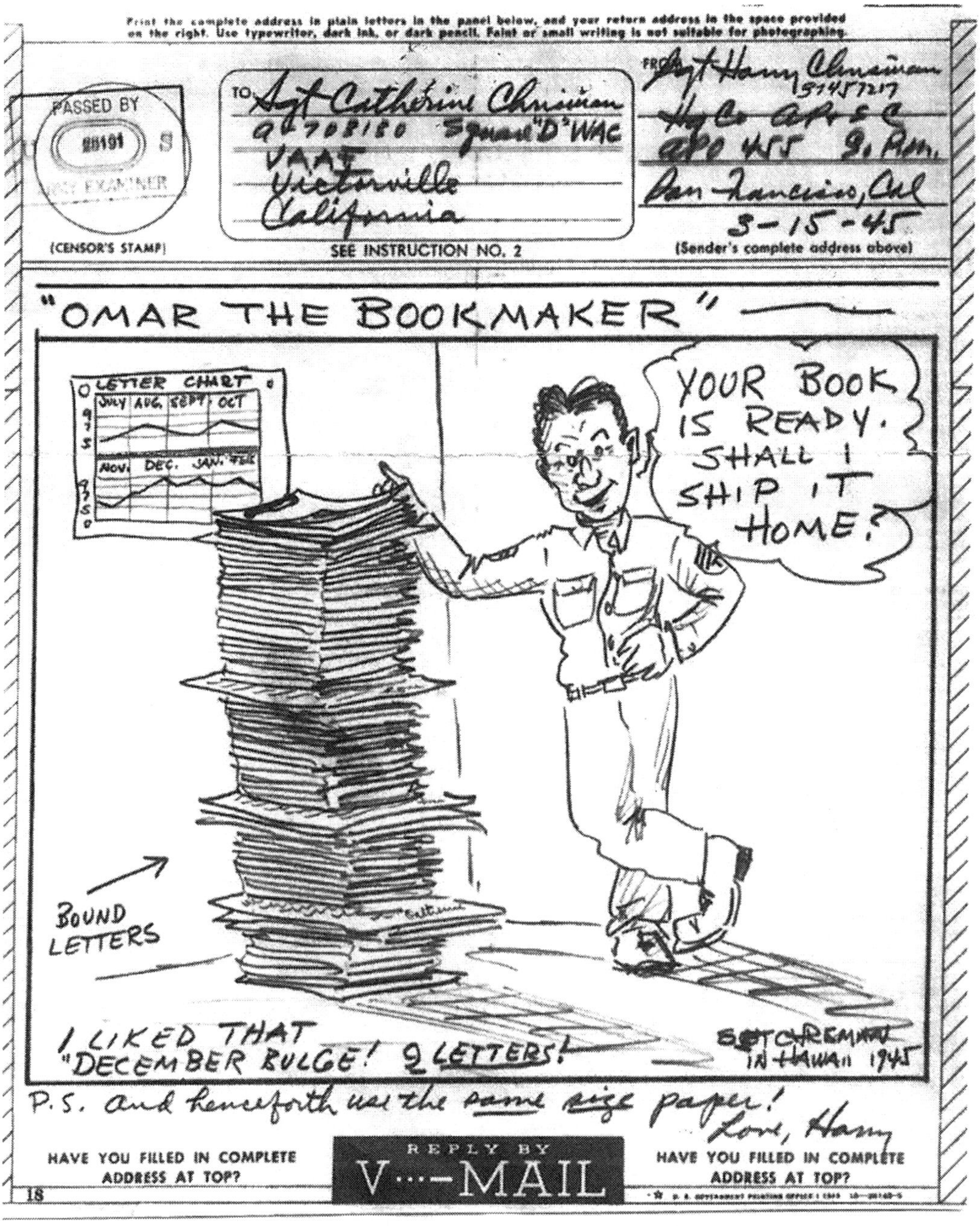
Print the complete address in plain letters in the panel below, and your return address in the space provided on the right. Use typewriter, dark ink, or dark pencil. Faint or small writing is not suitable for photographing.
PASSED BY
(CENSOR'S STAMP)
TO:
SEE INSTRUCTION NO. 2
FROM:
3-15-45
(Sender's complete address above)
"OMAR THE BOOKMAKER"
LETTER CHART
JULY AUG. SEPT. OCT
NOV. DEC. JAN. FEB
YOUR BOOK IS READY. SHALL I SHIP IT HOME?
BOUND LETTERS
I LIKED THAT "DECEMBER BULGE! 9 LETTERS!
IN HAWAII 1945
P.S. and henceforth use the same size paper!
Love, Harry
HAVE YOU FILLED IN COMPLETE ADDRESS AT TOP?
REPLY BY V-MAIL
HAVE YOU FILLED IN COMPLETE ADDRESS AT TOP?
18

Omar the Bookmaker 3-15-45

This poem was one written by the Japanese poet Ono No Yoshiki, taken from a book Harry found in the library in Honolulu, Anthology of World Poetry. *Harry was well read and often used the writings of others, but always gave them credit just as he wanted credit when he began writing his non-fiction books of the Old West. (S)*

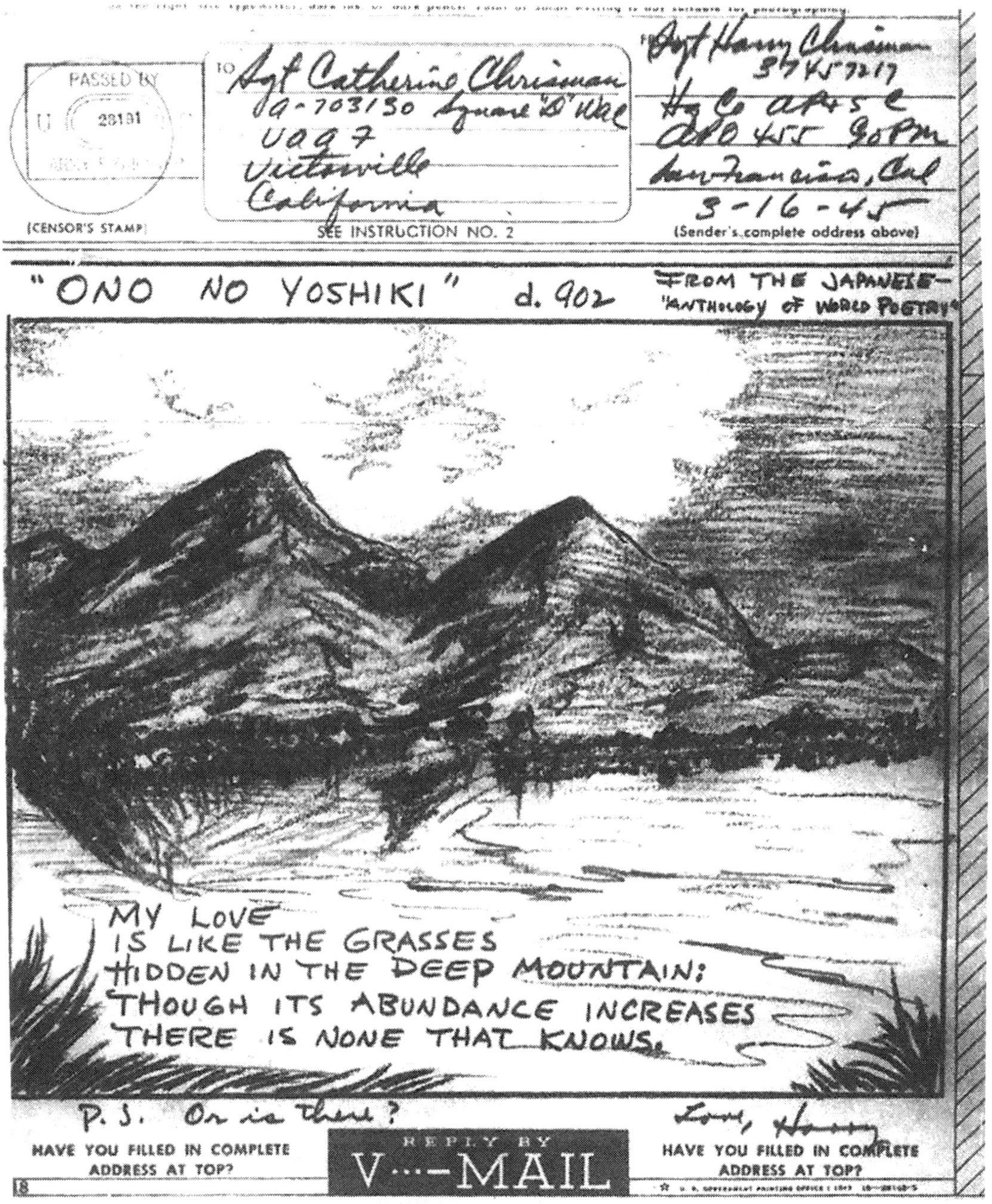
PASSED BY
(CENSOR'S STAMP)
TO Sgt Catherine Chrisman
Victorville
California
SEE INSTRUCTION NO. 2
San Francisco, Cal
3-16-45
(Sender's complete address above)
"ONO NO YOSHIKI" d. 902
FROM THE JAPANESE—
"ANTHOLOGY OF WORLD POETRY"
MY LOVE
IS LIKE THE GRASSES
HIDDEN IN THE DEEP MOUNTAIN;
THOUGH ITS ABUNDANCE INCREASES
THERE IS NONE THAT KNOWS.
P.S. Or is there?
Love, Harry
HAVE YOU FILLED IN COMPLETE ADDRESS AT TOP?
REPLY BY V---MAIL
HAVE YOU FILLED IN COMPLETE ADDRESS AT TOP?

Ono No Yoshiki 3-16-45

Cathy's dread of public speaking at Orientations Sessions brought about this V-Mail. (H)

Catherine was quiet and shy. After Harry's death she was asked to make a presentation to a group of senior citizens about her book. I took her, we had lunch, and proceeded to the meeting place. I ended up doing the session. She just sat quietly by me and nodded her head in agreement. But we sold about 20 of her books! (S)

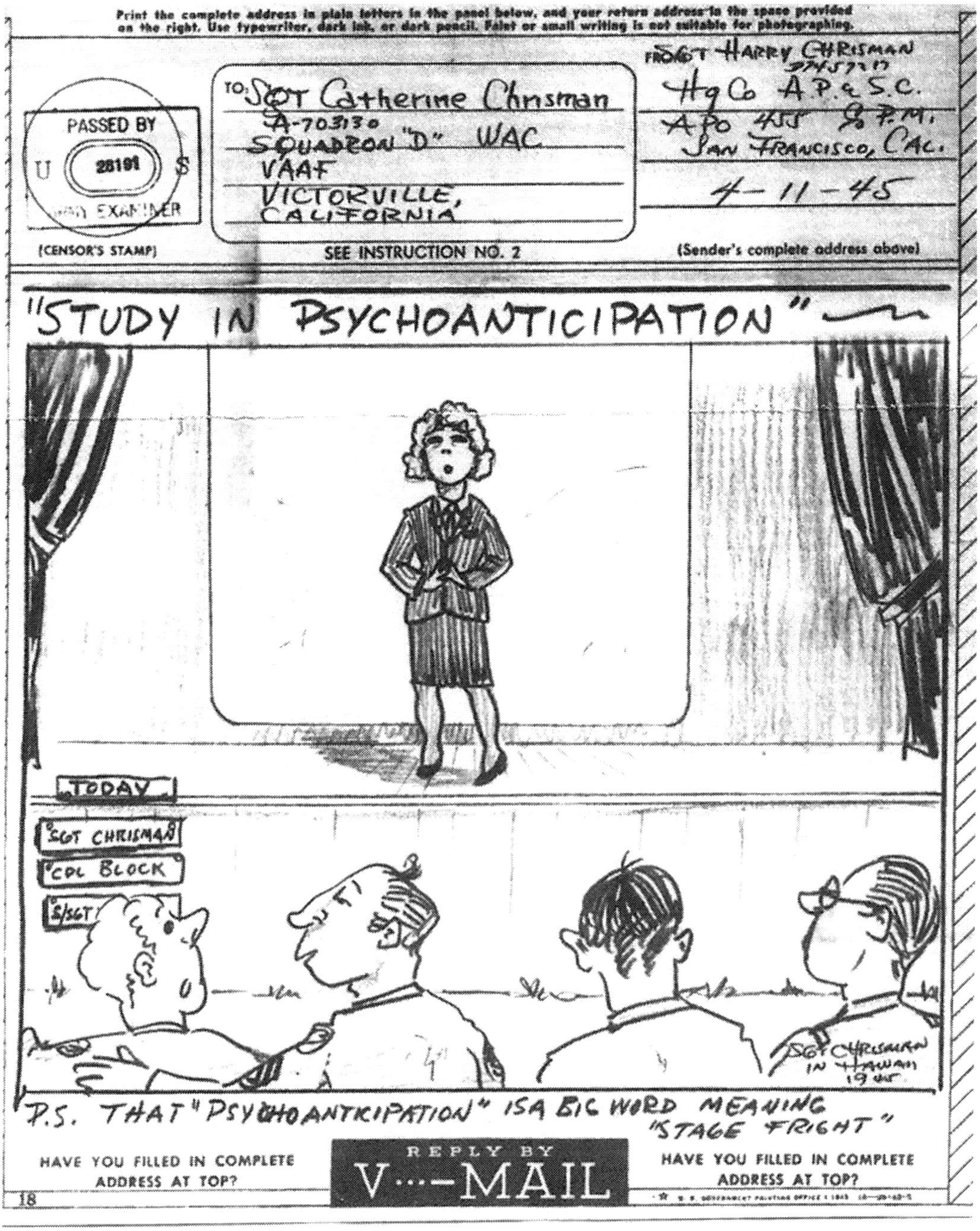
Print the complete address in plain letters in the panel below, and your return address in the space provided on the right. Use typewriter, dark ink, or dark pencil. Faint or small writing is not suitable for photographing.
TO: SGT Catherine Chrisman
A-703130
SQUADRON "D" WAC
VAAF
VICTORVILLE,
CALIFORNIA
SEE INSTRUCTION NO. 2
PASSED BY
28191
EXAMINER
(CENSOR'S STAMP)
FROM: SGT HARRY CHRISMAN
HqCo A.P.&S.C.
APO 455 % P.M.
SAN FRANCISCO, CAL.
4-11-45
(Sender's complete address above)
"STUDY IN PSYCHOANTICIPATION"
TODAY
SGT CHRISMAN
CPL BLOCK
S/SGT
SGT CHRISMAN IN HAWAII 1945
P.S. THAT "PSYCHOANTICIPATION" IS A BIG WORD MEANING "STAGE FRIGHT"
HAVE YOU FILLED IN COMPLETE ADDRESS AT TOP?
REPLY BY V-–MAIL
HAVE YOU FILLED IN COMPLETE ADDRESS AT TOP?
18

Stagefright 4-11-45

Just a dig at Catherine and her hectic job with the Radio Division. She was now a secretary for the commander and kept very busy. She often wrote to Harry about how much she enjoyed her job, but how very demanding it was. (S)

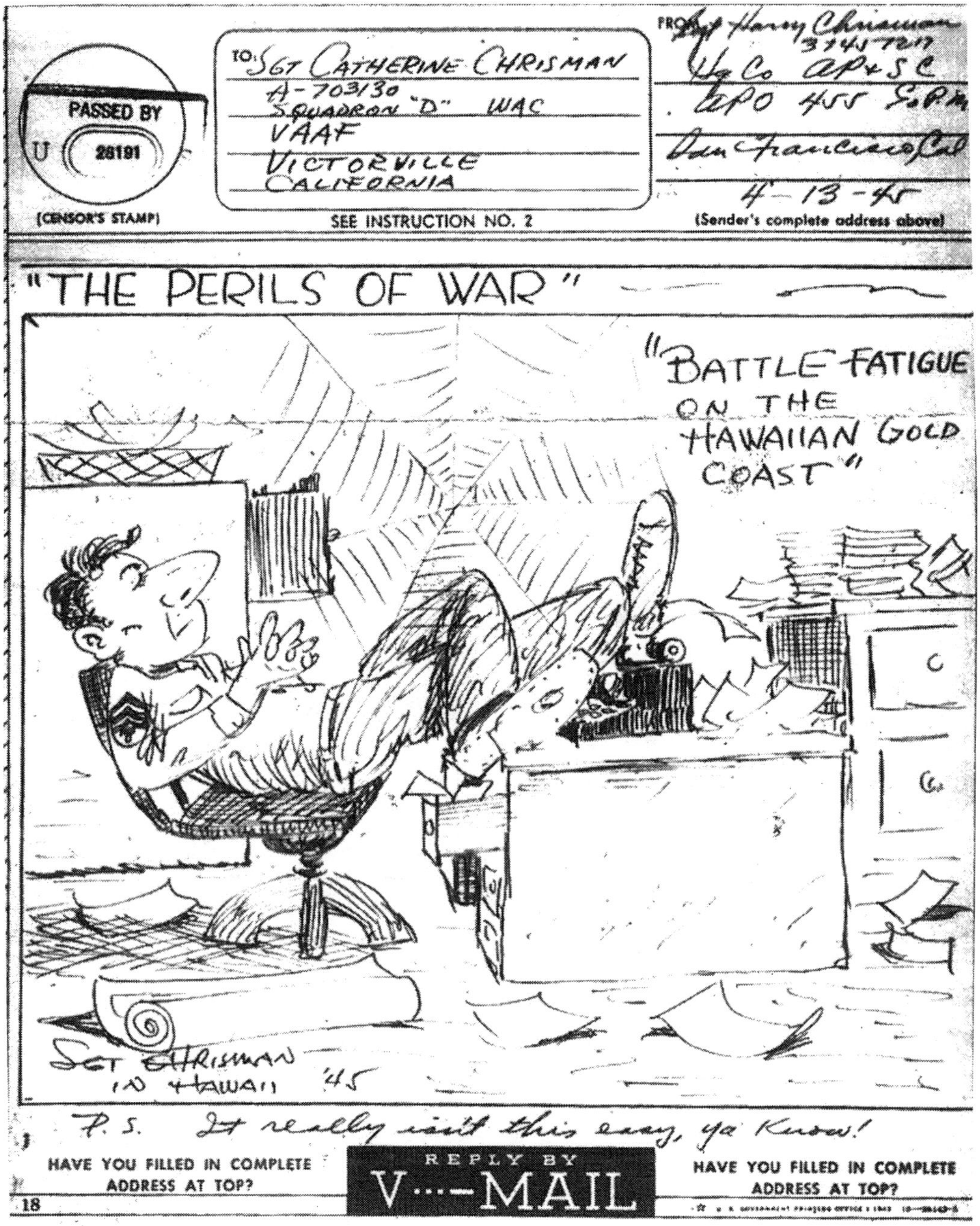
PASSED BY
U 28191
(CENSOR'S STAMP)
TO: SGT CATHERINE CHRISMAN
A-703130
SQUADRON "D" WAC
VAAF
VICTORVILLE
CALIFORNIA
SEE INSTRUCTION NO. 2
FROM
Hq Co
San Francisco Cal
4-13-45
(Sender's complete address above)
"THE PERILS OF WAR"
"BATTLE FATIGUE ON THE HAWAIIAN GOLD COAST"
SGT CHRISMAN IN HAWAII '45
P.S. It really isn't this easy, ya Know!
HAVE YOU FILLED IN COMPLETE ADDRESS AT TOP?
REPLY BY
V---MAIL
HAVE YOU FILLED IN COMPLETE ADDRESS AT TOP?
18

Perils of War 4-13-45

A lovely poem for Catherine since Harry could not deliver a May Basket to her on this May Day. We often talked about how we would deliver May Baskets containing flowers and candy to neighbors and friends on May 1st. We would put the basket on the front porch and ring the doorbell and then run so the person would not know who delivered the basket. Harry and Catherine both remember doing that when they were young as did I. It seemed a special thing to do. (S)

... Use typewriter, dark ink, or dark pencil. Faint or small writing is not suitable for photographing.

PASSED BY
28191
(CENSOR'S STAMP)

TO: Sgt Catherine Chrisman
A-103130
Squadron D WAC
WAAF
VICTORVILLE,
CALIFORNIA

SEE INSTRUCTION NO. 2

FROM: Sgt HARRY CHRISMAN
37457277
Hq Co APG C
APO 455 c/o P.M.
San Francisco, Cal
1 MAY 1945
(Sender's complete address above)

"MAY DAY — LEI DAY" —

Flowers woven into bright leis —
Carnation, pikake, gardenia —
Their blossoms sending out their fragrance
Over the busy streets.
This is a trade of Honolulu
In war as in peace —
A custom that never grows old
Whose newness stays ever-fresh
As the blossoms with which Leis
are fashioned.

Barefoot children gather blossoms;
Old men, fat women fashion them;
But the Lei, to be sold properly
Is handled by a shy wahine;
For the Lei, in Honolulu, means "Kiss."

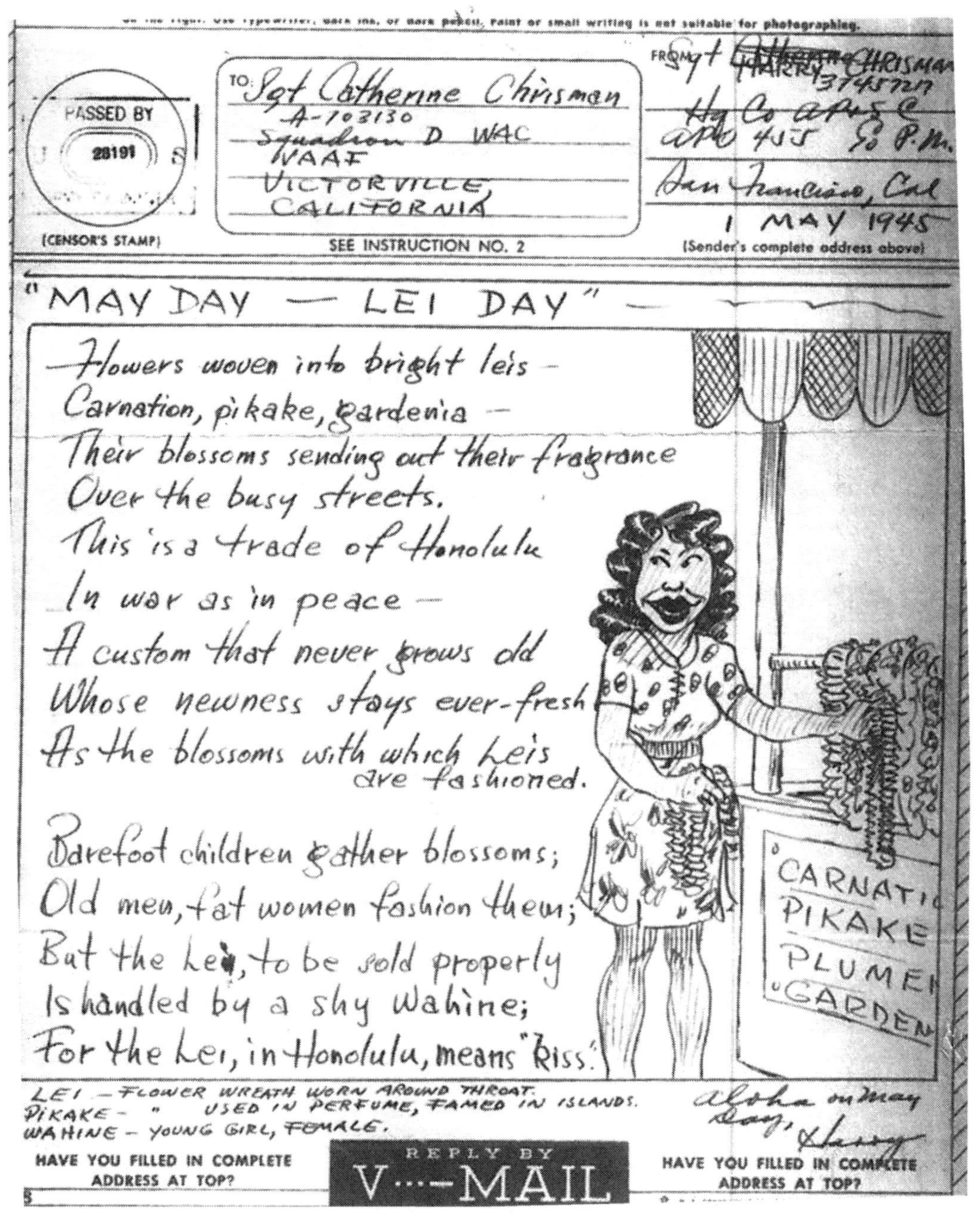

CARNATI
PIKAKE
PLUMEI
GARDEN

LEI — FLOWER WREATH WORN AROUND THROAT.
PIKAKE — " USED IN PERFUME, FAMED IN ISLANDS.
WAHINE — YOUNG GIRL, FEMALE.

Aloha on May Day,
Harry

HAVE YOU FILLED IN COMPLETE ADDRESS AT TOP?

REPLY BY V···—MAIL

HAVE YOU FILLED IN COMPLETE ADDRESS AT TOP?

Lei Day 5-1-45

A couple of years before she died on April 2, 2000, Catherine gave me their dog tags and told me to hang them on to my fireplace mantel and to pass them down to whatever son, then grandson, would want them. They hang there today in a place of honor and will go to our grandson, Erik, who is in the 82nd Airborne at Ft. Bragg, North Carolina. Erik also inherits Harry's fireplace bellows made from American Bison hide. Harry would play with the bellows with Erik, blowing air at him. Erik would laugh and laugh, and Harry said he would like for Erik to have them. They now reside by my fireplace. Erik was three when Harry died, but surprisingly enough, he remembers him. Perhaps because we talk about him so often, and of course he has a copy of Volume I of the V-Mail books! (S)

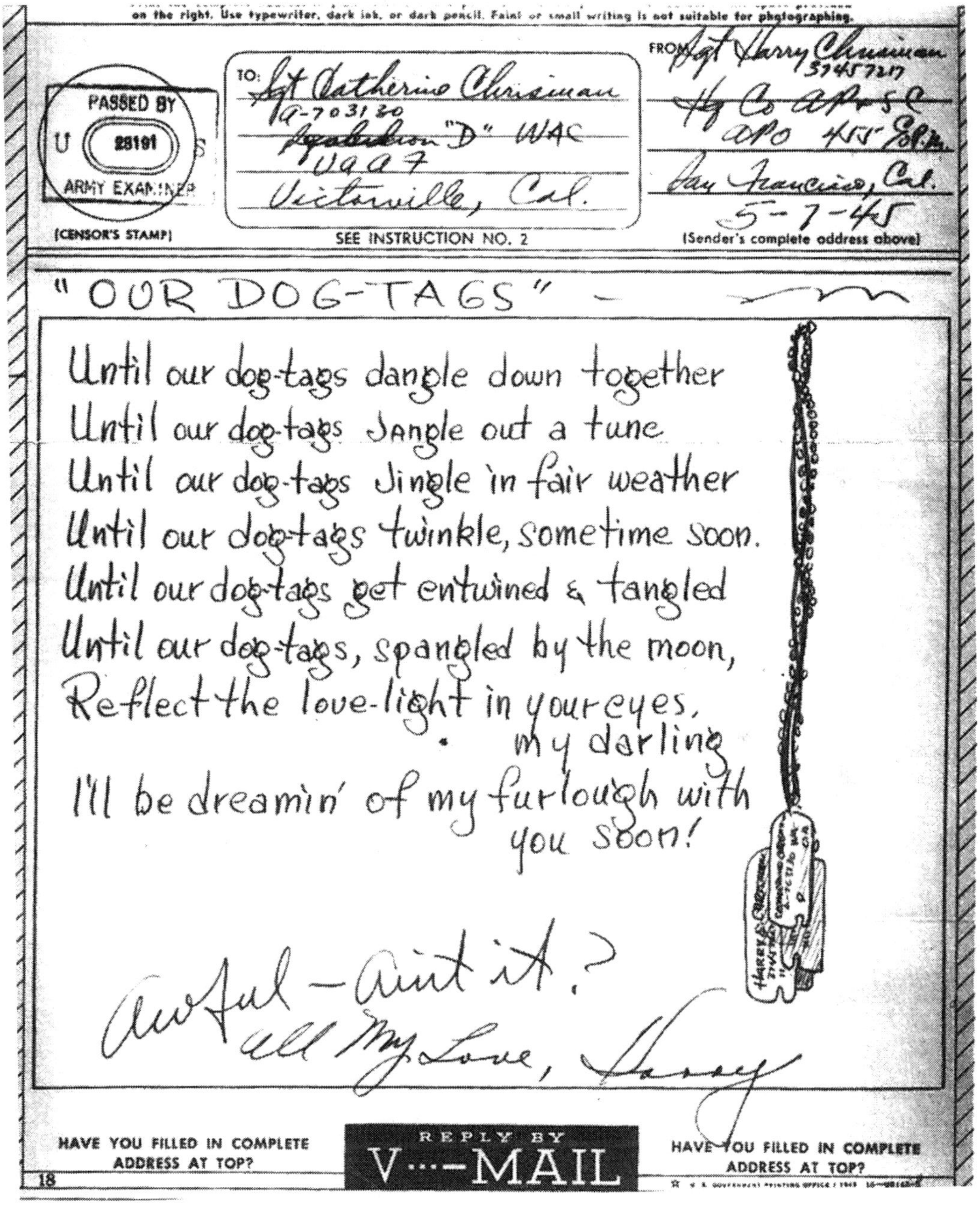

on the right. Use typewriter, dark ink, or dark pencil. Faint or small writing is not suitable for photographing.

TO: Sgt Catherine Chrisman
A-703130
Squadron "D" WAC
UAAF
Victorville, Cal.

SEE INSTRUCTION NO. 2

FROM Sgt Harry Chrisman
37457217
Hq Co APOSC
APO 455 %PM
San Francisco, Cal.
5-7-45

(Sender's complete address above)

PASSED BY
U 28191 S
ARMY EXAMINER
(CENSOR'S STAMP)

"OUR DOG-TAGS" —

Until our dog-tags dangle down together
Until our dog-tags jangle out a tune
Until our dog-tags jingle in fair weather
Until our dog-tags twinkle, sometime soon.
Until our dog-tags get entwined & tangled
Until our dog-tags, spangled by the moon,
Reflect the love-light in your eyes, my darling
I'll be dreamin' of my furlough with you soon!

Awful — aint it?
All My Love, Harry

HAVE YOU FILLED IN COMPLETE ADDRESS AT TOP?

REPLY BY V---MAIL

HAVE YOU FILLED IN COMPLETE ADDRESS AT TOP?

18

Dog Tags 5-7-45

YOU ARE MY SUNSHINE

PART TWO

NATURAL HISTORY

YOU ARE MY SUNSHINE

Harry's Natural History of the Pacific

HARRY WAS FASCINATED BY THE NATURAL HISTORY OF OUR WORLD and in January of 1944 began to draw both plants and animals he saw around him and often used as political allegories. He was especially enamored with the sea life he observed. He loved the variety of flora and fauna in the Pacific and told me he often thought how he had grown up in a land teeming with life and never thought a thing about it. He said he became much more observant and aware of the natural history of America and often recorded his thoughts about the land and its inhabitants while doing research for his books on the Old West. His huge *Webster's Dictionary* sits on its stand by my desk and there are news clippings about such things as whales and draft horses, and even an oak leaf held within its pages.

The oak leaf is from what Harry and Catherine called "The Lincoln Oak." On one of their journeys they stopped in Springfield, Illinois, to see Lincoln's grave. Harry reached down and picked up an acorn that was sprouting. Catherine kept that acorn in a foam cup of water on the dash of their Buick all the way home. They planted it in their yard and there it is today, merrily growing in Lakewood, Colorado.

The following Natural History V-Mails are self-explanatory and all were sent to Catherine who was also fascinated with the world around her. She noticed and was interested in everything!

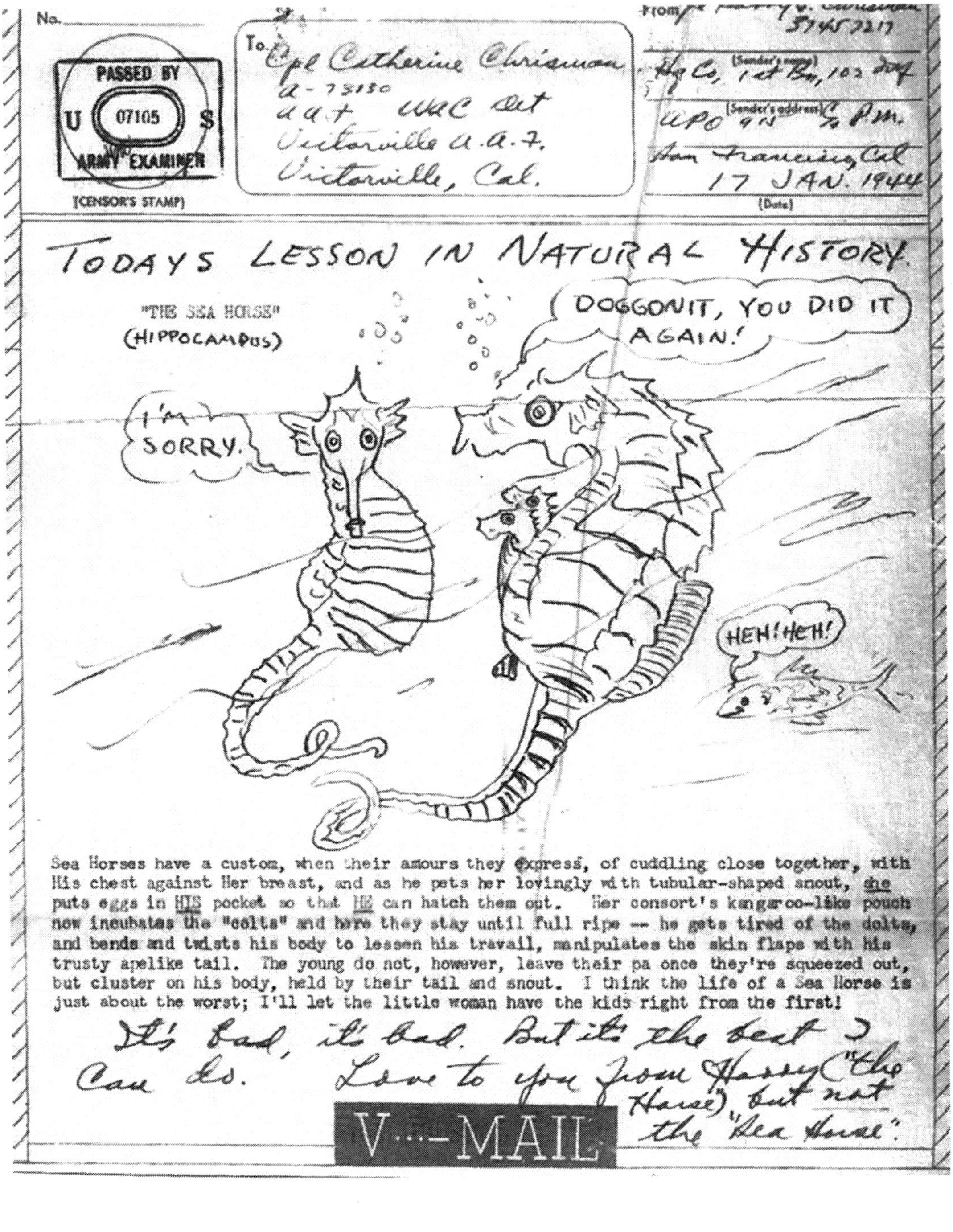

No.

PASSED BY
U 07105 S
ARMY EXAMINER
(CENSOR'S STAMP)

To: Cpl Catherine Chrisman
A-73130
A.A.F. WAC Det
Victorville A.A.F.
Victorville, Cal.

From
37457217
(Sender's name)
Hq Co, 1st Bn, 103 Inf
(Sender's address)
APO 43 c/o P.M.
San Francisco, Cal
17 JAN. 1944
(Date)

TODAYS LESSON IN NATURAL HISTORY

"THE SEA HORSE"
(HIPPOCAMPUS)
DOGGONIT, YOU DID IT AGAIN!
I'M SORRY.
HEH! HEH!

Sea Horses have a custom, when their amours they express, of cuddling close together, with His chest against Her breast, and as he pets her lovingly with tubular-shaped snout, she puts eggs in HIS pocket so that HE can hatch them out. Her consort's kangaroo-like pouch now incubates the "colts" and here they stay until full ripe -- he gets tired of the dolts, and bends and twists his body to lessen his travail, manipulates the skin flaps with his trusty apelike tail. The young do not, however, leave their pa once they're squeezed out, but cluster on his body, held by their tail and snout. I think the life of a Sea Horse is just about the worst; I'll let the little woman have the kids right from the first!

It's bad, it's bad. But it's the best I can do. Love to you from Harry ("the Horse"), but not the "Sea Horse".

V-MAIL

Sea Horse 1-17-44

To

Cpl Catherine Chrisman, A-703130
AAF Det WAC
VAAF
Victorville,
California

From Cpl Harry Chrisman
37457217
Hqs 1st Bn 182nd Inf
APC #915 care of
Postmaster San Francisco,
Cal.

21 Jan 1944
(Date)

TODAY'S LESSON IN NATURAL HISTORY

"THE PRIZZLE BEEST"

The Prizzle Beest, a funny cuss, around this island struts, it feeds on tortoise eggs and fish, and sometimes coconuts. You'd think with such a diet, and to conform to it's lot, the Prizzle Beest would need a build unlike the one it's got — for coconuts grow high in trees, fish live down in the sea, and tortoise eggs lie buried, unseen by folks like me. But, note the "fishline" tail that's worn by funny Prizzle Beest, with that he pulls whales from the sea — well, cuttlefish, at least. And see the spade-like feet he has to dig with in the ground; that's what he digs his eggs with — yes, friend Prizzle gets around. Sometimes I envy Prizzle Beests the tools they've been provided, to live with on a coral atoll, and I've about decided, that all of Nature's children have a very happy lot if they just would be contented with the million things they've got; if they'd stay at home and live their lives, be happy and be free, by using their million assets like the Prizzle uses three.

Love from an old Prizzle
fancier,

Harry

V---MAIL

The Prizzle Beast 1-21-44

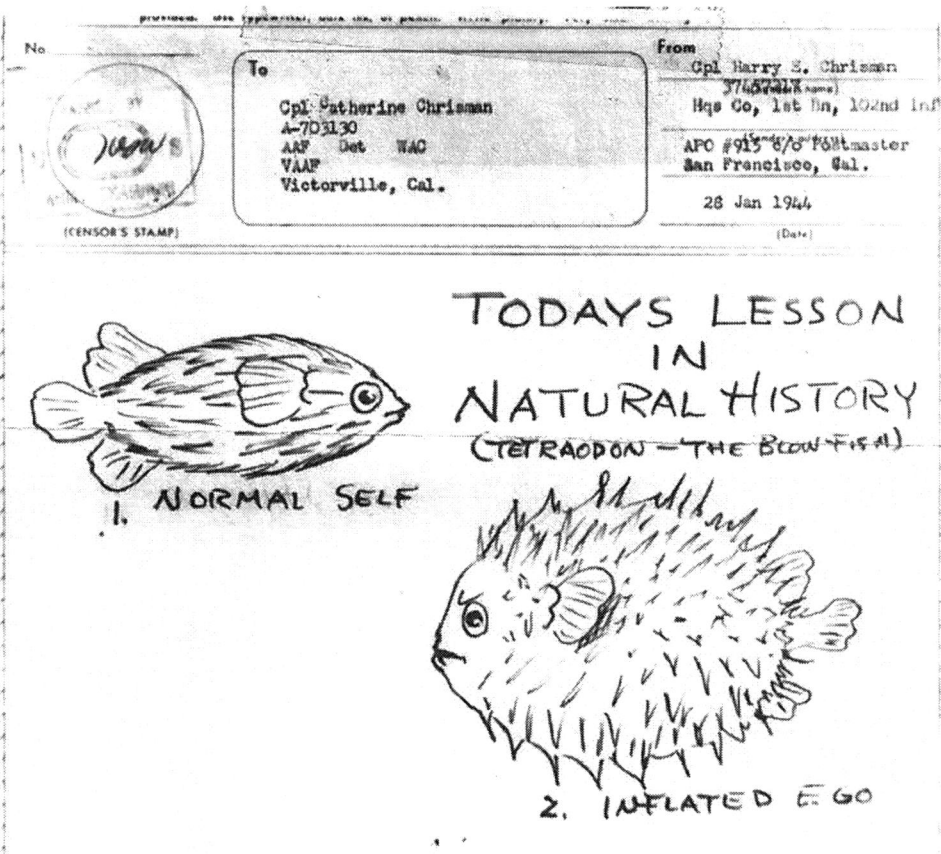

TODAYS LESSON IN NATURAL HISTORY
(TETRAODON — THE BLOW FISH)

1. NORMAL SELF

2. INFLATED EGO

TETRAODON

Tetraodon, the Puffer Fish, has many times recalled, to mind a politician who
was fat and loud and bald; and like Tetraodon, when irked, would swell in size,
and lecture from a balcony with big, and fierce-told, lies. But like Tetraodon
this man, so greatly overrated is just a "spineless" sad-eyed "fish" since he has
been deflated. I think you'll find all Dictators and stuffed shirts of that species,
are much like Tetraodon and the similar Blow Fishes. For only by expansion of their
ego, and their girth can they make themselves feel equal to the other men on earth.

Love, Harry

Puffer Fish 1-28-44

provided. Use typewriter, dark ink or pencil. Write plainly. Very small writing is not suitable.

No.

PASSED BY
U.S.
ARMY EXAMINER
(CENSOR'S STAMP)

To Cpl Catherine Chrisman
A-703130
A.A.F. Det., WAC
V.A.A.F.,
Victorville,
California

From Cpl Harry E. Chrisman
37457217
(Sender's name)
Hqs Co, 1st Bn, 102 Inf
APO 915 c/o PM
(Sender's address)
San Francisco, Cal
12 Feb 1944
(Date)

TODAYS LESSON
IN
NATURAL HISTORY
—
"THE STING-RAY"
(RAIA)

THIS ODDITY, THE STING-RAY, WEARS
OUT A VERTABRAE
AND GROWS ANOTHER FULL-LENGTH SPINE WITH
WHICH TO STING ITS PREY.
TOO BAD A MAN, LIKE STING-RAY, CAN'T GROW
ANOTHER SPINE—
I'M SURE I'D GET A STIFFER ONE THAN THIS
WEAK ONE OF MINE!

V---MAIL

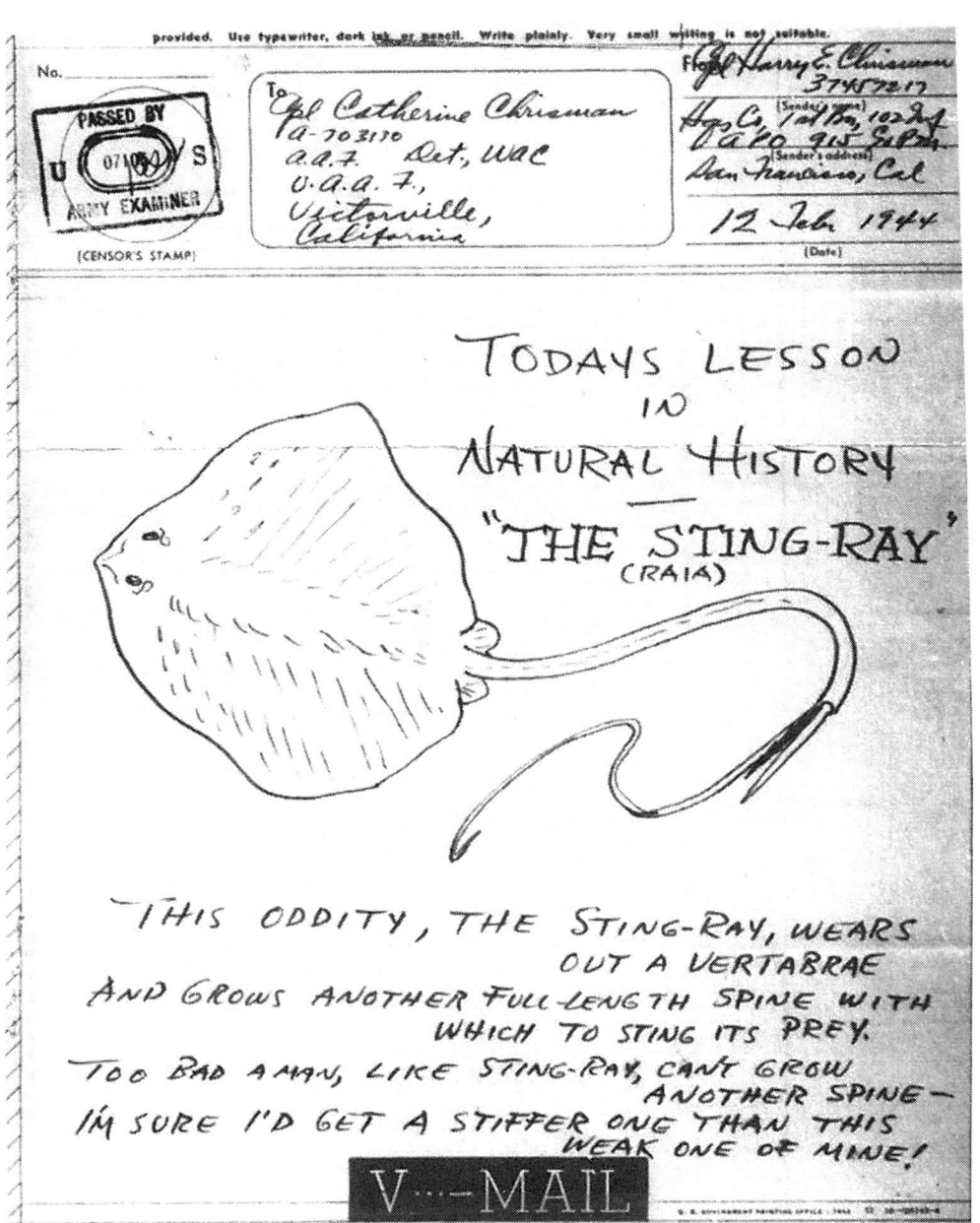

Sting Ray 2-12-44

provided. Use typewriter, dark ink, or pencil. Write plainly. Very small writing is not suitable.

No.

PASSED BY
U 07106 S
ARMY EXAMINER
(CENSOR'S STAMP)

To: Cpl Catherine Chrisman
A-703130 Det WAC
AG7
V.A.A.F.
Victorville
California

From: Cpl Harry Chrisman 37457217
(Sender's name)
Hq Co, 1st Bn, 102 Inf
APO #915
(Sender's address)
c/o P.M. San Francisco, Cal
13 Feb 1944
(Date)

BURP!
BEFORE DINING
AFTER DINING
TODAYS LESSON IN NATURAL HISTORY

"THE SWALLOWER" (CHIASMODON)

THE "SWALLOWER" REMINDS ME OF A MAN I KNEW BACK HOME;
HE'D BUY A 6 POUND T-BONE STEAK, AND EAT ALL BUT THE BONE.
THOUGH FISH AND MAN BOTH GORGE THEMSELVES UNTIL THEIR TUMMIES HURT
I NEVER SAW A "SWALLOWER" TAKE "SECONDS" ON DESSERT!

Do you KNOW WHO I MEAN?

V---MAIL

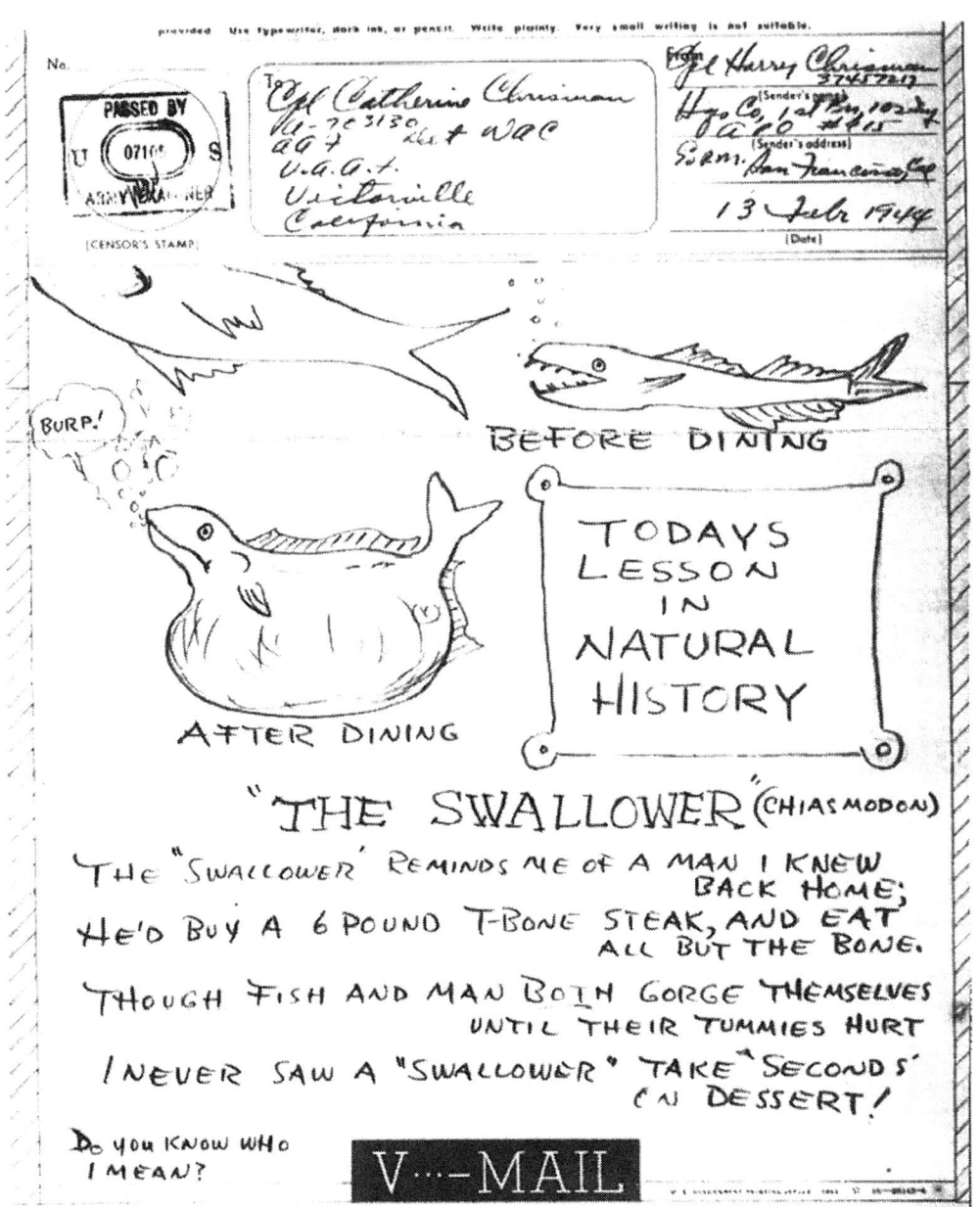

The Swallower 2-13-44

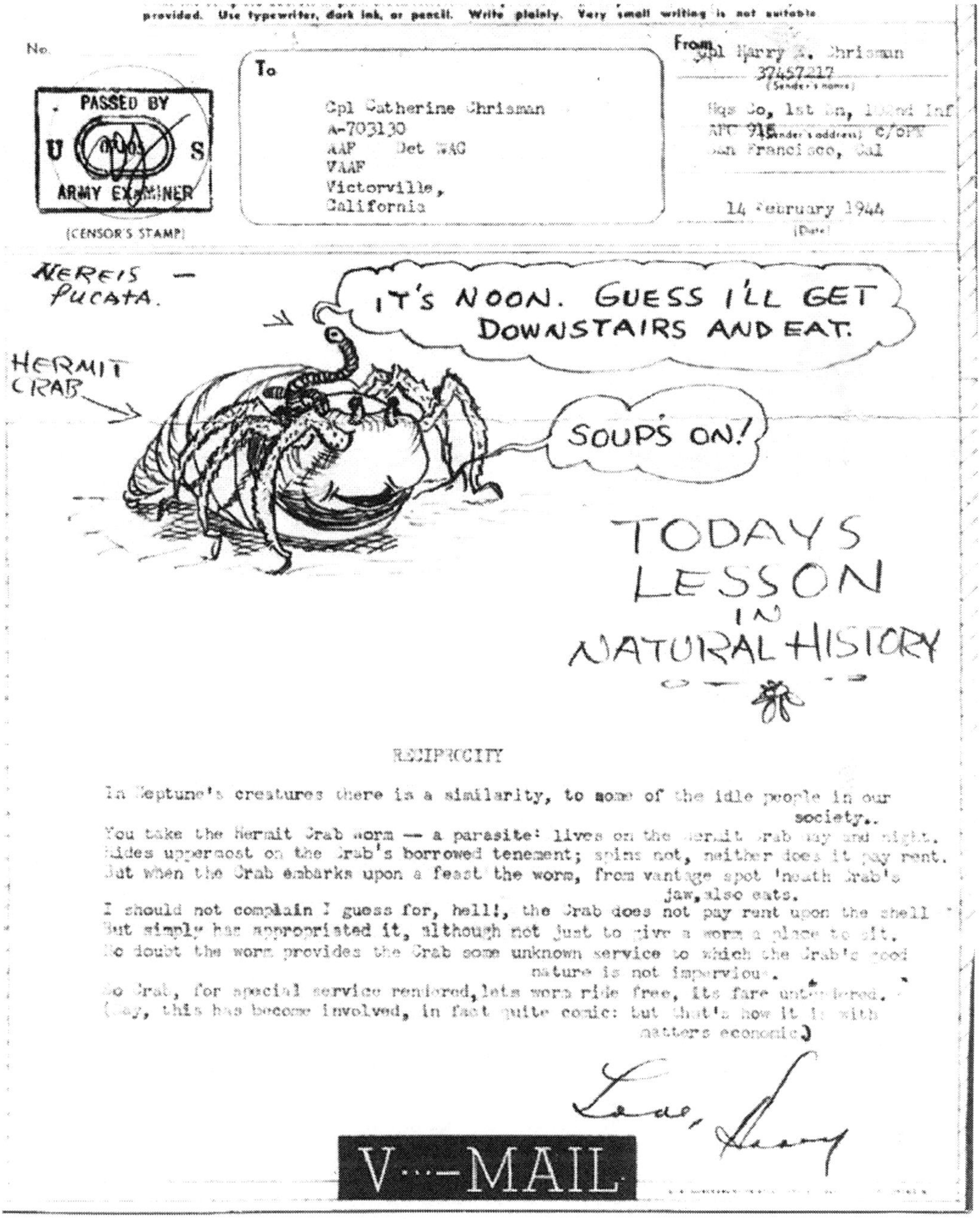

provided. Use typewriter, dark ink, or pencil. Write plainly. Very small writing is not suitable

No.

PASSED BY
U.S.
ARMY EXAMINER
(CENSOR'S STAMP)

To

Cpl Catherine Chrisman
A-703130
AAF Det WAC
VAAF
Victorville,
California

From Cpl Harry [illegible]. Chrisman
37457217
(Sender's name)

Hqs Co, 1st Bn, 102nd Inf
APO 715 (Sender's address) C/OPM
San Francisco, Cal

14 February 1944
(Date)

NEREIS — PUCATA.
HERMIT CRAB
IT'S NOON. GUESS I'LL GET DOWNSTAIRS AND EAT.
SOUPS ON!

TODAYS LESSON IN NATURAL HISTORY

RECIPROCITY

In Neptune's creatures there is a similarity, to some of the idle people in our society..
You take the Hermit Crab worm — a parasite: lives on the Hermit Crab day and night.
Rides uppermost on the Crab's borrowed tenement; spins not, neither does it pay rent.
But when the Crab embarks upon a feast the worm, from vantage spot 'neath Crab's jaw, also eats.
I should not complain I guess for, hell!, the Crab does not pay rent upon the shell
But simply has appropriated it, although not just to give a worm a place to sit.
No doubt the worm provides the Crab some unknown service to which the Crab's good nature is not impervious.
So Crab, for special service rendered, lets worm ride free, its fare untendered.
(Say, this has become involved, in fact quite comic: but that's how it is with matters economic.)

Love, Harry

V---MAIL

Hermit Crab 2-14-44

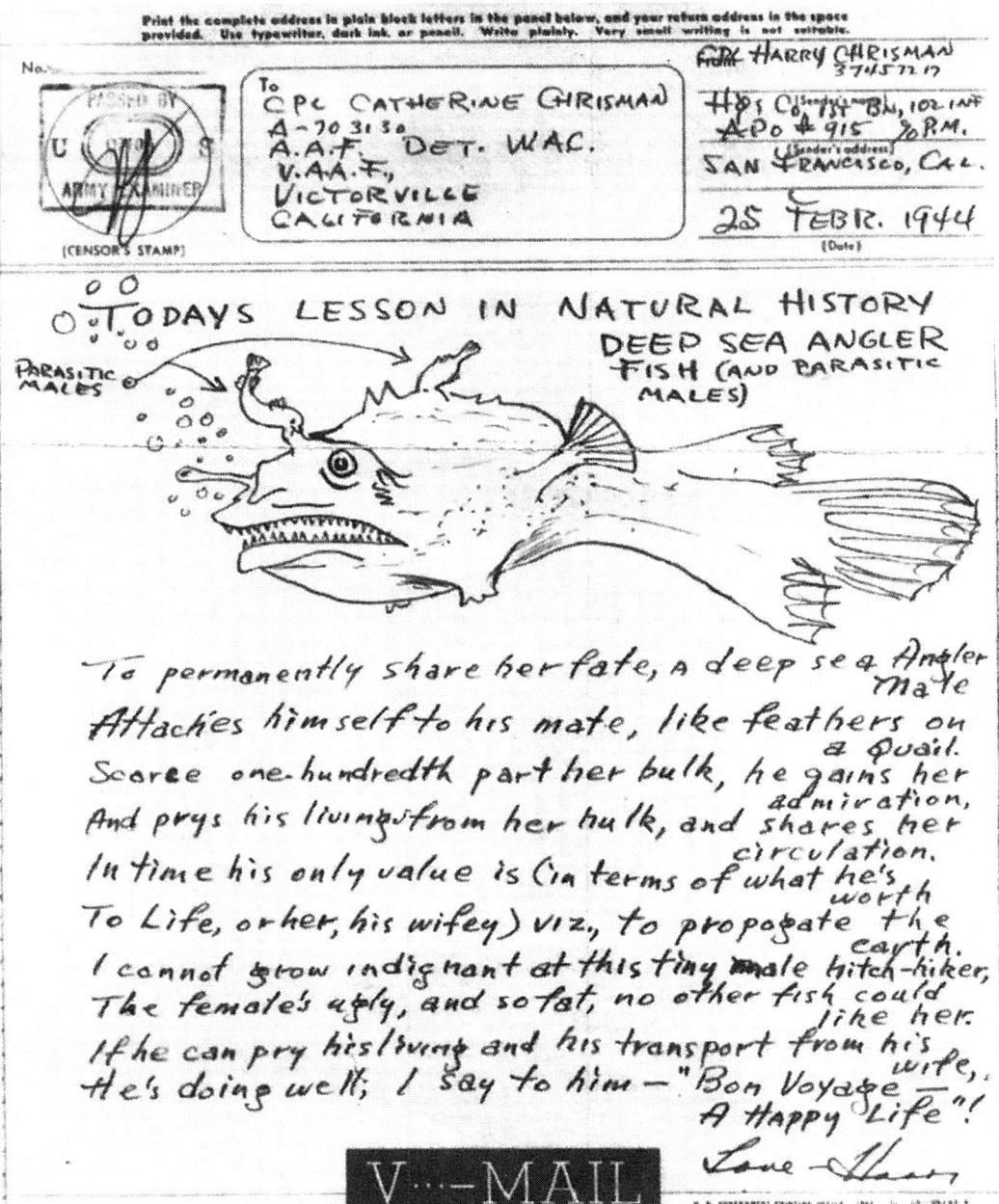

To permanently share her fate, a deep sea Angler male
Attaches himself to his mate, like feathers on a Quail.
Scarce one-hundredth part her bulk, he gains her admiration,
And prys his livings from her bulk, and shares her circulation.
In time his only value is (in terms of what he's worth
To Life, or her, his wifey) viz., to propagate the earth.
I cannot grow indignant at this tiny male hitch-hiker,
The female's ugly, and so fat, no other fish could like her.
If he can pry his living and his transport from his wife,
He's doing well; I say to him — "Bon Voyage — A Happy Life"!

Love Harry

Angler 2-25-44

168

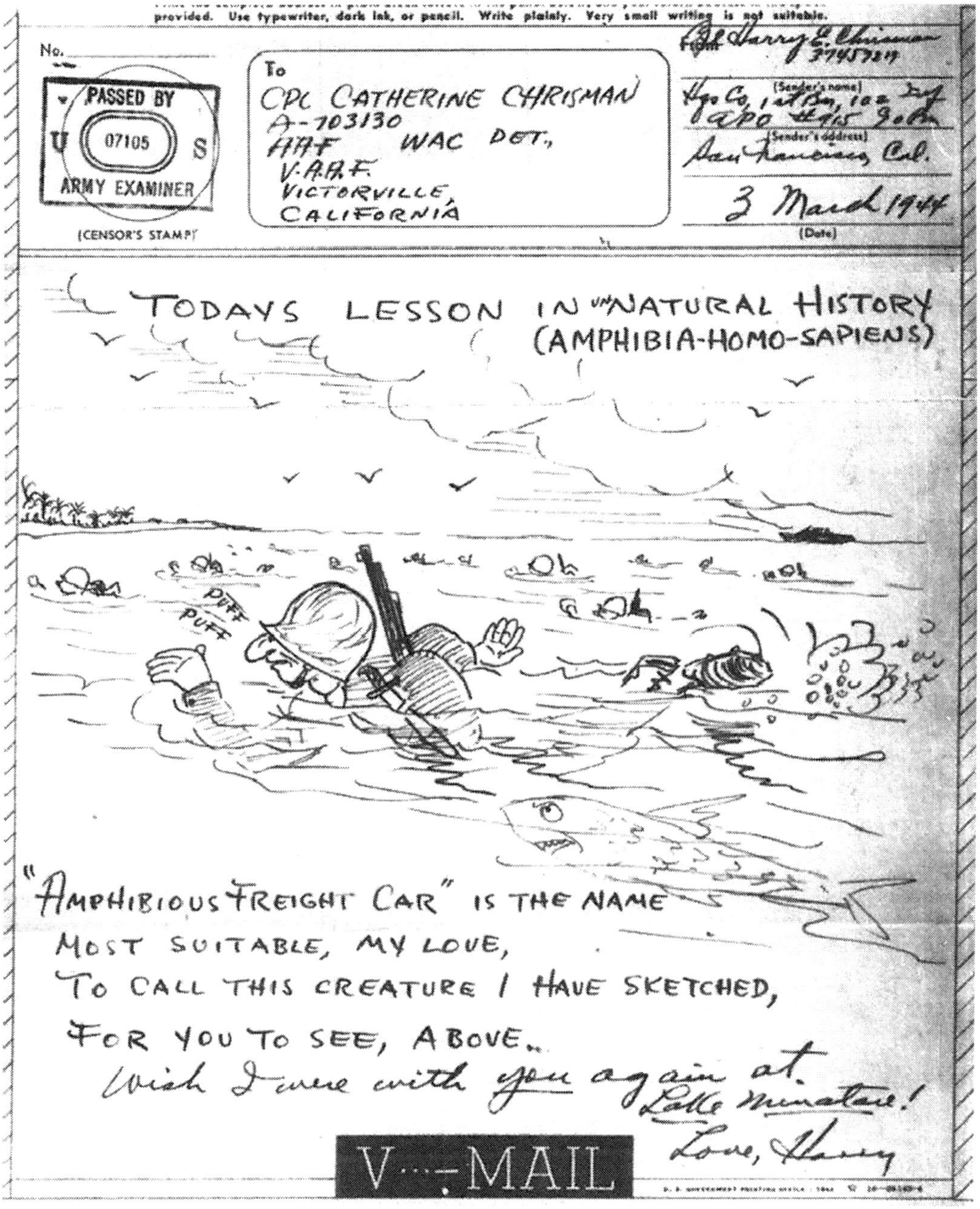

provided. Use typewriter, dark ink, or pencil. Write plainly. Very small writing is not suitable.

No.

PASSED BY
U 07105 S
ARMY EXAMINER

(CENSOR'S STAMP)

To
CPL CATHERINE CHRISMAN
A-703130
AAF WAC DET.,
V.A.A.F.
VICTORVILLE,
CALIFORNIA

From Cpl Harry E. Chrisman
37457214
(Sender's name)
Hq Co, 1st Bn, 102 Inf
APO #915 % P.M.
(Sender's address)
San Francisco, Cal.

3 March 1944
(Date)

TODAYS LESSON IN UNNATURAL HISTORY
(AMPHIBIA-HOMO-SAPIENS)

PUFF
PUFF

"AMPHIBIOUS FREIGHT CAR" IS THE NAME
MOST SUITABLE, MY LOVE,
TO CALL THIS CREATURE I HAVE SKETCHED,
FOR YOU TO SEE, ABOVE..
Wish I were with you again at Lake Minatare!
Love, Harry

V---MAIL

Freight Car 3-3-44

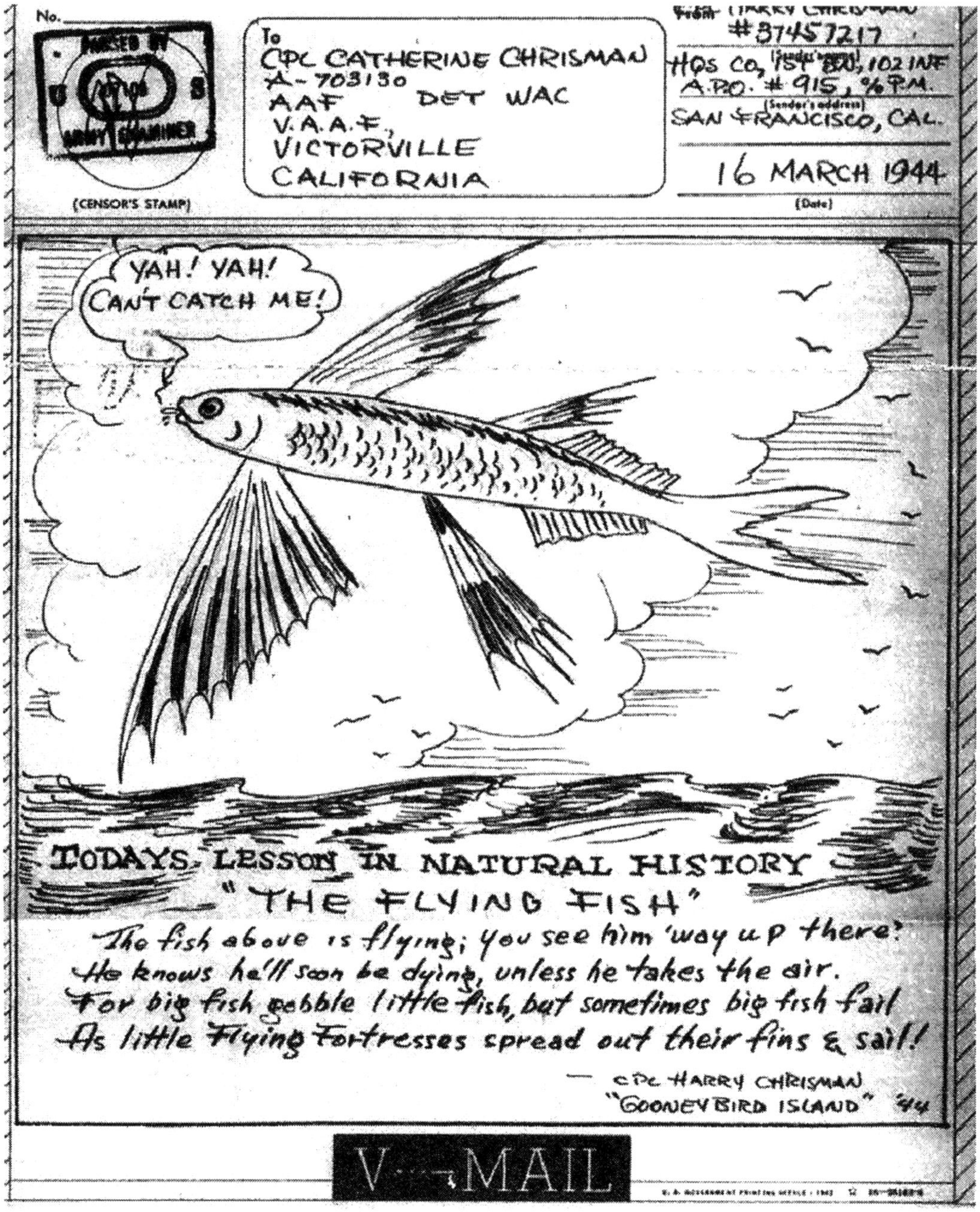
No.
(CENSOR'S STAMP)
To
CPL CATHERINE CHRISMAN
A-703130
AAF DET WAC
V.A.A.F.,
VICTORVILLE
CALIFORNIA
#37457217
HQs Co, 1st Bn, 102 INF
A.P.O. #915, % P.M.
(Sender's address)
SAN FRANCISCO, CAL.
16 MARCH 1944
(Date)
YAH! YAH! CAN'T CATCH ME!
TODAYS LESSON IN NATURAL HISTORY
"THE FLYING FISH"
The fish above is flying; you see him 'way up there!
He knows he'll soon be dying, unless he takes the air.
For big fish gobble little fish, but sometimes big fish fail
As little Flying Fortresses spread out their fins & sail!
— CPL HARRY CHRISMAN
"GOONEYBIRD ISLAND" '44
V-MAIL

Flying Fish 3-16-44

No. _____

PASSED BY
ARMY EXAMINER
(CENSOR'S STAMP)

To
Cpl Catherine Chrisman
A-703130
AAF   Det WAC
VAAF
Victorville,
California.

From Cpl Harry Chrisman
37457217
Hqs Co 2nd Bn 302 Inf
APO 915 c/o Postmaster
San Francisco, Cal.
(Sender's address)

19 March 1944
(Date)

TODAYS LESSON IN NATURAL HISTORY

THE SEA GHERKIN
(OTHERWISE KNOWN AS "CUCUMARIA" OR THE 'SEA CUCUMBER')

A quaint sea animale that is afflicted by a parasitic fish that swims in and out of the Sea Gherkins body cavity, thereby robbing Gherkin of his food and making a general damn nuisance of himself.
Sea Cucumbers are excellent to eat and resemble the taste of oysters. When served they are called "Beche de Mer" and are a great delicacy in the East.

Sea Gherkin is a homely chap with warts upon his back,
His awkward star-shaped head is sure attention to attract.
By swallowing the coral rocks, mixed with his stomache juice
He vomits up a limestone mess that makes poor soils produce.
Sea Gherkin has a parasite (a most obnoxious lout)
Who, from the Gherkins stomacke can swim both in and out;
The Gherkin does not seem to mind who shares his meager plate,
He keeps on masticating rocks for his commensal mate.
But all producers, like friend "Jerk", seem for the poorhouse slated
So long as idlers take the wealth that workers have created.
So long as there's a parasite, and creature dumb, like Gherkin,
There'll always be a loafer, and a fellow creature workin'
To keep that idler happy and a silk hat on his head,
While the workin' stiff gets callouses and the loafer gets the bread.

From your Coral-Bound Baby, Harry

V---MAIL

Sea Gherkin 3-19-44

Print the complete address in plain block letters in the panel below, and your return address in the space provided. Use typewriter, dark ink, or pencil. Write plainly. Very small writing is not suitable.

No.

PASSED BY
U 0710 S
ARMY EXAMINER
(CENSOR'S STAMP)

To
Cpl Catherine Chrisman
A-703130
AAF   Det WAC
VAAF
Victorville, California.

From
Cpl Harry Chrisman
37457217
Hqs Co 1st Bn 102nd Inf
APO 915 c/o Postmaster
San Francisco, Calif.

24 March 1944
(Date)

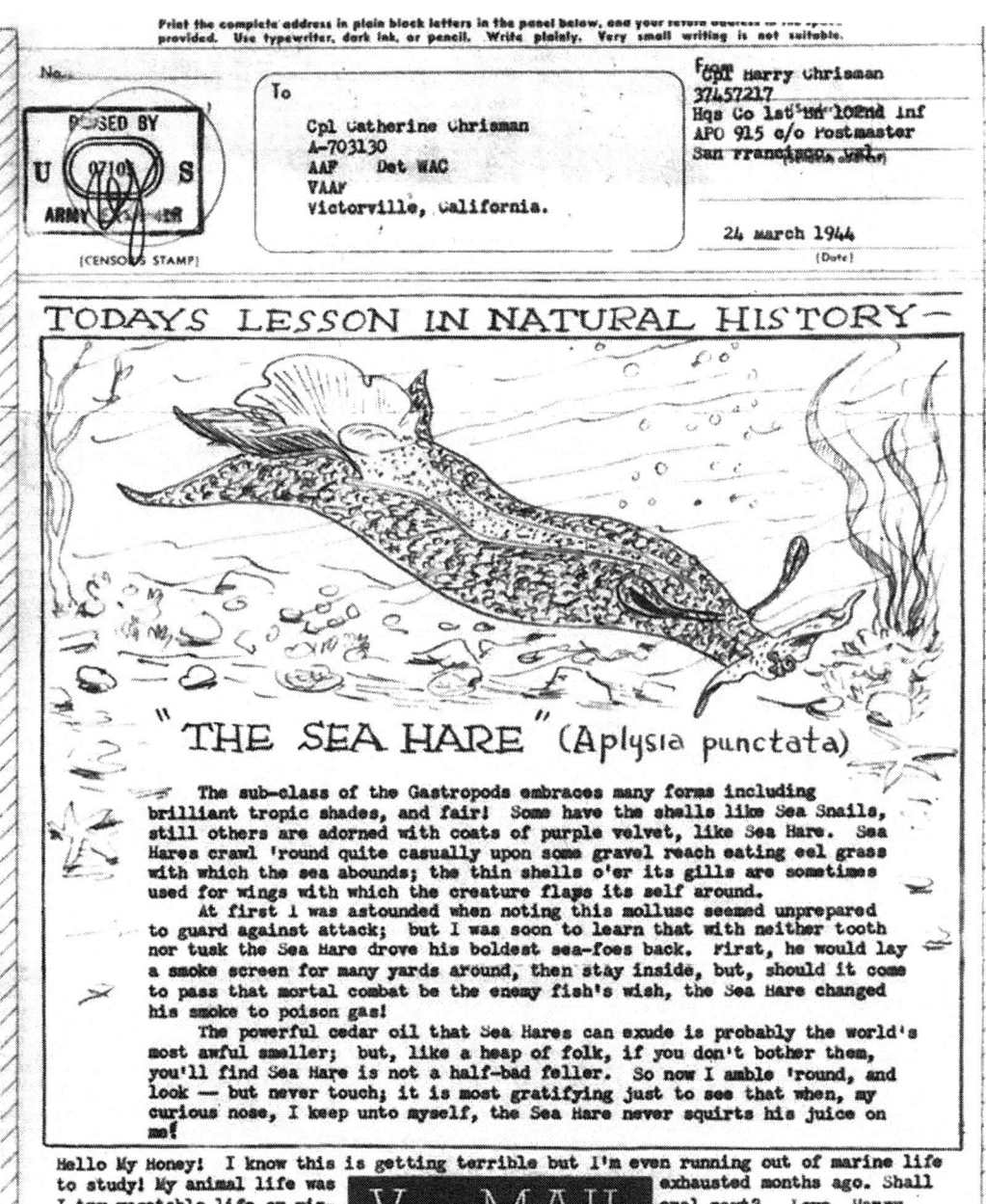

TODAYS LESSON IN NATURAL HISTORY—

"THE SEA HARE" (Aplysia punctata)

The sub-class of the Gastropods embraces many forms including brilliant tropic shades, and fair! Some have the shells like Sea Snails, still others are adorned with coats of purple velvet, like Sea Hare. Sea Hares crawl 'round quite casually upon some gravel reach eating eel grass with which the sea abounds; the thin shells o'er its gills are sometimes used for wings with which the creature flaps its self around.

At first I was astounded when noting this mollusc seemed unprepared to guard against attack; but I was soon to learn that with neither tooth nor tusk the Sea Hare drove his boldest sea-foes back. First, he would lay a smoke screen for many yards around, then stay inside, but, should it come to pass that mortal combat be the enemy fish's wish, the Sea Hare changed his smoke to poison gas!

The powerful cedar oil that Sea Hares can exude is probably the world's most awful smeller; but, like a heap of folk, if you don't bother them, you'll find Sea Hare is not a half-bad feller. So now I amble 'round, and look — but never touch; it is most gratifying just to see that when, my curious nose, I keep unto myself, the Sea Hare never squirts his juice on me!

Hello My Honey! I know this is getting terrible but I'm even running out of marine life to study! My animal life was exhausted months ago. Shall I try vegetable life or min- eral next? Love, Harry

V···— MAIL

Sea Hare 3-24-44

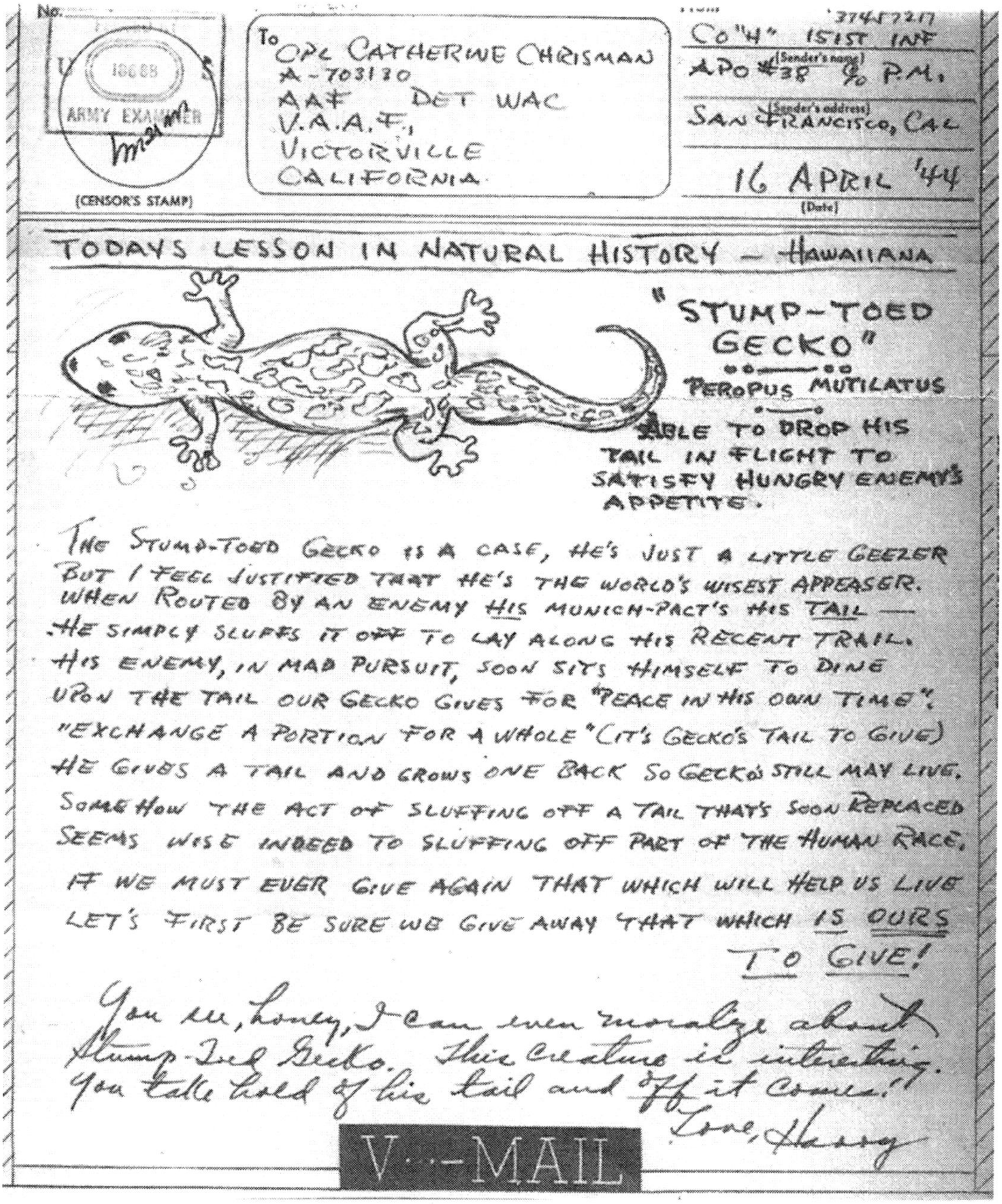

No.

ARMY EXAMINER 18688

(CENSOR'S STAMP)

To CPL CATHERINE CHRISMAN
A-703130
AAF DET WAC
V.A.A.F.,
VICTORVILLE
CALIFORNIA

37457217
Co "H" 151ST INF
(Sender's name)
APO #38 c/o P.M.
(Sender's address)
SAN FRANCISCO, CAL

16 APRIL '44
(Date)

TODAYS LESSON IN NATURAL HISTORY – HAWAIIANA

"STUMP-TOED GECKO"
PEROPUS MUTILATUS

ABLE TO DROP HIS TAIL IN FLIGHT TO SATISFY HUNGRY ENEMY'S APPETITE.

THE STUMP-TOED GECKO IS A CASE, HE'S JUST A LITTLE GEEZER
BUT I FEEL JUSTIFIED THAT HE'S THE WORLD'S WISEST APPEASER.
WHEN ROUTED BY AN ENEMY HIS MUNICH-PACT'S HIS TAIL —
HE SIMPLY SLUFFS IT OFF TO LAY ALONG HIS RECENT TRAIL.
HIS ENEMY, IN MAD PURSUIT, SOON SITS HIMSELF TO DINE
UPON THE TAIL OUR GECKO GIVES FOR "PEACE IN HIS OWN TIME".
"EXCHANGE A PORTION FOR A WHOLE" (IT'S GECKO'S TAIL TO GIVE)
HE GIVES A TAIL AND GROWS ONE BACK SO GECKO'S STILL MAY LIVE.
SOME HOW THE ACT OF SLUFFING OFF A TAIL THAT'S SOON REPLACED
SEEMS WISE INDEED TO SLUFFING OFF PART OF THE HUMAN RACE.
IF WE MUST EVER GIVE AGAIN THAT WHICH WILL HELP US LIVE
LET'S FIRST BE SURE WE GIVE AWAY THAT WHICH IS OURS
TO GIVE!

You see, honey, I can even moralize about Stump-Toed Gecko. This creature is interesting. You take hold of his tail and off it comes!

Love, Harry

V-MAIL

Gecko 4-16-44

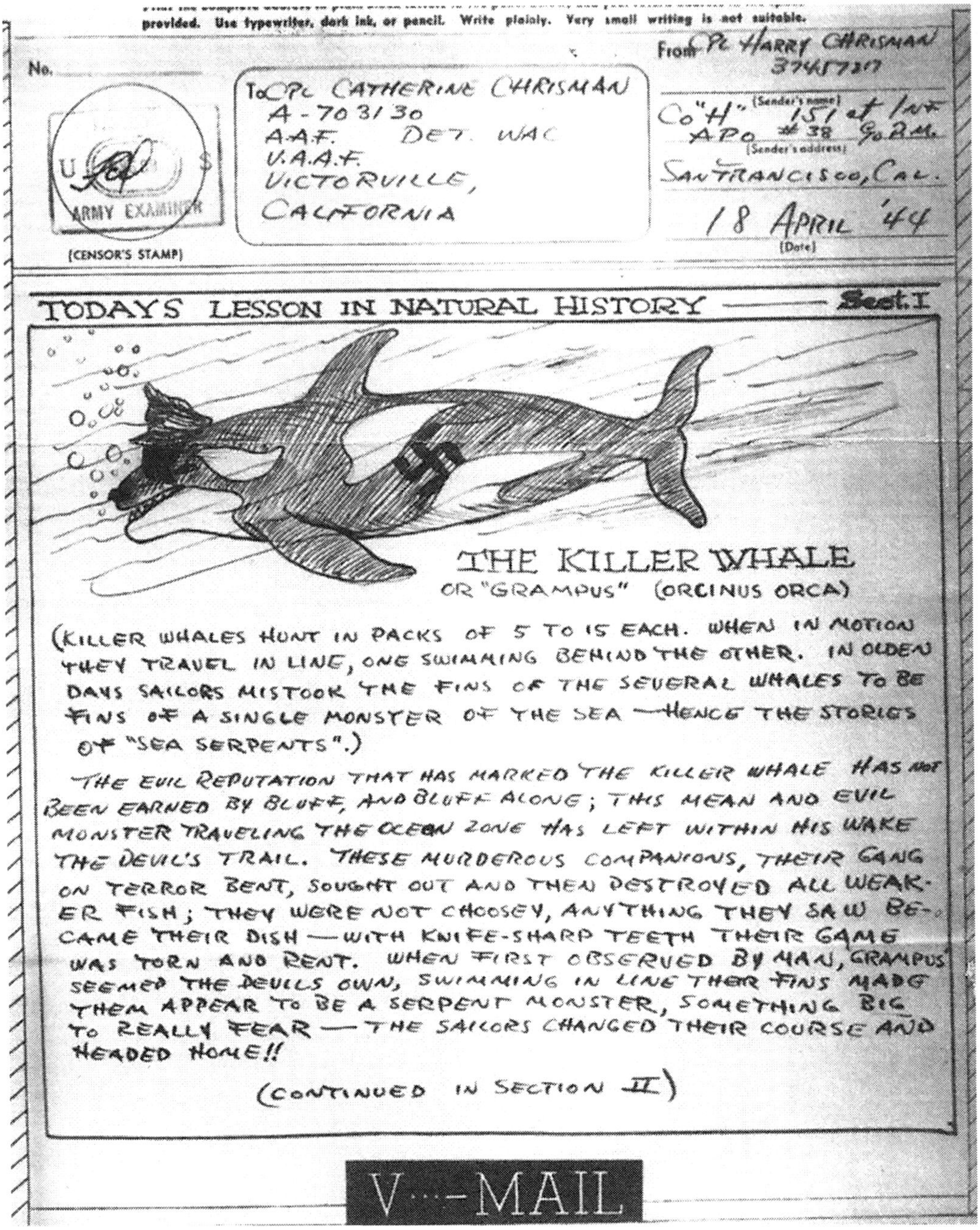

provided. Use typewriter, dark ink, or pencil. Write plainly. Very small writing is not suitable.

No.

To CPL CATHERINE CHRISMAN
A-703130
A.A.F. DET. WAC
V.A.A.F.
VICTORVILLE,
CALIFORNIA

From CPL HARRY CHRISMAN
37457217
(Sender's name)
Co "H" 151st Inf
APO #38 % P.M.
(Sender's address)
SAN FRANCISCO, CAL.
18 APRIL '44
(Date)

U.S. ARMY EXAMINER
(CENSOR'S STAMP)

TODAYS LESSON IN NATURAL HISTORY — Sect. I

THE KILLER WHALE
OR "GRAMPUS" (ORCINUS ORCA)

(KILLER WHALES HUNT IN PACKS OF 5 TO 15 EACH. WHEN IN MOTION THEY TRAVEL IN LINE, ONE SWIMMING BEHIND THE OTHER. IN OLDEN DAYS SAILORS MISTOOK THE FINS OF THE SEVERAL WHALES TO BE FINS OF A SINGLE MONSTER OF THE SEA — HENCE THE STORIES OF "SEA SERPENTS".)

THE EVIL REPUTATION THAT HAS MARKED THE KILLER WHALE HAS NOT BEEN EARNED BY BLUFF, AND BLUFF ALONE; THIS MEAN AND EVIL MONSTER TRAVELING THE OCEAN ZONE HAS LEFT WITHIN HIS WAKE THE DEVIL'S TRAIL. THESE MURDEROUS COMPANIONS, THEIR GANG ON TERROR BENT, SOUGHT OUT AND THEN DESTROYED ALL WEAKER FISH; THEY WERE NOT CHOOSEY, ANYTHING THEY SAW BECAME THEIR DISH — WITH KNIFE-SHARP TEETH THEIR GAME WAS TORN AND RENT. WHEN FIRST OBSERVED BY MAN, GRAMPUS SEEMED THE DEVILS OWN, SWIMMING IN LINE THEIR FINS MADE THEM APPEAR TO BE A SERPENT MONSTER, SOMETHING BIG TO REALLY FEAR — THE SAILORS CHANGED THEIR COURSE AND HEADED HOME!!

(CONTINUED IN SECTION II)

V-MAIL

Killer Whale 4-18-44

Print the complete address in plain letters in the panel below, and your return address in the space provided on the right. Use typewriter, dark ink, or dark pencil. Faint or small writing is not suitable for photographing.

TO: CPL CATHERINE CHRISMAN
A-703130

A.A.F.   DET. WAC
V.A.A.F.,
VICTORVILLE,
CALIFORNIA

FROM: Pc HARRY CHRISMAN
3745721?
Co "H"   151st INF
APO #38   ?, P.M.
SAN FRANCISCO, CAL

18 APRIL 44

[CENSOR'S STAMP]   SEE INSTRUCTION NO. 2   (Sender's complete address above)

TODAYS LESSON IN NATURAL HISTORY — SECT. II

"THE KILLER WHALE" —(CONTINUED)

KILLER WHALES SWIMMING.

NAZIS GOOSE-STEPPING

CAN YOU RECALL THE MARCHING, GOOSE-STEPPING FEET IN GERMANY, AND, TOO, THAT EVER-BUSY TONGUE THAT EVER-MORE CONTENDED THAT THE FINS GREW BUT ON ONE — AND IN THAT ONE WAS SUPERMAN COMPLETE? WELL, THAT'S THE WAY WITH 'GRAMPUS', EVENTUALLY 'TWAS FOUND THAT HE WAS NOT A DRAGON — OR A FLEA, BUT, WITH HIS GANG OF HOOLIGANS, WOULD BULLY ALL THE SEA UNLESS SOME WAY WAS FOUND TO SLAP HIM DOWN. SO WHALING SHIPS NOW HAVE HARPOONS TO STICK INTO HIS RUMP, AND FRIENDLY MEN PROTECT THE WEAKER FISH; AND 'GRAMPUS' NOW HIDES OUT, UPON HIS TONGUE THIS WISH — THAT HE'D NOT MADE HIMSELF THE "SUPER-CHUMP".

So, until my next "lesson" I am, with all my love to you my darling,
Your husband, Harry

Yes.

HAVE YOU FILLED IN COMPLETE ADDRESS AT TOP?

REPLY BY V····MAIL

Yes Sir!

HAVE YOU FILLED IN COMPLETE ADDRESS AT TOP?

Killer Whale, cont. 4-18-44

Print the complete address in plain letters in the panel below, and your return address in the space provided on the right. Use typewriter, dark ink, or dark pencil. Faint or small writing is not suitable for photographing.

PASSED BY U S (CENSOR'S STAMP)

TO CPL CATHERINE CHRISMAN
A-703130
AAF DET WAC
VAAF
VICTORVILLE
CALIFORNIA

SEE INSTRUCTION NO. 2

FROM CPL HARRY CHRISMAN
37457217
CO "H" 151st INF
APO #38 % P.M.
SAN FRANCISCO, CAL
21 APRIL '44

(Sender's complete address above)

TODAYS LESSON IN NATURAL HISTORY

"THE WALLABY"
(ORDER MARSUPALIA)

I SWEAR I'M NOT A KANGAROO!
JUST COUNT ME IN ON THAT OATH, TOO!

YOU THINK THIS IS A KANGAROO,
I KNOW; BECAUSE I THOUGHT SO TOO!
THEY'RE CALLED THE "WALLABY" YOU SEE –
THOUGH WHY YOU CANNOT LEARN FROM ME.

THE WALLABY, THEY'LL SAY TO YOU, IS JUST
A PINT-SIZED KANGAROO.
IT SEEMS TO ME THE WALLABY DESERVES A
WELL-EARNED HOLIDAY IF SHE MUST LONGER
HAVE TO PACK THAT FAT SON IN HER HAVERSACK
THIS BORES ME JUST AS MUCH AS YOU –
LET'S CALL THE THING A KANGAROO!

Love from your old man, Harry

YES ✓ HAVE YOU FILLED IN COMPLETE ADDRESS AT TOP?

REPLY BY V---MAIL

✓ YES SIR! HAVE YOU FILLED IN COMPLETE ADDRESS AT TOP?

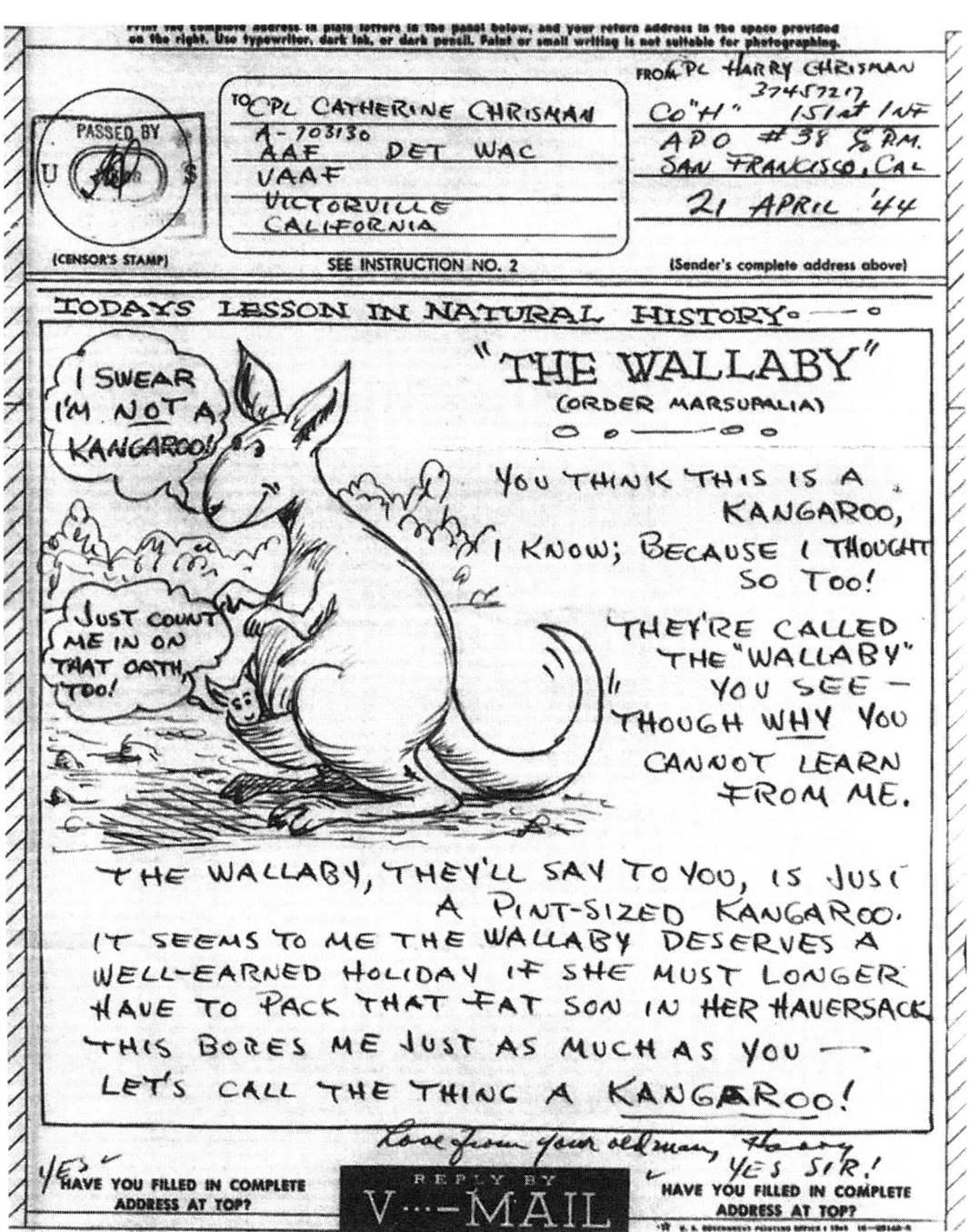

Wallaby 4-21-44

No. _____

[CENSOR'S STAMP]
PASSED BY
U ☐ 18688 S
ARMY EXAMINER

To CPL CATHERINE CHRISMAN
A-703130
AAF   DET WAC
V.A.A.F.,
VICTORVILLE,
CALIFORNIA

From CPL HARRY CHRISMAN
37457217
Co "H" (Sender's name) 151ST INF
APO #38 Po P.M.
(Sender's address)
SAN FRANCISCO, CAL.

27 APRIL '44
[Date]

TODAYS LESSON IN NATURAL HISTORY

"THE DOG"

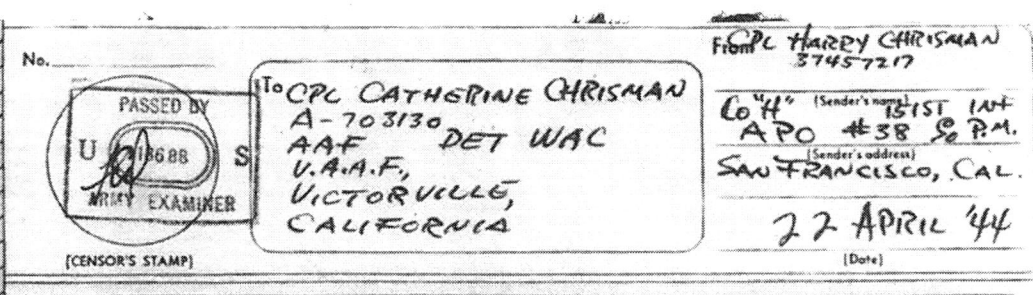

ANCIENT HAWAIIAN DOG.
"EXCEEDINGLY SLUGGISH..."
—CAPT. COOK

MODERN ARMY DOG.
"EXCEEDINGLY SPIRITED"
—CPL CHRISMAN

HAWAIIAN DOGS ARE BLESSED WITH WEALTH OF HAPPINESS,
AND SPLENDID HEALTH, WHEN YOU COMPARE THEIR PRESENT
LIFE TO ALL THE CANINES ANCIENT STRIFE, A CENTURY
OR TWO AGO. FOR AT THAT TIME THE POOR CANINE WAS
RAISED JUST AS WE NOW RAISE SWINE. HIS MASTER BROT
HIM UP ON POI; A GAIN IN WEIGHT BROUGHT SMILES OF
JOY. AND WHEN THE FEAST DAY ROLLED AROUND HIS
MASTER HURRIED TO THE "POUND", SELECTED FOR THE
BIG LUAU THE BIGGEST DOG AND FATTEST SOW, A
CENTURY OR TWO AGO. THEY DIDN'T PUT THEM ON A SPIT,
BUT ROASTED THEM DOWN IN A PIT, AND COVERED O'ER
THE FLESH WITH LEAVES (TO SPICE IT UP AS WE SALT
BEEVES). WHEN IT WAS DONE THEY GATHERED 'ROUND AND
SPREAD THE FEAST UPON THE GROUND WITH MANGOES, POI,
BREAD FRUIT, WINE, THE GROUP ASSEMBLED THERE TO DINE.
THE DOG, IT SEEMS, WAS UTILIZED FAR BETTER THEN —AND IN
MY EYES HIS CONTRIBUTION TO MANKIND WAS GREATER IN
THAT ANCIENT TIME. FOR NOW THEY FOLLOW ARMY CAMPS;
THEY'RE WHELPS AND CURS, AND MOSTLY SCAMPS. BUT DO YOU
THINK WE'D GIVE CURS UP? HELL NO! NOT EVEN ONE
SMALL PUP!

V----MAIL

Love, Harry

Dog 4-22-44

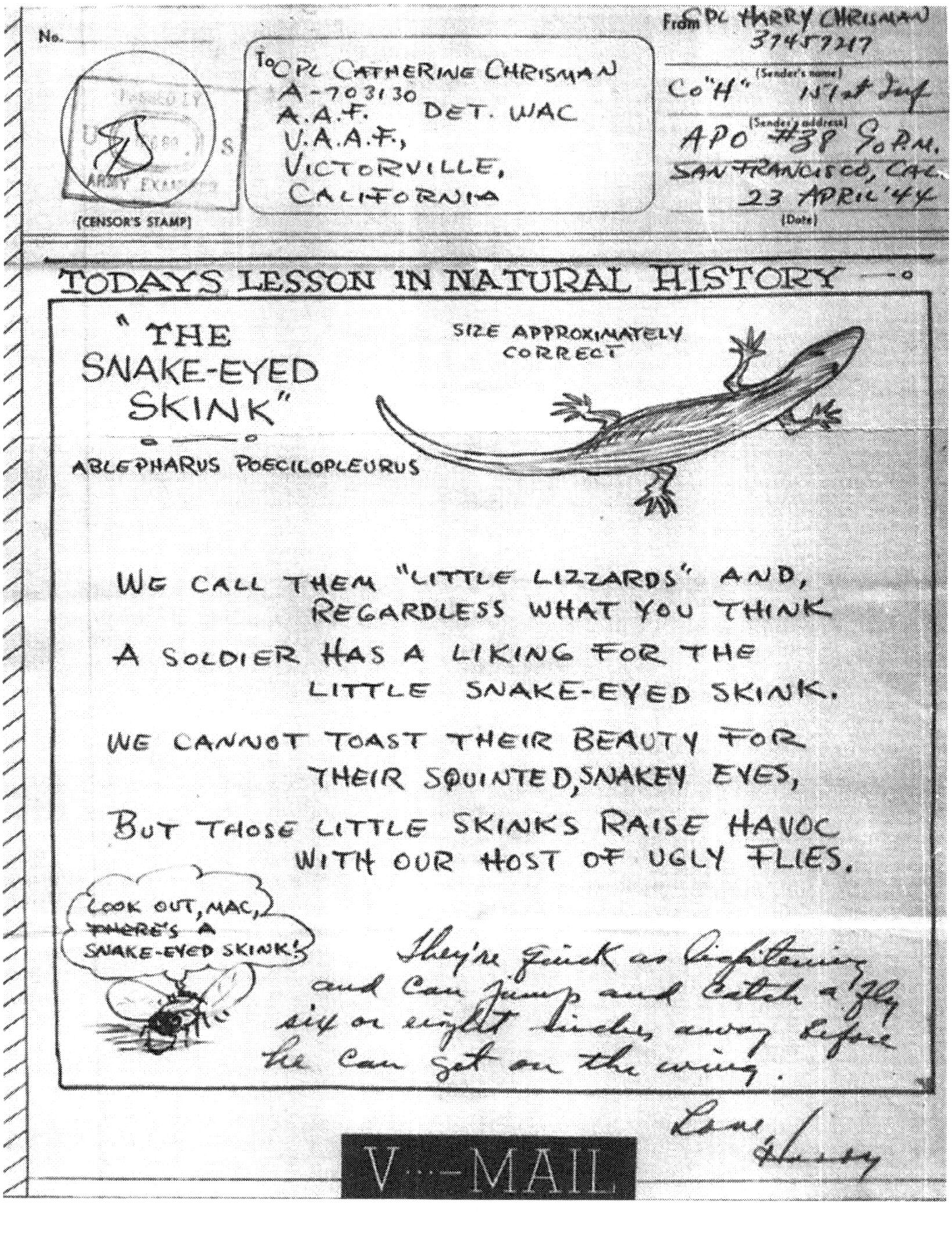

No.

From CPL HARRY CHRISMAN
37457217
(Sender's name)
Co "H" 151st Inf
(Sender's address)
APO #38 % P.M.
SAN FRANCISCO, CAL.
23 APRIL '44
(Date)

To CPL CATHERINE CHRISMAN
A-703130
A.A.F. DET. WAC
V.A.A.F.,
VICTORVILLE,
CALIFORNIA

ARMY EXAMINER
(CENSOR'S STAMP)

TODAYS LESSON IN NATURAL HISTORY

"THE SNAKE-EYED SKINK"

ABLEPHARUS POECILOPLEURUS

SIZE APPROXIMATELY CORRECT

WE CALL THEM "LITTLE LIZZARDS" AND,
REGARDLESS WHAT YOU THINK
A SOLDIER HAS A LIKING FOR THE
LITTLE SNAKE-EYED SKINK.
WE CANNOT TOAST THEIR BEAUTY FOR
THEIR SQUINTED, SNAKEY EYES,
BUT THOSE LITTLE SKINKS RAISE HAVOC
WITH OUR HOST OF UGLY FLIES.

LOOK OUT, MAC,
THERE'S A
SNAKE-EYED SKINK!

They're quick as lightening and can jump and catch a fly six or eight inches away before he can get on the wing.

Love,
Harry

V-MAIL

Skink 4-23-44

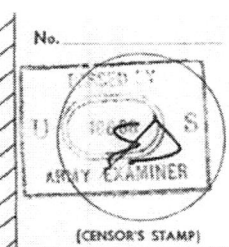

To CPL CATHERINE CHRISMAN
A-703130
A A F   DET WAC
V A A F
VICTORVILLE
CALIFORNIA

From: PC MAKKY CHRISMAN
37457217

Co "H" (Sender's name) 151ST INF

APO # 38 S. P.M. (Sender's address)
SAN FRANCISCO, CAL.
24 APR. '44
(Date)

TODAYS LESSON IN NATURAL HISTORY —

"THE
BAT"
(LASIURUS SEMOTUS)
CALLED
"OPEA PEA"

RARE, AND BELIEVED
TO BE THE ONLY NATIVE
LAND MAMMAL IN THE
HAWAIIAN ISLANDS. FIRST
SEEN AT KONA, HAWAII
(LITTLE GRASS SHACK AT
KEALAKEKUA) BY PEALE,
AMERICAN NATURALIST, IN
1838-42.

THERE'S LITTLE TO BE SAID ABOUT
            THE BAT
EXCEPT HE'S JUST A BAT FOR A THAT
            'N A THAT;
HIS HOURS ARE SOMETHING I'D APPRECIATE,
TO SLEEP ALL DAY, ALL NIGHT TO
            DRINK AND EAT.
The bat and I have one thing in common—
i. e. were *both* nocturnal in our habits!

V····MAIL

Love, Harry

Bat 4-22-44

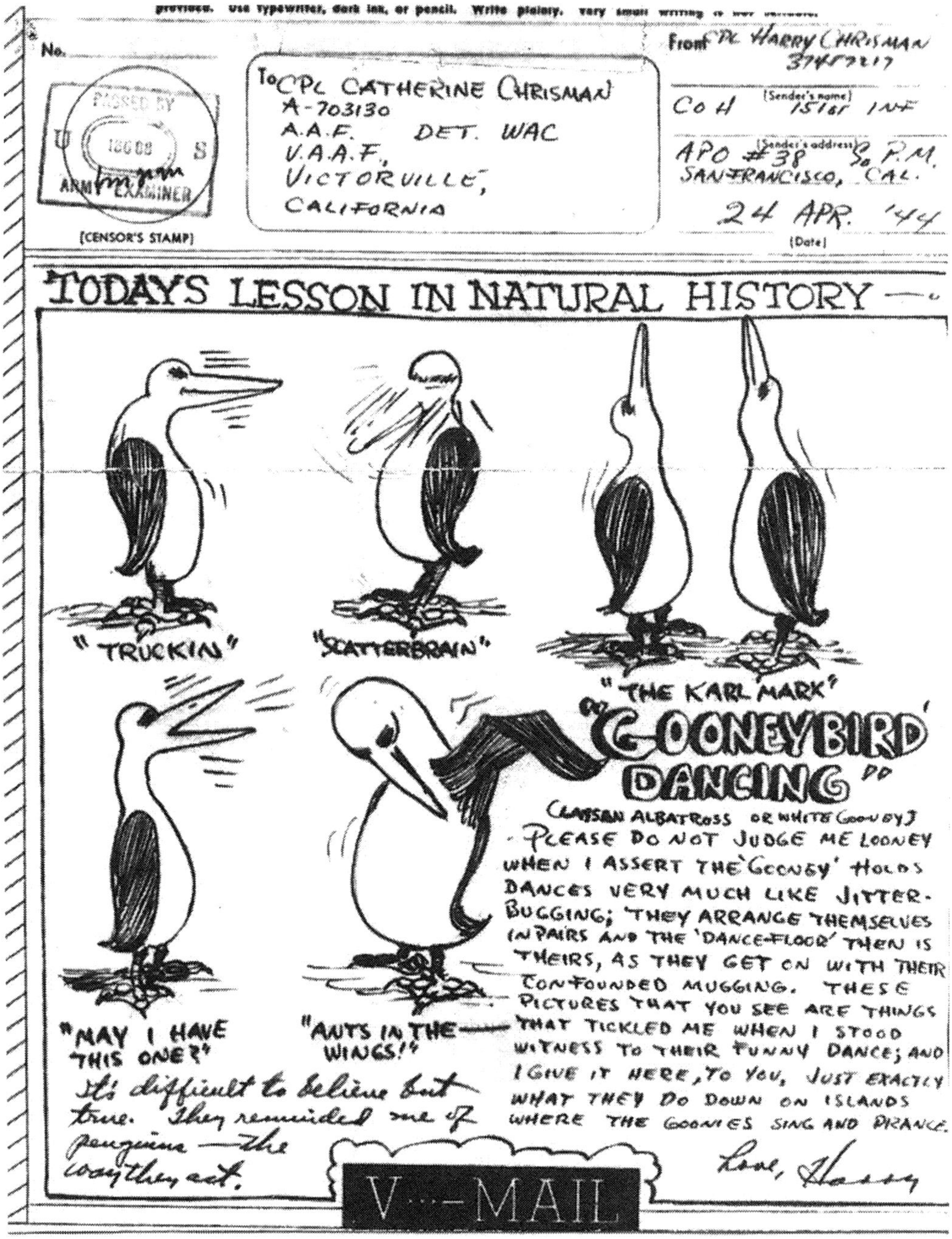

provided. Use typewriter, dark ink, or pencil. Write plainly. Very small writing is not suitable.

No.

PASSED BY U.S. ARMY EXAMINER

(CENSOR'S STAMP)

To CPL CATHERINE CHRISMAN
A-703130
A.A.F. DET. WAC
V.A.A.F.,
VICTORVILLE,
CALIFORNIA

From CPL HARRY CHRISMAN
37457217
(Sender's name)
CO H 151ST INF
(Sender's address)
APO #38 % P.M.
SAN FRANCISCO, CAL.
24 APR. '44
(Date)

TODAYS LESSON IN NATURAL HISTORY —

"TRUCKIN"

"SCATTERBRAIN"

"THE KARL MARX"

"MAY I HAVE THIS ONE?"

"ANTS IN THE WINGS!"

"GOONEYBIRD DANCING"

(LAYSAN ALBATROSS OR WHITE GOONEY)

PLEASE DO NOT JUDGE ME LOONEY WHEN I ASSERT THE 'GOONEY' HOLDS DANCES VERY MUCH LIKE JITTER-BUGGING; THEY ARRANGE THEMSELVES IN PAIRS AND THE 'DANCE-FLOOR' THEN IS THEIRS, AS THEY GET ON WITH THEIR CONFOUNDED MUGGING. THESE PICTURES THAT YOU SEE ARE THINGS THAT TICKLED ME WHEN I STOOD WITNESS TO THEIR FUNNY DANCE; AND I GIVE IT HERE, TO YOU, JUST EXACTLY WHAT THEY DO DOWN ON ISLANDS WHERE THE GOONIES SING AND PRANCE.

It's difficult to believe but true. They reminded me of penguins — the way they act.

Love, Harry

V—MAIL

Gooney Dance 4-24-44

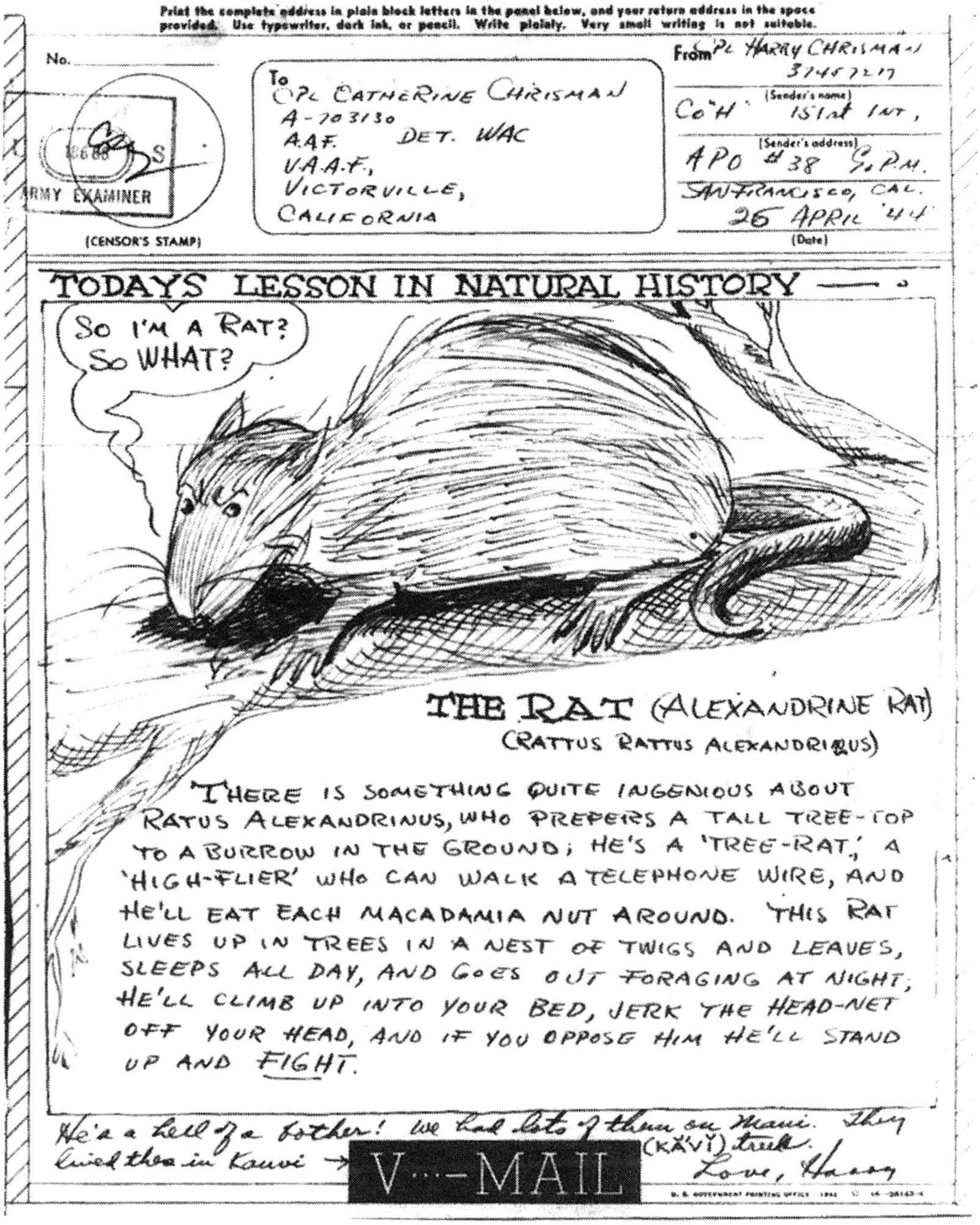

Print the complete address in plain block letters in the panel below, and your return address in the space provided. Use typewriter, dark ink, or pencil. Write plainly. Very small writing is not suitable.
No.
ARMY EXAMINER
(CENSOR'S STAMP)
To CPL CATHERINE CHRISMAN
A-703130
A.A.F. DET. WAC
V.A.A.F.,
VICTORVILLE,
CALIFORNIA
From CPL HARRY CHRISMAN
31457217
(Sender's name)
Co "H" 151st INT,
(Sender's address)
APO #38 % P.M.
SAN FRANCISCO, CAL.
26 APRIL '44
(Date)
TODAYS LESSON IN NATURAL HISTORY
SO I'M A RAT? SO WHAT?
THE RAT (ALEXANDRINE RAT)
(RATTUS RATTUS ALEXANDRINUS)
THERE IS SOMETHING QUITE INGENIOUS ABOUT RATUS ALEXANDRINUS, WHO PREFERS A TALL TREE-TOP TO A BURROW IN THE GROUND; HE'S A 'TREE-RAT,' A 'HIGH-FLIER' WHO CAN WALK A TELEPHONE WIRE, AND HE'LL EAT EACH MACADAMIA NUT AROUND. THIS RAT LIVES UP IN TREES IN A NEST OF TWIGS AND LEAVES, SLEEPS ALL DAY, AND GOES OUT FORAGING AT NIGHT; HE'LL CLIMB UP INTO YOUR BED, JERK THE HEAD-NET OFF YOUR HEAD, AND IF YOU OPPOSE HIM HE'LL STAND UP AND FIGHT.
He's a hell of a bother! We had lots of them on Maui. They lived there in Kauai → (KĂVY) truck.
Love, Harry
V-MAIL

Rat 4-26-44

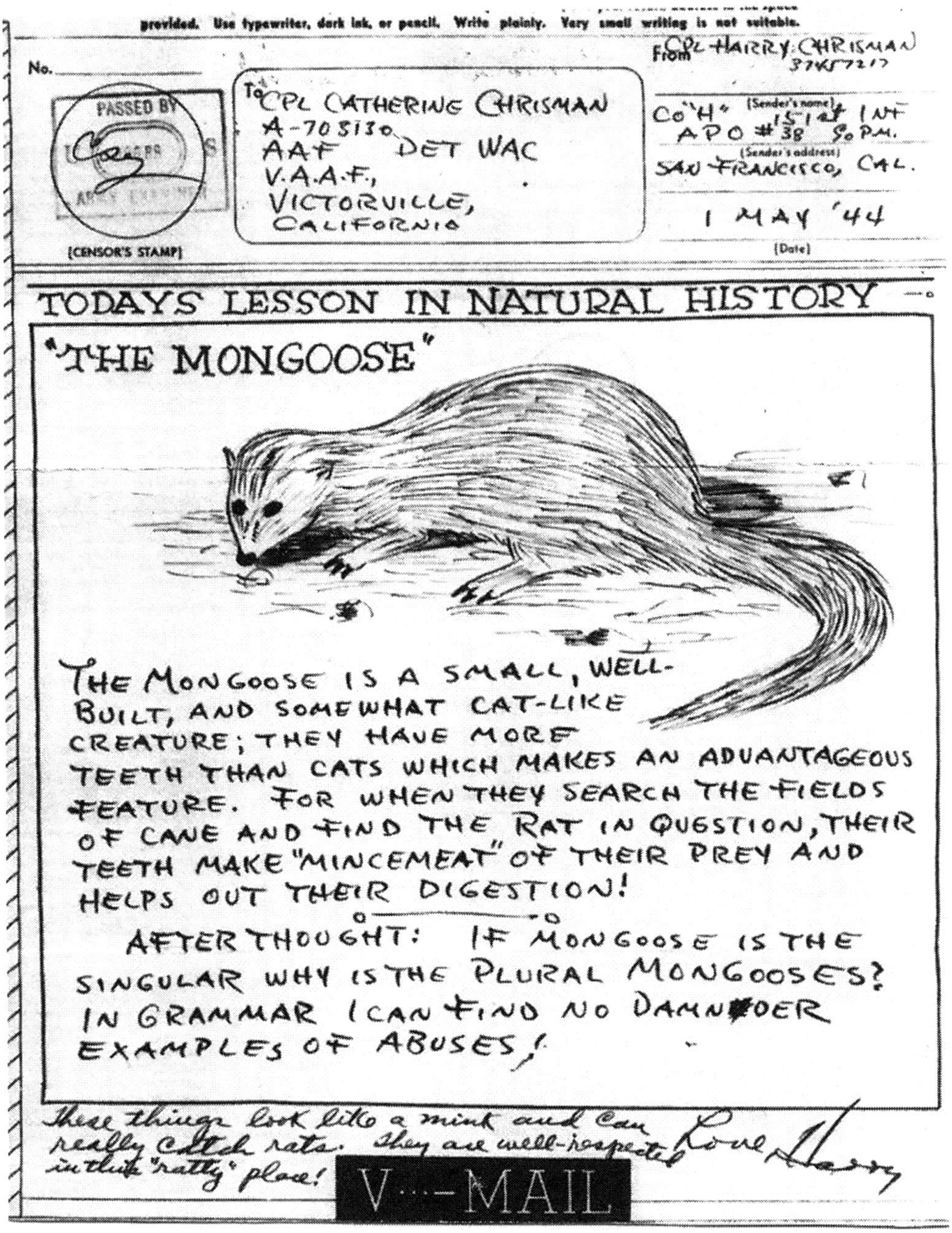
provided. Use typewriter, dark ink, or pencil. Write plainly. Very small writing is not suitable.

No.

From CPL HARRY CHRISMAN
37K57217

PASSED BY
ARMY EXAMINER
(CENSOR'S STAMP)

To CPL CATHERINE CHRISMAN
A-705130
AAF DET WAC
V.A.A.F.,
VICTORVILLE,
CALIFORNIA

CO "H" 151st INF (Sender's name)
APO #38 % P.M. (Sender's address)
SAN FRANCISCO, CAL.

1 MAY '44
(Date)

TODAYS LESSON IN NATURAL HISTORY

"THE MONGOOSE"

THE MONGOOSE IS A SMALL, WELL-BUILT, AND SOMEWHAT CAT-LIKE CREATURE; THEY HAVE MORE TEETH THAN CATS WHICH MAKES AN ADVANTAGEOUS FEATURE. FOR WHEN THEY SEARCH THE FIELDS OF CANE AND FIND THE RAT IN QUESTION, THEIR TEETH MAKE "MINCEMEAT" OF THEIR PREY AND HELPS OUT THEIR DIGESTION!

AFTERTHOUGHT: IF MONGOOSE IS THE SINGULAR WHY IS THE PLURAL MONGOOSES? IN GRAMMAR I CAN FIND NO DAMNDER EXAMPLES OF ABUSES!

These things look like a mink and can really catch rats. They are well-respected in this "ratty" place!

Love Harry

V-MAIL

Mongoose 5-1-44

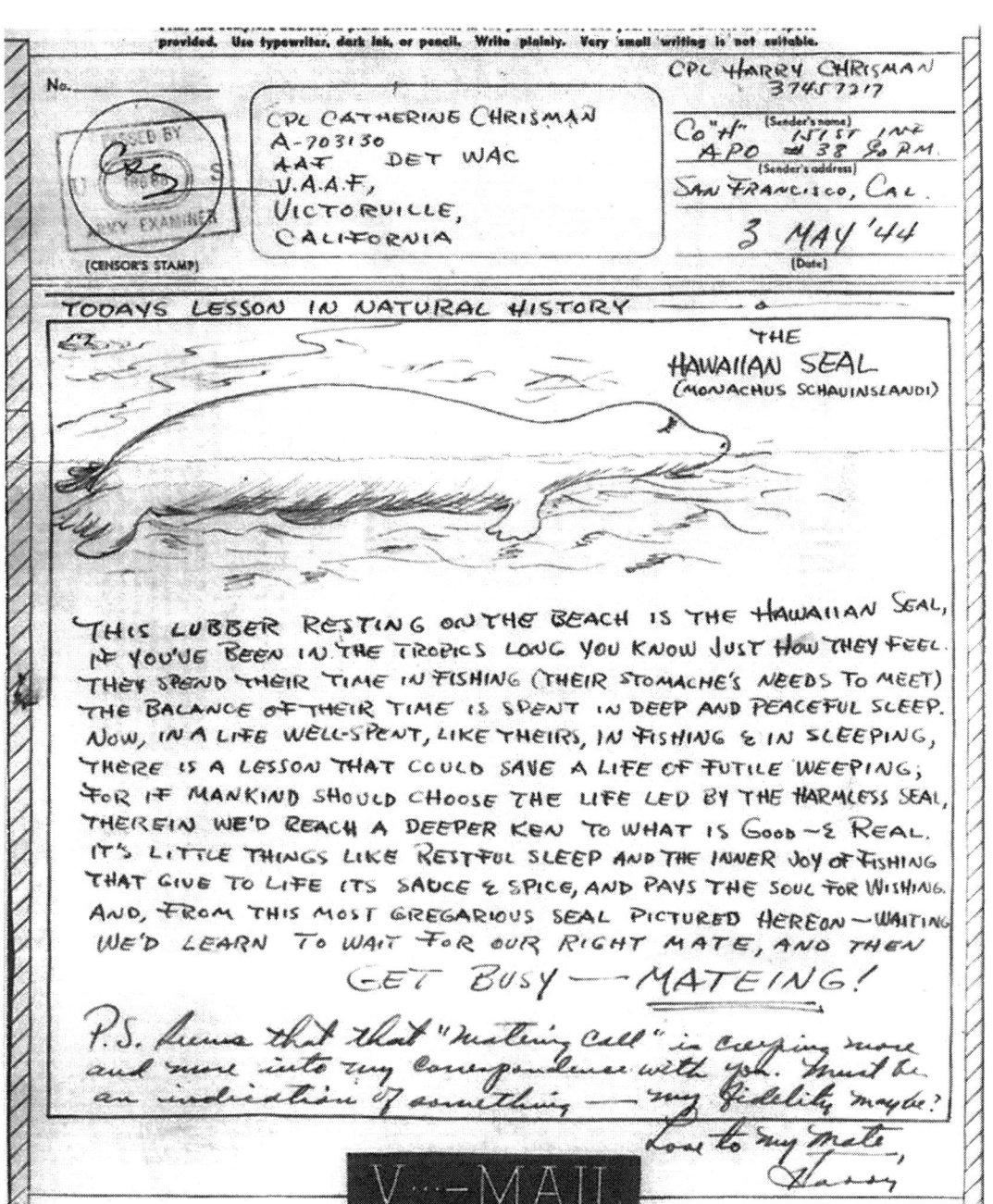

provided. Use typewriter, dark ink, or pencil. Write plainly. Very small writing is not suitable.

No.

CPL CATHERINE CHRISMAN
A-703130
AAF   DET WAC
V.A.A.F,
VICTORVILLE,
CALIFORNIA

(CENSOR'S STAMP)

CPL HARRY CHRISMAN
37457217

Co "H"   (Sender's name)
          151st INF
APO # 38 % P.M.
          (Sender's address)
SAN FRANCISCO, CAL.

3 MAY '44
(Date)

TODAYS LESSON IN NATURAL HISTORY

THE
HAWAIIAN SEAL
(MONACHUS SCHAUINSLANDI)

THIS LUBBER RESTING ON THE BEACH IS THE HAWAIIAN SEAL,
IF YOU'VE BEEN IN THE TROPICS LONG YOU KNOW JUST HOW THEY FEEL.
THEY SPEND THEIR TIME IN FISHING (THEIR STOMACHE'S NEEDS TO MEET)
THE BALANCE OF THEIR TIME IS SPENT IN DEEP AND PEACEFUL SLEEP.
NOW, IN A LIFE WELL-SPENT, LIKE THEIRS, IN FISHING & IN SLEEPING,
THERE IS A LESSON THAT COULD SAVE A LIFE OF FUTILE WEEPING;
FOR IF MANKIND SHOULD CHOOSE THE LIFE LED BY THE HARMLESS SEAL,
THEREIN WE'D REACH A DEEPER KEN TO WHAT IS GOOD & REAL.
IT'S LITTLE THINGS LIKE RESTFUL SLEEP AND THE INNER JOY OF FISHING
THAT GIVE TO LIFE ITS SAUCE & SPICE, AND PAYS THE SOUL FOR WISHING.
AND, FROM THIS MOST GREGARIOUS SEAL PICTURED HEREON — WAITING
WE'D LEARN TO WAIT FOR OUR RIGHT MATE, AND THEN
     GET BUSY — MATEING!

P.S. Seems that that "mateing call" is creeping more
and more into my correspondence with you. Must be
an indication of something — my fidelity maybe?

Love to my mate,
Harry

V····MAIL

Hawaiian Seal 5-3-44

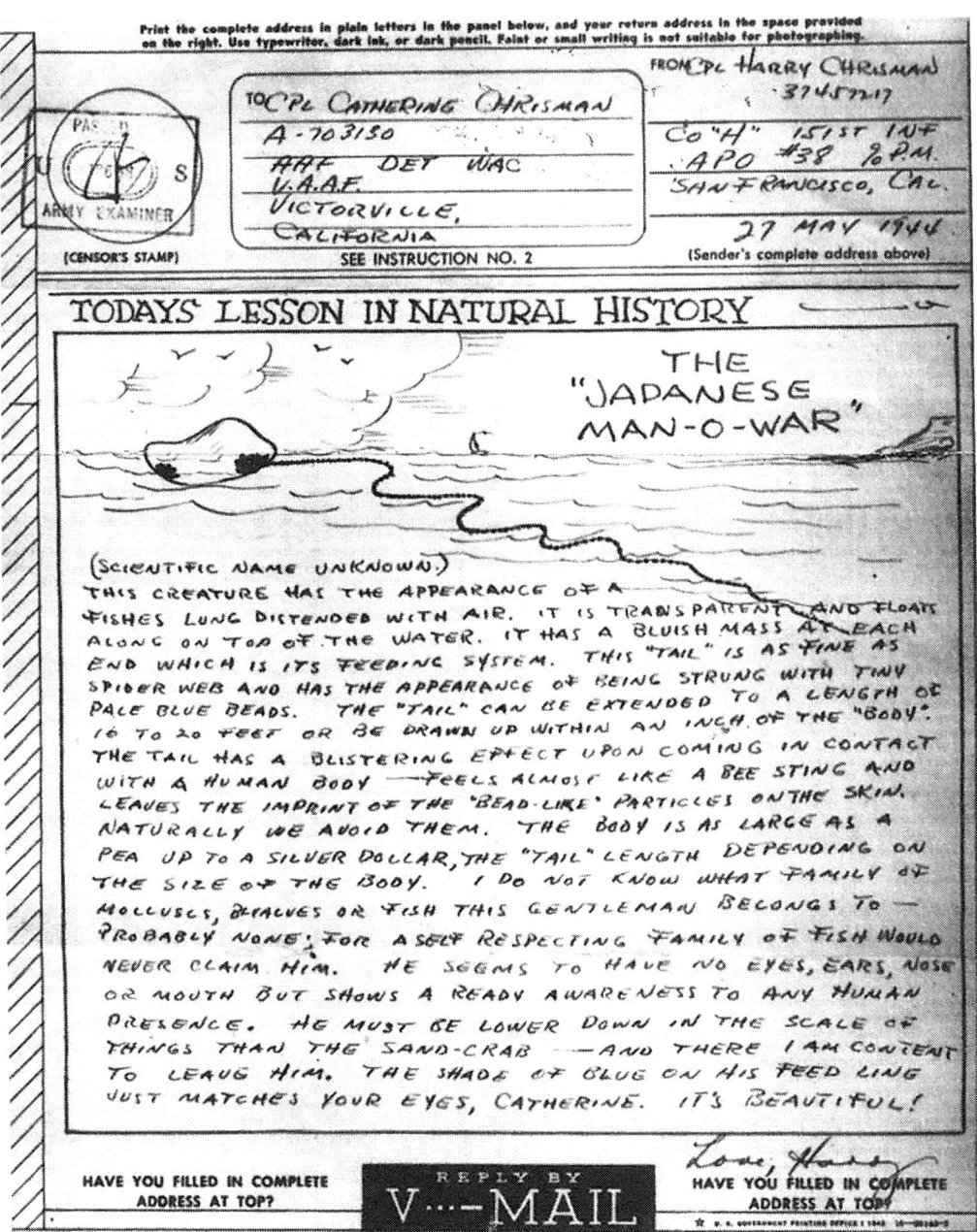

Print the complete address in plain letters in the panel below, and your return address in the space provided on the right. Use typewriter, dark ink, or dark pencil. Faint or small writing is not suitable for photographing.

TO CPL CATHERING CHRISMAN
A-703150
AAF DET WAC
V.A.A.F.
VICTORVILLE,
CALIFORNIA
SEE INSTRUCTION NO. 2

FROM CPL HARRY CHRISMAN
37457217
Co "H" 151ST INF
APO #38 % P.M.
SAN FRANCISCO, CAL.
27 MAY 1944
(Sender's complete address above)

(CENSOR'S STAMP)   PASSED BY ARMY EXAMINER

TODAYS LESSON IN NATURAL HISTORY

THE "JAPANESE MAN-O-WAR"

(SCIENTIFIC NAME UNKNOWN.)
THIS CREATURE HAS THE APPEARANCE OF A
FISHES LUNG DISTENDED WITH AIR. IT IS TRANSPARENT AND FLOATS
ALONG ON TOP OF THE WATER. IT HAS A BLUISH MASS AT EACH
END WHICH IS ITS FEEDING SYSTEM. THIS "TAIL" IS AS FINE AS
SPIDER WEB AND HAS THE APPEARANCE OF BEING STRUNG WITH TINY
PALE BLUE BEADS. THE "TAIL" CAN BE EXTENDED TO A LENGTH OF
16 TO 20 FEET OR BE DRAWN UP WITHIN AN INCH OF THE "BODY".
THE TAIL HAS A BLISTERING EFFECT UPON COMING IN CONTACT
WITH A HUMAN BODY — FEELS ALMOST LIKE A BEE STING AND
LEAVES THE IMPRINT OF THE "BEAD-LIKE" PARTICLES ON THE SKIN.
NATURALLY WE AVOID THEM. THE BODY IS AS LARGE AS A
PEA UP TO A SILVER DOLLAR, THE "TAIL" LENGTH DEPENDING ON
THE SIZE OF THE BODY. I DO NOT KNOW WHAT FAMILY OF
MOLLUSCS, BIVALVES OR FISH THIS GENTLEMAN BELONGS TO —
PROBABLY NONE; FOR A SELF RESPECTING FAMILY OF FISH WOULD
NEVER CLAIM HIM. HE SEEMS TO HAVE NO EYES, EARS, NOSE
OR MOUTH BUT SHOWS A READY AWARENESS TO ANY HUMAN
PRESENCE. HE MUST BE LOWER DOWN IN THE SCALE OF
THINGS THAN THE SAND-CRAB — AND THERE I AM CONTENT
TO LEAVE HIM. THE SHADE OF BLUE ON HIS FEED LINE
JUST MATCHES YOUR EYES, CATHERINE. IT'S BEAUTIFUL!

Love, Harry

HAVE YOU FILLED IN COMPLETE ADDRESS AT TOP?
REPLY BY V····MAIL
HAVE YOU FILLED IN COMPLETE ADDRESS AT TOP?

Japanese Man-O-War 5-27-44

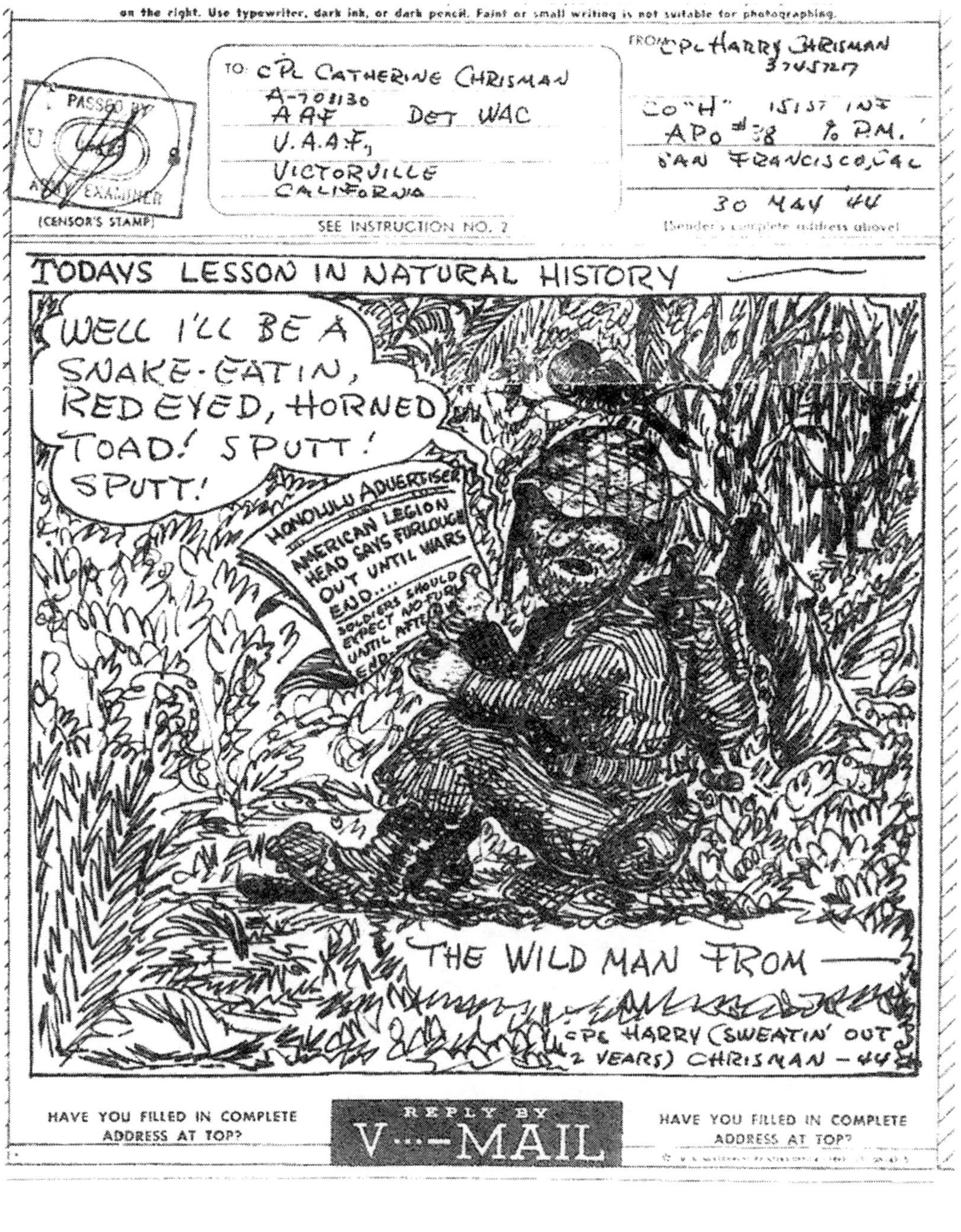
on the right. Use typewriter, dark ink, or dark pencil. Faint or small writing is not suitable for photographing.
PASSED BY ARMY EXAMINER
(CENSOR'S STAMP)
TO: CPL CATHERINE CHRISMAN
A-708130
AAF DET WAC
U.A.A.F.,
VICTORVILLE
CALIFORNIA
SEE INSTRUCTION NO. 2
FROM: CPL HARRY CHRISMAN
CO "H" 151ST INF
APO #38 % P.M.
SAN FRANCISCO, CAL
30 MAY 44
(Sender's complete address above)
TODAYS LESSON IN NATURAL HISTORY
WELL I'LL BE A SNAKE-EATIN, REDEYED, HORNED TOAD! SPUTT! SPUTT!
HONOLULU ADVERTISER
AMERICAN LEGION HEAD SAYS FURLOUGH OUT UNTIL WARS END....
SOLDIERS SHOULD EXPECT NO FUR... UNTIL AFTER... END
THE WILD MAN FROM ——
CPL HARRY (SWEATIN' OUT 2 YEARS) CHRISMAN - 44
HAVE YOU FILLED IN COMPLETE ADDRESS AT TOP?
REPLY BY V-MAIL
HAVE YOU FILLED IN COMPLETE ADDRESS AT TOP?

Wild Man 5-30-44

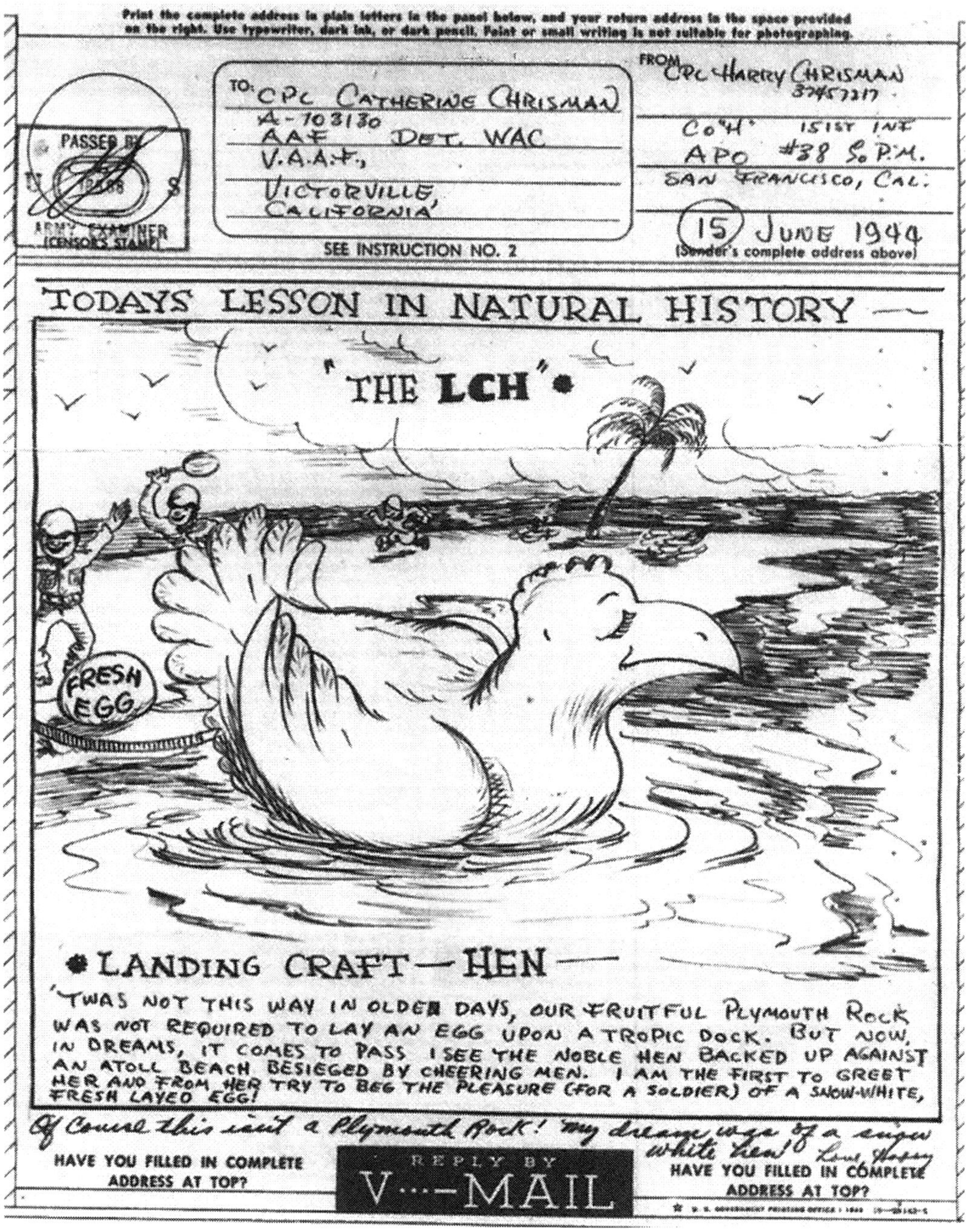
Print the complete address in plain letters in the panel below, and your return address in the space provided on the right. Use typewriter, dark ink, or dark pencil. Faint or small writing is not suitable for photographing.
TO: CPL CATHERINE CHRISMAN
A-703130
AAF DET. WAC
V.A.A.F.,
VICTORVILLE,
CALIFORNIA
FROM CPL HARRY CHRISMAN
37457217
CO "H" 151ST INF
APO #38 % P.M.
SAN FRANCISCO, CAL.
15 JUNE 1944
(Sender's complete address above)
PASSED BY
ARMY EXAMINER
(CENSOR'S STAMP)
SEE INSTRUCTION NO. 2
TODAYS LESSON IN NATURAL HISTORY
"THE LCH"
FRESH EGG
LANDING CRAFT—HEN
'TWAS NOT THIS WAY IN OLDEN DAYS, OUR FRUITFUL PLYMOUTH ROCK WAS NOT REQUIRED TO LAY AN EGG UPON A TROPIC DOCK. BUT NOW, IN DREAMS, IT COMES TO PASS I SEE THE NOBLE HEN BACKED UP AGAINST AN ATOLL BEACH BESIEGED BY CHEERING MEN. I AM THE FIRST TO GREET HER AND FROM HER TRY TO BEG THE PLEASURE (FOR A SOLDIER) OF A SNOW-WHITE, FRESH LAYED EGG!
Of Course this isn't a Plymouth Rock! My dream was of a snow white hen!
HAVE YOU FILLED IN COMPLETE ADDRESS AT TOP?
REPLY BY
V...—MAIL
HAVE YOU FILLED IN COMPLETE ADDRESS AT TOP?

The LCH 6-15-44

Appendix

Harry drew this picture during his first furlough in July 1945, when he and Catherine got to spend it together at their favorite lake in Nebraska, Lake Minatare. He meant it for Catherine's fellow WACs back in Victorville, teasing them about having to be hard at work while he and Catherine were hard at play! The poem he wrote reads:

> At Victorville the work piles up
> And causes fear and anguish—
> While on a beach, far out of reach
> A WAC and soldier languish.

YOU ARE MY SUNSHINE

About Harry Chrisman

HARRY EUGENE CHRISMAN WAS BORN on February 7, 1906 in a Sod House on land homesteaded by his father, Eugene Chrisman, and mother, Berna Hunter Chrisman. The Edom Ranch was near Broken Bow, Nebraska, and Harry, the last of four children, lived there until he was eleven when the prolonged illness of his father forced the family to move into Broken Bow. He went to school there until his father bought the livery stable in Scottsbluff, Nebraska and moved the family there.

When Harry was a sophomore in high school he recalls, "We were studying Beowulf and I thought to myself, 'What in the hell am I going to do with Beowulf?'"

Harry left school, worked with his father who also raised mules for the Army, became a traveling salesman, met Catherine Bell, became the main support of his mother and father, married Catherine, joined the Army and was inducted on October 9, 1942.

Immediately after basic training at Ft. Logan, Colorado he was sent to the Pacific. There he continued Basic Training at Schofield Barracks on Oahu, was assigned to L Company of the 108th Infantry, 40th Division and spent Jan to March of 1943 helping to set up defenses along the beaches of Maui.

He volunteered for the Birch Task Force and was sent to Christmas Island to help defend the Line Islands against the Japanese should they decide to use those islands as fueling points.

Harry was then with the 102nd Infantry, but spent most of his time in the Clerk's Hut. Few men had his multiple skills. He could write, type, draw, sing, entertain, etc. He started a newsletter at every post and in addition to The Christmas Times he also helped establish and run the island radio station. And he drew over 300 V-Mail cartoons designed to lift the spirits of those he left at home. He also drew hundreds of cartoons for the men in his units.

Harry on Maui, March 1943. At this point he was with L. Company, 108th Infantry, 40th Division.

He was transferred to the Army Port and Service Command on Oahu in June of 1944. In July of 1945 he was re-assigned to the Separation Center at Ft. Leavenworth, Kansas and was given an honorable discharge in November of that year.

He then took advantage of the G. I. Bill as did his wife Catherine, the second WAC from the state of Nebraska. They attended the Rochester Institute of Technology and graduated with teletype degrees.

Harry spent the next twenty years as a newspaperman. During those years he began to write about the Old West. After retirement he and Catherine moved to Denver, Colorado, because, according to Harry, "The Denver Public Library has the best Western section for research of any library!"

Harry published and/or edited fourteen books during his lifetime. All reflect life in the Old West. His first major book, Ladder of Rivers was the story of I. Print Olive, the first cattleman to drive herds north from Texas and graze them on the grasslands of Nebraska before driving them back to Dodge City, Kansas for shipment east.

Harry died on December 17, 1993 in Lakewood, Colorado and is buried at Ft. Logan National Cemetery in Denver.

BOOKS BY HARRY E. CHRISMAN

The Ladder of Rivers: the Story of I. P (Print) Olive, 1962, 1964,1983
Chariot of the Sun, 1964 (With Mrs. Catherine Ward Allen)
Butcher's History of Custer County, Nebraska (Edited by HEC), 1965, 1976
Fifty Years on the Owl Hoot Trail (with Jim Herron, Sr.), 1969, 1972
When You and I Were Young, Nebraska! (With Berna Hunter Chrisman), 1971, 1976
The Fighting Railroad Mayor, by Earl Walker (edited by HEC)
Boss Neff in the Okla-Tex Panhandle, by Boss Neff, (2nd edition edited by HEC) 1969
The 1001 Most-Asked Questions About the American West, 1962
Tales of the Western Heartland, 1984
The Call of the High Plains: The Autobiography of Charles E. Hancock (Re-written and Edited by HEC), 1989

Harry and Catherine, 1988.

YOU ARE MY SUNSHINE

About Sheryl Jones

I WAS BORN AND RAISED IN THE FLINT HILLS OF eastern Kansas. I loved tramping through the woods with my father and writing about it afterwards. And I loved to read! My mother belonged to the Book of the Month Club and purchased the Book of Knowledge from a traveling salesman. I would read the fairy tales and other interesting tidbits to my little sister, Judy, usually after listening to our favorite after school radio shows: "Batman," "The Lone Ranger," "Superman," "Buster Brown," and the "Green Hornet."

I wrote my first story when I was eight and have never stopped. I taught writing for twenty-three years and hope some of my love of the written word rubbed off on one or two of those students.

My husband, Don, is my best editor and fan. My sister, Judy, wonders why I am not rich and famous. My sister, Debbie, illustrates the children's books I write for Sea Turtle, Inc. in South Padre, Texas. And all those stories my father told me about growing up on a ranch in Oklahoma encouraged me write the Rowdy Stories and to apply for membership in the Cherokee Nation, and I'm proud to say I am now a member of that nation.

Here is a partial list of the children's stories I have written, some of which are published, all of which I loved writing!

FOR SEA TURTLE, INC.
> *Swim, Allison, Swim!*
> *Smile and Say "Lettuce!"*
> *Fred, the Lopsided Loggerhead*
> *MJ and Her Secret Friend.*

THE ROWDY STORIES

A Young Boy's Adventures in the Old West:

Life on the Circle C

The Secret of the Gypsy Horse

Where in the World is John Bobbie D.?

Saving Sadie Mae

THE JONES BOYS MYSTERIES

The Strange Disappearance of Mr. Noah

The Ghosts of Cougar Pass

The Case of the Missing Musket

The Family in the Forest.

THE JERALDINE JOSEPHINE SERIES

Jeraldine Josephine and the Topknots

Jeraldine Josephine and the Kachina Doll

Jeraldine Josephine and the Tiki God

Jeraldine Josephine and Tookie Bean.

The author at a sea turtle presentation, 2013.

List of Harry E. Chrisman's V-Mails

PART ONE

LOVE, ROMANCE AND THE WAC

WAC Love Letter
WACs in a Line 12-25-42
What Does a WAC Look Like? 1-27-43
When It's Two AM 3-7-43
Item of 1898 3-7-43
On Pacific Island 3-30-43
See Here 6-6-43
Music/Radio 8-4-43
New Radio 8-4-43
Well I Can Dream 8-7-43
Dream About Your Own Girl 9-12-43
Rose Aisenberg, Camp Sweetheart 1943
Things We Could Be Doing 9-14-43
Military Millennium 9-24-43
Packages 10-4-43
Snowing a Gooney 10-20-43
Gremlins 10-28-43
You'll Be Sorry 11-11-43
Mistletoe 12-25-43
Call of the Wolf 12-25-43
Madame Ennui 12-26-43
The Day of the Chevron Shower 1-6-44
Catherine Drawn From Memory 1-16-44
Hand Salute 1-21-44
World 1-29-44
Valentine 1-9-44
We Don't Get It 2-2-44
Snow Job 2-5-44
WAC '64 2-23-44
Furlough 3-5-44
To Hawaii 3-13-44
Maps 3-15-44
One Sweet Letter 3-17-44
Fifth Freedom 3-20-44
Squealer 3-23-44

Sex Hygiene 3-27-44
Letter to Rose 4-18-44
He–She 4-23-44
Mail Mule 4-26-44
Ode to WAC 5-1-44
Tents Again 5-4-44
With The WACs in Hawaii 5-22-44
The Nose Knows 5-27-44
Love Over the Pacific 6-5-44
Old Friends 6-17-44
Sundial 6-25-44
The Rain 6-26-44
My Aching Back 6-2-44
Morale 6-16-44
Feast or Famine 7-17-44
Descent of Man 7-24-44
Furlough Bird 8-15-44
Pagan Love Song 9-5-44
Dotage 9-12-44
Dog In the Manger 9-24-44
Phone Call 10-28-44
Letter Saver 11-11-44
The Adjuster 11-12-44
Resident Soldier 11-12-44
Teeter-Totter 12-1-44
April Showers 23-6-44
Maytime 12-6-44
Civilian Worker 12-10-44
Life of Riley 12-19-44
Mail Squawl 1-1-45
Rec Hall 1-3-45
Pops on Oahu 1-14-45
Manifesto to the WAC 1-15-45
Types 1-16-45
Our Army 1-25-45
Grandmas 1-27-45
Buckin' for a Rocker 2-12-45
Shopper 2-17-45
Omar the Bookmaker 3-15-45

Ono No Yoshiki 3-16-45
Stage Fright 4-11-45
Perils of War 4-13-45
Lei Day 5-1-45
Dog Tags 5-7-45
Sunbath at Minatare 5-11-45

PART TWO
NATURAL HISTORY
Seahorse 1-17-44
Prizzle Beast 1-21-44
Puffer Fish 1-28-44
Sting Ray 2-12-44
Swallower 2-13-44
Hermit Crab 2-14-44
Polyps 2-16-44
Angler 2-25-44
Freight Car 3-3-44
Flying Fish 3-16-44
Sea Gherkin 3-19-44
Sea Hare 3-24-44
Gecko 4-16-44
Killer Whale 4-18-44 A
Killer Whale 4-18-44 B
Wallaby 4-21-44
Dog 4-22-44
Skink 4-23-44
Bat 4-24-44
Gooney Dance 4-24-44
Rat 4-26-44
Mongoose 5-1-44
Hawaiian Seal 5-3-44
Japanese Man-O-War 5-27-44
Wild Man 5-30-44
The LCH 6-15-44

53322935R00118

Made in the
USA
Lexington, KY